Direct Democracy

The International IDEA Handbook

INTERNATIONAL
IDEA
INSTITUTE FOR
DEMOCRACY AND
ELECTORAL
ASSISTANCE

Direct Democracy

The International IDEA Handbook

Lead Writers and Editors

Virginia Beramendi
Andrew Ellis
Bruno Kaufman
Miriam Kornblith
Larry LeDuc
Paddy McGuire
Theo Schiller
Palle Svensson

Contributors

Jennifer Somalie Angeyo
Nadja Braun
Mugyenyi Silver Byanyima
Algis Krupavicius
Humberto de la Calle Lombana
Krisztina Medve
Alfred Lock Okello Oryem
Rodolfo Gonzáles Rissotto
Daniel Zovatto

Handbook Series

The International IDEA Handbook Series seeks to present comparative analysis, information and insights on a range of democratic institutions and processes. Handbooks are aimed primarily at policy makers, politicians, civil society actors and practitioners in the field. They are also of interest to academia, the democracy assistance community and other bodies.

International IDEA publications are independent of specific national or political interests. Views expressed in this publication do not necessarily represent the views of International IDEA, its Board or its Council members. The map presented in this publication does not imply on the part of the Institute any judgement on the legal status of any territory or the endorsement of such boundaries, nor does the placement or size of any country or territory reflect the political view of the Institute. The map is created for this publication in order to add clarity to the text.

Applications for permission to reproduce or translate all or any part of this publication should be made to:
International IDEA
SE -103 34 Stockholm
Sweden

International IDEA encourages dissemination of its work and will promptly respond to requests for permission to reproduce or translate its publications.

Cover design by: Helena Lunding
Map design: Kristina Schollin-Borg
Graphic design by: Bulls Graphics AB
Printed by: Bulls Graphics AB

ISBN: 978-91-85724-50-5

Foreword

Democracy has different faces. This Handbook considers whether, when and how the use of electoral direct democracy mechanisms is conducive to enhancing democratic systems. It gives an overview of the usage of direct democracy in all regions of the world, and examines six countries – Hungary, Switzerland, Uganda, the United States (Oregon), Uruguay and Venezuela.

Direct Democracy: The International IDEA Handbook provides recommendations and best practices, offering a critical analysis for those who may be considering the adoption of one or more instruments of direct democracy, or for those who may be seeking to make existing institutions and processes perform more effectively.

Switzerland opted for the system of direct democracy. The right of optional referendums, incorporated into the Swiss constitution in 1874, allows citizens to have the ultimate say on laws enacted by the parliament. In 1891, a modification to the constitution further introduced the popular initiative which allows citizens to request that a partial revision be made to the constitution. These two instruments of direct democracy exist at the federal and local levels.

Direct democracy can sometimes be perceived as slowing down social progress, and has shown its limits when used by political parties to introduce, for instance, xenophobic measures under cover of the protection of national sovereignty and cultural identity. It is, however, a unique mechanism which, by encouraging citizen participation and popular freedom of speech, contributes to avoiding social conflict and permits the launch of political debate on given themes.

With this new Handbook, International IDEA offers policy makers and actors engaged in the democractic reform process some thoughts and reflections on the enhanced participation of citizens in building democracy in an evolving society.

Micheline Calmy-Rey
Minister of Foreign Affairs, Switzerland

Democracy indicates an involvement of the people in the functioning of their government. A wide range of democratic practices exist in order to further engage citizens in making political and institutional decisions. The level to which this engagement occurs is mandated either by the constitution or by individual governments through legislation and through the choice and design of the electoral system. While some countries offer more provisions for direct citizen participation within the constitutional framework, others have tighter restrictions.

This Handbook explores four mechanisms of direct democracy designed to give the electorate increased opportunities to involve themselves in the running of their governments – referendums, citizens' initiatives, agenda initiatives and recall. The Handbook also surveys the range of uses for each of these four mechanisms and, by highlighting best practices, notes when and how each mechanism can best be used. The case studies throughout the book offer a unique comparison of the various direct democracy mechanisms and how they have been tailored to the needs of individual countries and contexts.

International IDEA aims to support democracy-building processes globally, and offers insights into the variety of ways in which democracy can be advanced. This Handbook addresses issues ranging from questions of institutional design and the initial adoption of any one or more direct democracy mechanisms, to their implementation and the potential obstacles that might be encountered during this phase. The target audience of this book is not only policy makers and practitioners but also those working in the field of democracy support and assistance, namely civil society, non-governmental organizations and academics.

This Handbook does not aim to resolve ongoing debates on direct democracy but rather aims to bring out the variety of potential participatory approaches and ways of realizing them that can be tailored to individual democracies as necessary.

In addition to the authors and contributors, International IDEA would like to thank all those who have assisted in the editing, assembly and production of the Handbook, in particular those mentioned in the acknowledgements.

Vidar Helgesen
Secretary-General
International IDEA

Acknowledgements

A great number of organizations and individuals have contributed to this work. In addition to the writers, editors and contributors we would like to acknowledge the support provided by Richard Sinnott, Oregon Secretary of State Bill Bradbury, Nitin Khanna, Gonzalo Arguello, David Altman, Hans-Urs Wili, Kristina Lemon, Volker Mittendorf, Zoltan Tibor Pallinger, Alexandra Panzarelli, Yume Kitasei, Florencia Enghel, Lisa Hagman and Ileana Aguilera.

Special thanks go to our copyeditor, Eve Johansson, for her patience and meticulous attention to detail. We also thank editorial anchors Mélida Jiménez and Shana Kaiser as well as the rest of the Management and Research Team who made this publication possible: Adhy Aman, Erika Beckman, Hanna Berheim, Ellie Greenwood, Paul Guerin, Stina Larserud and Ola Pettersson.

We also acknowledge with gratitude the valuable contribution of all the Electoral Management Bodies worldwide that have taken the time to answer our surveys, thereby contributing to the comparative country information in this Handbook, and to all of the research centres who have worked with International IDEA gathering the comparative country information:

African Centre for Economic Growth (ACEG)
Al Urdun Al Jadid Research Center (UJRC)
Association of Central and Eastern European Election Officials (ACEEEO)
Australian Election Commission (AEC)
Centre d'études et de documentation sur la démocratie directe, Universität Zürich
Centre for Democratic Governance (CDD)
Centre for Electoral Reform (CETRO)
Centre pour la Governance Démocratique (CGD)
Commission Electorale Independante (CENI)
Elections Canada
Electoral Institute of Southern Africa (EISA)
Gorée Institute
Initiative and Referendum Institute, University of Southern California
Institute for Education in Democracy (IED)
Instituto Federal Electoral (IFE)
National Jury of Elections (JNE)
Resource Building Institute in Democracy Governance and Elections (RBI)
Servicio Electoral de Chile (SERVEL)
The Arab NGO Network for Development (ANND)
The Centre for the Study of Developing Societies (CSDS)
The Pacific Islands, Australia and New Zealand Electoral Administrators Network (PIANZEA).

Additional thanks go to Helena Catt, Ramlan Surbakti and David Kupferschmidt for their work in reviewing the Handbook and to IDEA's Publications Manager, Nadia Handal Zander, for succesfully managing the production of this Handbook.

Contents

Figures

Boxes

Acronyms and abbreviations

AUD	Australian dollars
CAPEL	Centro de Asesoría y Promoción Electoral (Center for Electoral Promotion and Assistance) (IIDH)
CNE	Consejo Nacional Electoral (National Electoral Council) (Venezuela)
EMB	electoral management body
EU	European Union
FC	federal constitution (Switzerland)
FLP	Federal Law on Political Rights (Switzerland)
IDASA	Institute for Democracy in South Africa
IDEA	(International) Institute for Democracy and Electoral Assistance
IIDH	Instituto Interamericano de Derechos Humanos (Inter-American Institute for Human Rights)
IRI Europe	Initiative and Referendum Institute Europe
MMP	Mixed Member Proportional (electoral system)
MP	member of parliament
NEC	National Electoral Committee (Hungary)
OAS	Organization of American States
PR	proportional representation
PRR	presidential recall referendum (Venezuela)
UK	United Kingdom
UN	United Nations
USD	US dollar

Introduction

Introduction

Introduction: direct democracy in political context

Discussions of the use of referendums, citizens' initiatives and recall votes often revolve around two opposing positions. Perhaps oversimplifying, one of these positions can be described as the strict representative approach – that direct voting of any kind undermines the principle of representative democracy and should ideally be avoided. Equally oversimplified, the other position is that of the direct democracy enthusiast – that there are few situations in which the use of the direct vote of the people is not an appropriate way to determine the will of the people. In the practical context which faces participants in democracy building and democratic institutional design, the alleged choice between these two opposing positions is not only restricting and unhelpful – it is fundamentally false. Direct democracy mechanisms and mechanisms of representative democracy can complement and enrich each other rather than being seen as opposed. The varied experience of the use of direct democracy mechanisms that has been gained in many countries and territories around the world provides a richness of knowledge and expertise, the sharing of which can be of great value.

This Handbook considers whether, when and how the use of electoral direct democracy mechanisms is appropriate to enhance democratic systems. By involving voters directly in decision-making processes, does the use of direct democracy increase voter participation? Does allowing voters the opportunity to initiate their own laws, to vote on laws proposed or enacted by others, or to propose and vote on the continuation in office of representatives whom they perceive as unsatisfactory increase their satisfaction that political outcomes more accurately reflect popular preferences? Does direct democracy reduce dissatisfaction with elected representatives? Does the existence of direct democracy mechanisms act as a discipline on the behaviour of elected representatives? Criteria by which the success of direct democracy as a component of a democratic system might be judged include levels of participation and engagement, and levels of satisfaction with the democratic system as a whole. Such judgements can only be made in the context of wider political realities, which differ between countries and localities, and also change over time. The Handbook therefore does not provide clear-cut answers to the questions asked above. It is intended to provide the background, the information and the tools to enable citizens themselves to debate and evaluate them.

Direct Democracy: The International IDEA Handbook concentrates on the design, implementation and impact of the electoral direct democracy mechanisms, making available, analysing and comparing experiences both in countries which have built these mechanisms into the fabric of their institutions and in countries where they are used much less frequently. It seeks to give an overview of various types of instruments, and looks in particular at the differences between those instruments where an initiative can be taken 'from below' and those which are initiated and dominated by governmental authorities. The Handbook does not address wider mechanisms of participatory democracy, or how direct and continuing citizen engagement in the process of government can be encouraged – a much wider question which engages debate about motivation, civic education and about a range of other issues. But in seeking to promote informed consideration and debate on the role of the electoral instruments of direct democracy, it lays a cornerstone for that important broader discussion to take place.

Direct votes are a political tool

As is true of any process of political change, it is a mistake to think of discussion and decisions about the use and the form of direct democracy mechanisms as a purely technical matter, in which best-practice answers can be laid down by lawyers or external technical experts. The political and institutional framework of a country or a municipality is a political decision, in which all citizens have a stake, and in which there are no 'best answers' that can be arrived at by independent arbiters.

The legitimacy of the political and institutional framework chosen is linked just as much to ownership of the decision-making process by the people as it is to the actual content of the decision, in which the various stakeholders will have a variety of interests. Some of these interests will appear to be served by the use of direct voting in some form, while others will not; and the approach to discussion and negotiation of the various stakeholders will be strongly coloured by these calculations. (This is of course just as true in relation to any other feature of institutional framework design.) The motivations of the decision makers will thus sometimes be visionary, long-term and altruistic – but may more often be short-term, sectoral, based on partisan advantage, or even venal.

As with design, so with implementation. Proponents of the direct voting mechanism may describe its outcomes as reflections of the will of the people, and they may well be right. But the participants in actual campaigns on referendums, citizens' initiatives or recall votes are not trying to determine what the will of the people is: they are campaigning to win a victory for their point of view, and will deploy arguments and tactics and use resources in order to do so. The principles of credible and legitimate elections – freedom, fairness, secrecy of the ballot, transparency, accountability and so on – apply just as much to direct democracy electoral processes. The principle of a level playing field for participants is just as valid and important for the conduct of direct democracy votes as it is for elections, and there are many questions on the detail of design and implementation of the mechanisms which will affect or indeed determine the extent to which a level playing field exists. Who poses the referendum or initiative question and in what terms, when and how an initiative question or a recall vote gets to the ballot, the relationship between whoever calls a referendum vote and whoever poses the question, and the regulations relating to campaign access and finance for all forms of direct votes are among many critical issues discussed in the Handbook.

Direct voting frameworks can change political choices

Political institutions matter: the outcome of decision making is dependent on the form of democratic institutions chosen. One of the criticisms often levelled at referendums is that the individual voters do not always vote on the merits of the question on the ballot paper: other issues, for example the general popularity of the incumbent government, may intervene. (Similar criticisms are also sometimes made of the motivation of voters in elections.) But even if every vote cast in a referendum reflected the view of the voter on the question that is posed rather than being influenced by other considerations not directly at issue, the availability of the referendum mechanism may change the decisions that emerge. Even though the views of every citizen remain the same, the decision made with one set of political institutions in place will not be the same as the decision made with another.

Inspired by the Finnish political scientist Hannu Nurmi, imagine a country in which the legislature is elected by proportional representation and with two political parties. Party A won the last general election with two-thirds of the vote, which remains the division of opinion in the country. The legislature thus has two-thirds of its members from Party A, and one-third from Party B. On a particular issue, however, Party A and its supporters are opposed to a proposal for change by a margin of 60 per cent : 40 per cent, whereas Party B and its supporters are 100 per cent in favour of this change. The figure compares what would happen if the decision were made by the legislature, where the legislators would follow the policy of their party, with what would happen if the decision were made by calling a referendum.

With voters holding and expressing exactly the same views, a proposal which fails by two-thirds in a legislature which fully reflects the preferences of the voters passes by 60 per cent to 40 per cent in a referendum of the same voters. As with political design generally, the outcome can depend on the institutional framework chosen. Institutional framework decisions reflect political choices and affect the political choices that are made.

Decision by Legislature

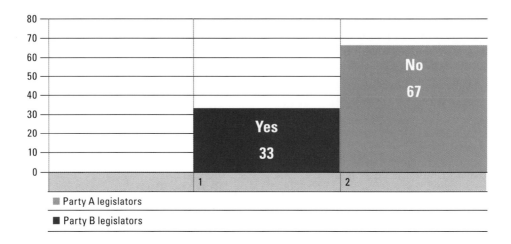

Decision by Referendum

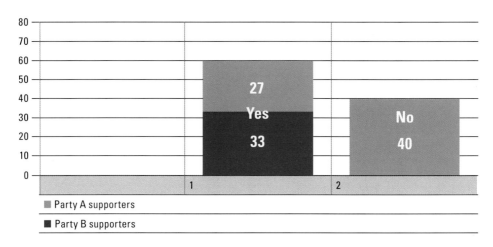

Effects of this kind do not only exist in the imaginings of political scientists. In Denmark, the Single European Act was passed in a referendum despite majority opposition in the parliament: and in another referendum some years later, the Maastricht Treaty on European integration was defeated despite the support of most of the political forces within the parliament.

Direct votes are a one-way street

There are few, if any, known cases where direct democracy mechanisms, once made part of the political framework, have later been abolished (although there are some countries where – contrary to the general worldwide trend – the use of referendums has become less frequent over time). This is not surprising: it would clearly be difficult to run a successful political campaign for a position easily portrayed by its opponents as 'taking the right to their say away from the people'. This means that designers of institutional frameworks, when they choose to include provisions for referendums, citizens' initiatives, an agenda initiative or recall votes, need to be sure that it is what they want to do: it is unlikely, short of a full revision of the constitution, that direct democracy provisions could be removed from an institutional framework once they were there.

Direct votes can help legitimize decisions – but not always

Even when direct democracy mechanisms are not regularly in use, referendums are often the tool of choice to adopt and legitimize new constitutions and other major institutional reforms. Such referendums may, however, not turn out the way in which politicians and those who conduct political negotiations envisage. The Irish rejection of the Lisbon Treaty on European integration issues in 2008 is just one prominent example.

Direct votes can help end conflict – but not always

Referendums are often proposed as part of a political process of transition after violent conflict, to gain or confirm popular consent for an element of a peace process. This may be a new or revised constitution, as for example in Chile, but need not be restricted to constitutions. It is not just the substance of such a process that matters, but the engagement of stakeholders and the timing and sequencing of the elements of the transition. There are examples where the referendum mechanism is widely acknowledged to have assisted the process, for example in Northern Ireland; but in other cases it has confirmed existing divisions. Even when the referendum leads to political change, its context and environment may produce undesirable side effects – as happened for example in Timor Leste in 1999.

The issues associated with the design and implementation of referendums are perhaps even more sensitive where sovereignty is an issue: there is a long history of referendums and proposals for referendums relating to disputes over territory. Questions over who can vote can be complex, involving geographical issues – where the conflict surrounds a proposal for separation, and whether the electorate be defined by the territory at issue or the whole country of which it is currently part – and sometimes also ethnic issues. The timing of electoral and other events in post-conflict transitions can be critical, and the nature of the choices posed by referendum questions can make the timing of the votes and their sequencing with other transitional events particularly sensitive.

What this Handbook is for

International IDEA is an intergovernmental organization with a single objective to its work – the strengthening of democratic institutions and processes worldwide. The work of IDEA seeks to achieve this objective through the provision of knowledge resources which can be used by participants in democratic reform processes worldwide, through policy development designed to provoke action and change in democracy building and democracy support policy, and through engagement in selected processes of democratic reform.

This Handbook adds to the range of IDEA knowledge resources on electoral process issues available to participants in democratic reform processes and to policy makers. It does not aim to encourage its users to either choose or reject the inclusion of some form of direct democracy mechanism in their political and institutional framework. Nor does it advocate one specific direct democracy option rather than another. It seeks to look at the many ways in which the views of citizens can be sought through an electoral process, to outline the many different alternatives available to countries and localities which are building or amending their democratic institutions, and to show the political and technical factors which are important in the design and implementation of direct votes. Most importantly, it seeks to do this in the context of the political realities which bear on the process of decision. Its value will be shown as it enables choices to be made through informed debate and discussion.

CHAPTER 1

CHAPTER 1

Overview

Introduction

1. This Handbook addresses the questions when and how direct democracy instruments might be employed to make certain types of political decisions. It considers a number of issues that arise in determining whether these mechanisms are appropriate in different political environments, and it draws on the experiences of political jurisdictions throughout the world in which the instruments and processes of direct democracy have been used at various times. Specifically, the Handbook examines four separate applications of direct democracy:

- referendums;
- citizens' initiatives;
- agenda initiatives; and
- recall.

Each of these four applications is discussed in detail in subsequent chapters of this Handbook, and a number of specific case studies of each type is used, in 'boxes' in the text and in the form of longer case studies after chapters 1, 4 and 7, to illustrate the operation of direct democracy processes.

2. The terminology used to describe the various instruments of direct democracy can vary between different jurisdictions, and different terms have sometimes been used to describe what are essentially the same institutions and processes. Referendums conducted by the government, for example, have sometimes been called plebiscites – a term that remains in use today in some jurisdictions. Citizens' initiatives – the term used in this Handbook – are sometimes also known as popular referendums or citizen-

initiated referendums, depending on the context in which the procedures are used. The meaning of some of the terms used to describe the different institutions and processes of direct democracy has changed over time, and is also subject to linguistic variations. The glossary at annex C clarifies some of these variations in terminology, and we will follow a consistent pattern in our usage of these terms throughout this Handbook.

3. *Referendums* are procedures which give the electorate a direct vote on a specific political, constitutional or legislative issue. As discussed in chapter 2 of this Handbook, referendums take place when a governing body or similar authority decides to call for a vote on a particular issue, or when such a vote is required by law under the terms of a constitution or other binding legal arrangement. In some cases, procedures also exist which allow citizens or a minority in a legislature to demand a referendum on an issue. The result of a referendum may be legally binding, as determined by the law or constitution under which it is called, or it may be used by the authorities for advisory purposes only. Case studies of both binding and consultative referendums are discussed in this Handbook.

4. *Citizens' initiatives* allow the electorate to vote on a political, constitutional or legislative measure proposed by a number of citizens and not by a government, legislature, or other political authority. To bring an issue to a vote, the proponents of the measure must gather enough signatures in support of it as the law under which the initiative is brought forward requires. As discussed in chapter 3, citizens' initiatives may deal with new proposals, existing laws or constitutional measures, depending on the jurisdiction in which they occur. As with referendums, the result of an initiative vote may be legally binding or advisory, depending on the provisions of the law under which such a vote takes place.

5. *Agenda initiatives* are procedures by which citizens can organize to place a particular issue on the agenda of a parliament or legislative assembly. As with citizens' initiatives, a minimum number of signatures is generally specified by law in order for the initiative to be brought forward to the legislature. Unlike the procedure followed for citizens' initiatives, no popular vote takes place when an agenda initiative is brought forward. The use of agenda initiatives at both the national and the sub-national level in a number of different countries, as well as proposed procedures for the use of agenda initiatives at the transnational level, are discussed in chapter 4 of this Handbook.

6. *Recall* procedures allow the electorate to vote on whether to end the term of office of an elected official if enough signatures in support of a recall vote are collected. Although the process of recall is often similar to that of citizens' initiatives, recall deals only with the question of removal of a person from public office, and the outcome is therefore always binding. The use of the recall process, together with appropriate case studies, is discussed in detail in chapter 5 of this Handbook.

The structure of the Handbook

7. The Handbook is organized to follow the steps which are generally involved in planning and then implementing a referendum, initiative or recall procedure. The first five chapters of the Handbook deal with questions of institutional design, and the potential implications of these. Agencies that may be considering the adoption of one or more instruments of direct democracy will need to decide the form that the institutions to be established will take, since once structures are put in place they are often difficult to change. In chapter 2 – 'When the authorities call a referendum: design and political considerations' – the various institutional forms of the referendum are examined. In particular, the differences between mandatory and optional referendums are discussed, illustrated by case studies in Europe, Africa, Asia and the Americas. In chapter 3 – 'When citizens take the initiative: design and political considerations' – institutional design issues that concern the use of citizens' initiatives are examined, drawing on short studies from Germany, Italy, Lithuania, New Zealand, Switzerland, Uruguay and California, as well as some of the US states. In chapter 4 – 'Agenda initiatives: when citizens can get a proposal on the legislative agenda' – issues are discussed that might apply to the use of agenda initiatives, in which citizens are able to bring an issue before a legislative body. Examples of the use of this instrument in Austria, Poland and Argentina are examined, as well as the features of a proposed agenda initiative for the European Union (EU). In chapter 5 – 'When citizens can recall elected officials' – questions of institutional design involving the use of a recall election are examined, drawing on case studies from Venezuela, California and Romania.

8. The next two chapters of the Handbook deal with the process involved in getting an issue on to the ballot and conducting a vote. Once particular institutions are put in place, how do they function in practice? Chapter 6 – 'How citizens get involved – step by step' – considers the process that citizens in various jurisdictions must follow in order for a proposal to qualify for a popular vote. Once an issue has qualified for a ballot, how does the electoral process function? What are the administrative procedures? What are the rules regarding campaign finance and the dissemination of information during the campaign? Chapter 7 – 'Direct democracy votes: information, campaigning and financing' – examines the special problems involved in administering, regulating and financing direct democracy campaigns, in disseminating the necessary information to the voters, and in providing for the fair use of the media. The advantages and disadvantages of a heavily regulated process, such as that used in the Republic of Ireland, are contrasted with those of a less regulated model such as that used in Uruguay. Finally, chapter 8 provides a comparative overview of direct democracy procedures through the various regions of the world; and chapter 9, on 'Recommendations and best practices', considers strategies that might be of relevance to those jurisdictions that are considering adopting one or more of the instruments of direct democracy or seeking to make existing institutions and processes perform more effectively. This chapter also incorporates conclusions that might be drawn regarding the applications of direct democracy in the world today, and discusses some of the considerations that might enter into the decision to adopt any particular model of direct democracy practices.

9. The Handbook draws extensively on a database of direct democracy processes and procedures compiled by the International IDEA research staff (see world survey, annex A). Here may be found information on the existing use of instruments of direct democracy in 214 countries and territories worldwide. For every country, the world survey provides information on the existing legal provisions for, and the use of, referendums, citizens' or agenda initiatives, and recall at the national, regional and/or local levels of government. The world survey provides detailed information on provisions for the conduct of referendums, citizens' initiatives, agenda initiatives and recall in each of the 214 countries and territories. The Handbook is accompanied by a map showing the spread of the use of these instruments of direct democracy throughout the world.

The forms of direct democracy

10. Direct democracy takes many forms and shows many variations. Our categorization in this Handbook of four broad types of direct democracy – referendums, citizens' initiatives, agenda initiatives and recall – also recognizes that there are variations within each type. Within each category, we define a number of variations concerning the specific circumstances under which they might take place, the extent to which the results are legally binding, the rules governing campaigns and finance, and a host of other issues. Throughout the Handbook, we explore the significance of some of these variations in form and practice with respect to each of the four main categories of direct democracy instruments considered here.

11. The subjects on which referendums are held vary widely in different parts of the world. In most of Europe and in Australia, referendums are most often conducted on issues of extraordinary political or constitutional significance (e.g. European integration, institutional changes, etc.), and referendums on more day-to-day policy questions are less frequent. Some examples include the referendums on the proposed European Union Constitutional Treaty held in 2005 in Spain, France, the Netherlands and Luxembourg, and the referendums on adoption of the euro held in Denmark in 2000 and in Sweden in 2003. In Latin America and the United States (at the state level), referendums often address a wider array of internal political issues. Referendums have been held in Latin America on subjects as diverse as constitutional reform, political amnesty and the privatization of state industries. In the Republic of Ireland, the constitution requires that any issue involving a transfer of sovereignty must be put to a referendum. In practice, this has meant that all the major EU treaties have been voted on in a referendum in the Republic of Ireland, while this has not been the case in many other EU member countries. In Switzerland, where several votes take place each year on citizens' initiatives or constitutional proposals (see the case study following this chapter), the subjects of recent votes have included issues as diverse as membership of the United Nations (UN), retirement age and refugee policies.

Box 1.1. Forms of direct democracy in Colombia

The constitution of Colombia provides for the following mechanisms of direct democracy.

A *plebiscite* is a vote of the people, convened by the president, by means of which a decision already taken by the executive is either supported or rejected. The official declaration of a plebiscite must bear the signature of all the ministers and be submitted to and approved by the Senate (the upper house). Neither a plebiscite nor a referendum can coincide with another election.

A *referendum* is an official call by the president or the Congress for the public to approve or reject a draft law or to repeal an existing law or possibly a new law that has not yet been passed. For a referendum to be valid, a minimum turnout equal to 25 per cent of registered electors is required, as well as a simple majority of those voting. The approved text then becomes legally enforceable and is binding.

By means of a *consultative referendum*, a question of a general nature on an issue of national, regional or local importance may be submitted to popular vote by the decision of the president, a governor or a mayor. In some cases the result may be binding. Measures concerning taxes or public expenditures, international treaties, the granting of amnesties or pardons, and issues of law and order cannot be submitted for consultative referendum.

The *agenda initiative* (also called the *popular legislative initiative*) is the political right of a group of citizens to present a bill (constitutional, statutory or local) to be debated and then approved, amended or refused by the official body concerned. The initiative is filed before the National Registrar of the Civil State if it collects the support of at least 5 per cent of citizens on the electoral register. If the agenda initiative is turned down, 10 per cent of citizens on the electoral register can call for a referendum on the issue.

The *mandate recall* is a political right by which the citizens can end the mandate that they have conferred on a governor or mayor. For recall to take place, the official concerned must have been in office for at least one year and the request must be signed by a number of people that is not less than 40 per cent of the total number of votes he or she received. If a majority of those voting vote for the official to be recalled, his or her successor must be elected within 30 days.

Table 1.1. The instruments of direct democracy and the organization of this Handbook

Substantive issues							Repre-sentatives
Referendums						Agenda initiatives	Recalls
Mandatory		Optional			Citizens' initiatives		
Predetermined issues	Predetermined situations	Executive	Institutional		Citizen's demand		
					New legislation	Old legislation	
			Legislative majority	Legislative minority	Rejective	Abrogative	
Chapter 2					Chapter 3		Chapter 4 / Chapter 5

12. Certain subjects may be constitutionally or legally excluded from being the subject of a referendum. In Uruguay, direct democracy instruments cannot be used in relation to laws concerning fiscal policy or laws applicable to the executive power (e.g. pension laws for civil servants) (see the case study following chapter 7). In Italy, tax and budget laws, amnesties and pardons, and international treaties cannot be submitted to a popular vote, and the Constitutional Court is empowered to determine whether a request for such a vote is legal. In countries where there has been a recent political transition, certain sensitive subjects may also be excluded from the referendum mechanism. In Colombia, for example, the issue of amnesty (as well as that of taxation) is excluded from being the subject of referendums (see box 1.1).

13. The instruments of direct democracy can be further subdivided according to the circumstances in which they might take place and the type of issue that each is designed to address (see table 1.1). A referendum, for example, may be *mandatory* because it concerns a certain type of issue or situation, as defined by law, or it may be *optional* when the government takes the decision to call a vote. Countries such as Switzerland require that important international treaties be submitted to a mandatory referendum. On the other hand, Sweden chose to hold a referendum on the adoption of the euro in 2003 even though it was not legally required to do so. In Australia, all proposed constitutional amendments must be submitted to a binding referendum, a provision also found in countries such as the Republic of Ireland and Switzerland. Most US states also require that constitutional amendments be submitted to a referendum, but there is no such provision at the national level in the United States.

14. Similarly, optional referendums can occur under different kinds of circumstances. Some, such as the Swedish example noted above, are initiated by the government for its own political reasons. There are also some jurisdictions in which a legislative minority of a sufficient size may demand a popular vote on an issue. In Denmark, for example, one-third of the members of the Folketing (parliament) can demand a referendum on an issue, even when it has been passed by a majority of the assembly. The Irish constitution has a similar provision, but it takes the form of a petition to the president to call a referendum, rather than an automatic procedure. In France, the decision to call a referendum rests with the executive – the president of the republic – alone, while in Brazil only the Congress is empowered to call for a popular vote on an issue. In Argentina, either the president or the Congress may authorize a 'consultative' vote.

15. The process by which citizens might demand a referendum varies according to whether the issue in question has already been passed into law. Where a referendum is demanded on pending legislation, the process is referred to as rejective – that is, citizens are given an opportunity within a certain period of time to reject a new law. Switzerland, for example, has a provision by which 50,000 citizens or the councils of eight or more cantons may demand a referendum on a law enacted by the Federal Assembly within 90 days of its passage. In Italy, 500,000 voters or five regional councils may trigger a similar process, but it can apply to any law, regardless of how long it has been in force. This procedure is known as an abrogative referendum.

16. Citizens' initiatives (chapter 3) or agenda initiatives (chapter 4) do not flow from or require any action by the government or other political institutions. Their use rests solely in the hands of citizens, generally determined by the number of signatures obtained in support of a proposal. But what happens after a document containing the legally specified number of valid signatures is filed can vary widely. Under the provisions of the EU agenda initiative contained in the Treaty of Lisbon, a proposal obtaining the signatures of 1 million EU citizens would require only that the European Commission 'consider' an issue. Austria has been one of the more frequent users of the agenda initiative. On obtaining 100,000 signatures in support of an initiative, the proposal must be debated in parliament. However, Austria does not have any provision requiring a direct popular vote on the issue presented. In Switzerland, by contrast, a proposed constitutional change put forward by 100,000 citizens must be submitted to a popular vote, the result of which is always binding. New Zealand's provision for citizen-initiated referendums permits citizens to force a vote on an issue, but the outcome of that vote is not binding on the government or parliament.

17. The final category of direct democracy discussed in this Handbook – recall (chapter 5) – is much rarer in practice than either citizens' initiatives or referendums, and its specific provisions and practices can also vary considerably from one jurisdiction to another. It may, for example, apply only to one or more members of the executive – such as the president – or it may extend to a wider range of public officials – legislators or judges, for example. It may involve simply removing an official from office, or it may provide for their replacement at the same time, thereby combining some elements of both representative and direct democracy in the same procedure. In California in 2003, the governor of the state was recalled, and his successor elected at the same time. Typically, a 'recall election' begins in the same manner as a citizens' initiative – with a petition containing a minimum number of signatures. In the California example noted above, the petition leading to the successful recall contained over 1.6 million signatures, more than meeting the legal requirement of 12 per cent of the votes cast for that office in the preceding election. In an attempted recall of the president of Venezuela in 2004, which was unsuccessful, the petition filed contained over 3.4 million signatures – over 1 million more than the minimum required to trigger the recall vote. However, the recall attempt failed in that instance, because 59 per cent of the voters in the following recall election said 'No' (see the case study following this chapter).

Rules and procedures

18. A number of important variations in rules and procedures may also exist within each of the categorizations of direct democracy practice shown in table 1.1. For example, the number of signatures required for a citizens' initiative or recall can vary considerably from one jurisdiction to another. Setting a high minimum will make it more difficult for the process to be used. A lower threshold, in contrast, is likely to result in more initiative votes or recalls being held, but it does not ensure that such efforts will be successful.

Generally, a jurisdiction that wishes to use these processes will want to set the bar low enough for them to be accessible to citizens but sufficiently high to discourage their frivolous use. Likewise, there are many variations regarding the rules and procedures that apply to campaigns conducted within each of these procedures. Turnout quorums exist in many jurisdictions, and these can vary widely. Italy, for example, requires that 50 per cent of its citizens vote in a referendum in order for the result to be valid. In Colombia, the quorum required is 25 per cent. Lithuania has two types of turnout and approval quorums, depending on the nature of the proposal (see box 1.2).

1. Overview

Box 1.2. Direct democracy procedures in Lithuania

A law on referendums was passed by the Supreme Soviet of the Lithuanian Soviet Socialist Republic on 3 November 1989. Article 9 of the constitution stated that 'the most urgent issues relating to the life of the State and the Nation shall be decided by a referendum'. The 1989 law covering referendums called by the Seimas (parliament) and those initiated by citizens was amended many times up to 2000, and was replaced by a new law on referendums in 2002.

Under the 2002 law, a referendum can be initiated by one-quarter of the members of the Seimas, or by 300,000 citizens (*c.* 11.5 per cent of registered electors).

There is a distinction between mandatory referendums and consultative referendums. Mandatory referendums are those which have to be called on specific constitutional issues, as well as those initiated by citizens 'with regard to other laws or provisions thereof'; their result is always binding. Consultative referendums, also initiated by 300,000 citizens, or the Seimas, may be held with respect to 'other issues of utmost importance to the State and the People'; their result is only advisory but must be deliberated in the Seimas.

Validity requirements for the referendum votes differ between the two types of referendums. For a mandatory referendum, in addition to a majority of the votes cast, the required approval quorum has been the approval of 50 per cent of all registered electors, since 2002 the turnout of one-half of the total electorate, and a 'Yes' vote of at least one-third of all registered electors. In a consultative referendum, the validity requirement is also a turnout of 50 per cent of all registered electors and a 'Yes' vote by at least half of the voters who participate (i.e. at least 25 per cent of the total electorate).

In addition, since 1998 a legislative initiative may be proposed by 50,000 registered electors to the Seimas which must consider this proposed law (agenda initiative).

In practice, citizens' initiatives on major issues of constitutional or economic transformation in Lithuania have not resulted in a valid vote. One feature has been strong party control of referendum initiatives. Because of the high level of citizen support required to initiate a referendum, only large political parties have been able to campaign successfully for a particular issue.

19. Double majorities or super majorities are also sometimes required in direct democracy votes. In Australia, for example, not only must a national referendum achieve an overall majority, but it must also obtain a majority in at least four of the six Australian states. In Switzerland, constitutional proposals must be supported by a majority of citizens both nationally and in a majority of the cantons in order to be successful. In a 2005 referendum on electoral reform in the Canadian province of British Columbia, and in a similar referendum in 2007 in Ontario, the referendum law specified that a total vote of 60 per cent of the total votes cast had to be obtained in favour of the proposal in order for the reform to be approved. It further specified that the proposal had to obtain a majority in 60 per cent of the voting constituencies. Thus, even though 57 per cent of voters in British Columbia supported the proposed change, it was deemed to have failed.

20. There are also a substantial number of administrative issues, such as the timing of a referendum or initiative vote (e.g. holding it to coincide with an election) and the wording of the question on the ballot paper (the ballot question). Votes on US ballot propositions, for example, are normally held on the same dates as other elections for public officials, and proposals often appear on the same ballot papers. In Switzerland, however, initiative and referendum votes are held at regular intervals three or four times a year and do not coincide with national elections. These decisions can affect turnout, as voters may be more likely to participate in a general election than in a separate issue vote. On the other hand, the US practice suggests that citizens do not always vote on propositions, even when they appear on the same ballot paper as other public offices. Furthermore, even when participation is higher due to turnout in a general election, a proposal may receive less attention if there are many other items on the ballot paper.

21. Campaign spending and access to the media are further administrative or regulatory issues that must be considered in enacting any initiative, referendum, or recall law. The amount of money spent on a campaign may be subject to regulation, or it may be left entirely to the discretion of those participating in the exercise. Arguments are commonly made in favour of both these views. Fewer restrictions on campaign activities are seen by some as providing for greater democratic freedom. However, others believe that limits on the amount of money that can be spent in support of or in opposition to a

proposal are necessary in order to ensure that the public is informed equally about both sides of an issue. Chapter 7 compares several jurisdictions that employ a 'maximum freedom' model with examples of more regulated regimes.

22. An updated electoral register is an important basis for a legitimate quorum (turnout or approval) in a referendum. Depending on the law, an electoral register may be updated continuously or periodically. An accurate electoral register should remove duplicate and deceased voters and add voters who have reached the minimum voting age. An inaccurate register could distort the voter turnout required for a quorum and thereby undermine the legitimacy of the referendum. In Colombia, the turnout quorum is 25 per cent. In the 2003 referendum, this was not reached, possibly because many people on the electoral register were either no longer alive or migrants who had left the country.

23. Some jurisdictions provide public assistance in the form of financial support for campaigns or free access to the media, while in others no subsidies or other forms of public support are made available to those participating in a referendum or initiative campaign. In some jurisdictions, the government or electoral authority assumes a role in providing information directly to the public, sometimes in the form of a pamphlet or brochure giving information on both sides of an issue. California and Oregon are two US states that have such a provision (see box 7.7 in chapter 7). In California, the state mails a pamphlet to each household summarizing the content of all ballot propositions and giving a synopsis of the arguments advanced by each side. In Oregon, any group or individual who wishes to do so may, on payment of a nominal fee or the filing of a petition, include a statement in the information booklet published by the state. Measures such as these help to neutralize somewhat the effects of disproportionate expenditure of private funds on campaign advertising and other activities.

The impact on representative democracy

24. Direct democracy is often contrasted with representative democracy, although in practice the two concepts are generally complementary to each other. Under pure representative democracy, voters choose which candidates and parties they want to elect and empower those representatives to make decisions on their behalf. Conversely, when direct democracy is used, citizens themselves are able to decide about specific laws and do not need to delegate the decision-making process solely to their elected representatives. For example, in referendums, voters rather than their elected representatives make decisions about constitutional or policy issues; when using citizens' initiatives, voters can actually seek to introduce constitutional or legislative measures themselves. With agenda initiatives, citizens may organize to bring a particular issue to the attention of a legislature or parliament, but no direct vote is held. Finally, the recall tool provides voters with a mechanism by which they can replace their elected representatives if they are not satisfied with their performance, or with the decisions that have been taken on their behalf.

25. Critics of direct democracy sometimes argue that these processes might weaken representative democracy by undermining the role and importance of elected representatives. Referendums can, in some circumstances, provide a means for allowing elected representatives to avoid the necessity of confronting difficult or contentious political issues. Recalls might involve the risk of creating something like permanent election campaigns, diverting the attention of representatives from the responsibilities of their elected office. Frequent use of referendums also acts to create precedents, even when the result of a referendum is non-binding. Once a referendum has been conducted on a particular type of issue, it is sometimes difficult to avoid holding a referendum when a similar issue arises in the future. However, supporters of the use of referendums and initiatives maintain that, in the context of increasing voter apathy and disenchantment, and declining voter turnout, direct democracy can help to re-engage voters in the democratic political process.

26. It is also argued that direct democracy can act as a useful discipline on the behaviour of elected representatives, ensuring that they fully consider the views of voters when taking decisions on their behalf, and that there will thus be a greater correspondence between the views of citizens and the decisions of their representatives. Referendums can provide greater transparency in political decision making. Criteria by which the success of direct democracy as a component of a democratic system might be judged include levels of participation and engagement, or levels of citizen satisfaction with the democratic system. Many advocates of direct democracy argue that greater use of initiatives and referendums can help to engage citizens in the democratic process in ways that elections often do not. However, direct democracy does not in itself guarantee greater citizen participation or engagement. While voter turnout and the quality of citizen participation in many referendums are quite comparable to those found in national elections, in other instances they may fall short of expectations. In other words, both representative and direct democracy can suffer from problems of voter apathy under certain circumstances.

The usage of direct democracy

27. The use of referendums and initiatives has increased dramatically, both in the number of countries employing such devices and in the number of issues being put to a direct vote. These trends have occurred at least partly in response to a growing sense of dissatisfaction with democratic performance in many countries, and to a decline in participation in democratic elections in some. One argument often advanced in favour of referendums is that they can be used to resolve difficult political problems, particularly where political parties are divided over an issue. In such circumstances, holding a referendum can help reach a solution on the issue without splitting the party. Similarly, initiatives may allow citizens to raise issues that may be difficult for a political party to deal with, particularly when its own members are divided on the issue. The use of a referendum in many European countries to determine whether or not to join the EU (nine of the ten countries that joined the EU in 2004 held referendums on the

issue) provides an example of this trend towards the use of direct democracy to resolve important political questions.

28. Referendums have also been important in some instances in establishing new democracies or in managing a transition from authoritarian to democratic rule. Conducting a direct vote on a new constitution, for example, provides a mechanism for legitimizing the document, both in the minds of a country's own citizens and in the international arena. Such votes, however, can also become caught up in party politics, or in questions of government popularity, as was the case in Kenya in its 2005 constitutional referendum (see box 1.3). Referendums might also provide a mechanism for resolving territorial or sovereignty issues, as in cases of secession or the creation of a new state. Many of the former Soviet republics conducted referendums to affirm their independent status following the dissolution of the Soviet Union in 1991. A referendum held in Montenegro in 2006 dissolved the union between Serbia and Montenegro, ending the last remaining ties between the states of the former Yugoslavia. Some referendums, such as that on devolution in Scotland in 1997, are conducted by the national government, while others, such as the two Quebec 'sovereignty' referendums of 1980 and 1995 are conducted by the provincial government. The US territory of Puerto Rico has held three referendums (in 1967, 1993 and 1998) dealing with the question of its political status. Occasionally, referendums are held under international supervision, as in the case of the UN-administered referendum in Timor Leste in 1999.

Box 1.3. Bananas or oranges?
The November 2005 referendum in Kenya on a new constitution

Kenya was ruled by the Kenya African National Union (KANU) as a one-party state from 1969 until 1991, when President Daniel arap Moi yielded to internal and external pressure for political liberalization and accepted multiparty elections. However, the ethnically divided opposition failed to remove KANU from power in elections in 1992 and 1997. In December 2002 President Moi stepped down and Mwai Kibaki, running as the candidate of the 'Rainbow' coalition, defeated the KANU candidate following a campaign that focused on fighting corruption and endorsing constitutional change. His coalition splintered in 2005 because of disagreement over amendment of the constitution, and government defectors joined with KANU to form a new opposition coalition, the Orange Democratic Movement.

On 21 November 2005, a referendum was held on the new constitution proposed by the government. This was the first referendum in Kenya and no previous legislation could be applied. Although the referendum was advisory rather than binding, the government chose to accept the result as if it were binding.

The referendum was organized by the Electoral Commission of Kenya (ECK). After the proposal for the new constitution was published on 22 August, the ECK registered referendum committees, respectively referred to as 'bananas' ('Yes') and 'oranges' ('No'). The question on the ballot paper was 'Are you for or against the ratification of the proposed new constitution?' and voters selected the symbol of a banana if they backed it or an orange if they did not. The ECK set a campaign period of one month, from 21 October to 19 November. The registration of voters lasted for two months, ending on 19 October, and coincided with the period of voter education conducted by the ECK. Both the bananas and the oranges started campaigning weeks before the official campaign period and were criticized for this by the ECK. The 'Oranges' mainly claimed that the proposal failed to limit the president's powers.

As President Kibaki campaigned for the adoption of the new constitution, it is likely in a country with high levels of illiteracy that many voters ignored the complex constitutional details and taken the vote simply as a vote of confidence in his leadership.

The proposed new constitution was rejected by 57 per cent of the votes cast. The voter turnout was 52.4 per cent. The assessment of international observers was that the referendum had been conducted in a peaceful and orderly manner, and that the poll represented the will of the Kenyan people through a process and a vote that were largely free and fair. The independent media covered both sides of the campaign in a balanced manner, but the state-controlled Kenya Broadcasting Corporation was biased in favour of the 'Yes' campaign, according to a report from the Chr. Michelsen Institute, in Bergen, Norway.

Citizen information and competence

29. Direct democracy demands from citizens a relatively high level of knowledge of issues that are sometimes complex. Concerns are often expressed that voters may not always have the capacity or information to make well-informed decisions about the issue at stake, and instead could make ill-considered decisions based on partial knowledge of an issue or the emotion of a campaign, or on the basis or unrelated factors such as feelings about a particular political party or personalities. In some jurisdictions, the government or an independent electoral authority assumes responsibility for providing citizens with detailed information concerning the issues on the ballot paper, while in others this task is left to those involved directly in the campaign. Propositions can be complex. A 2004 California proposal supporting stem cell research, for example, contained within a single measure proposals to establish a new research institute, prohibit cloning, and fund a bond issue (see box 3.3 in chapter 3). Voters therefore had either to accept or reject the entire package.

30. In jurisdictions where direct democracy is common practice, voters are often asked to consider a number of different propositions at the same time. In the United States, the most common complaints from voters about ballot propositions are the sheer number of items appearing on the ballot papers and the sometimes confusing or complex question wording. Arizona voters in the 2006 US congressional elections faced no fewer than 19 ballot propositions, dealing with subjects as diverse as property tax limitation, immigrant rights, smoking bans and same-sex marriage. Swiss voters typically consider three or four proposals at a time, at specific intervals over the course of a year. Even the most conscientious voters may find it difficult to be well informed on a large array of proposals, particularly in jurisdictions where they are competing with candidates in an election for the attention of the electorate.

31. The tactics employed in a referendum or initiative campaign can sometimes inhibit public deliberation of an issue rather than promote it. Opposing sides in an initiative or referendum campaign, whether they be political parties, interest groups, or umbrella committees, aim to win the contest, not always to foster careful deliberation of an issue. The amount of money spent on a campaign may be a factor, particularly when funds are used disproportionately by one side to purchase large amounts of television and print advertising in support of their position. Voters in referendums sometimes complain about insufficient information, confusing question wording, or contradictory lines of argument regarding the possible consequences of a referendum vote. However, referendums also promote greater public responsibility for political decisions, and encourage citizens to become better informed about important issues.

Concerns about minority rights

32. Modern democracy theorists are generally positive about the use of initiatives and referendums to foster greater citizen participation and improve the quality of democracy, but they also raise some warnings. Referendums, and particularly initiatives, could possibly threaten the civil rights of vulnerable minorities or exacerbate racial or ethnic tensions in some societies. Popular majorities might, either deliberately or inadvertently, use the processes of initiative or referendum to deprive unpopular minorities of certain rights. Divided societies may find that the victory of one side over another in a referendum could re-ignite old grievances or create new divisions. In some circumstances, it could be necessary to provide safeguards against the unmitigated power of electoral majorities through protection by the courts or by the specification of majorities other than a simple '50 per cent plus one' of those voting in a referendum. The requirement of double majorities or super majorities is sometimes directed towards protecting minorities.

33. It can also be argued that the existence of instruments of direct democracy can empower minorities, because direct democracy processes provide alternative ways to raise issues that are not necessarily favoured by the majority, particularly the majority within a legislature or parliament. Citizens' initiatives can often be triggered by a small minority of the electorate. In some countries, initiative campaigns are sometimes begun by smaller political parties or groups that have little or no representation in a legislative

assembly. When such an initiative succeeds, it can demonstrate that the power of majorities is not absolute. Thus, the majority/minority question is complex when applied to the instruments of direct democracy. However, it is clear that these instruments are more appropriate in some societies than in others, and their possible consequences for the rights and protection of minorities must be weighed carefully.

Other concerns

34. While most jurisdictions that practise direct democracy do so in an effort to facilitate greater democratic participation of citizens in deciding important issues, and to give political decisions greater democratic legitimacy, other motives are sometimes present. On occasion, referendums or 'plebiscites' have also been employed by authoritarian rulers, either to create a veneer of democratic legitimacy for their actions or to counter domestic political opposition. In authoritarian polities where pressures for democratization exist, referendums might provide, intentionally or unintentionally, an alternative outlet for genuine democratic expression. In modern times, referendums have been employed by regimes such as those of Augusto Pinochet in Chile, Ferdinand Marcos in the Philippines, or Park Chung Hee in South Korea, for purposes that would have been considered at the time to be anti-democratic. Yet it can be argued that some referendums may have actually accelerated the process of democratization. Pinochet unexpectedly lost the 1988 referendum which was intended to extend his term of office, and his regime collapsed shortly thereafter.

35. Initiatives may sometimes be put forward by powerful groups, acting to promote their own economic or social interests, or they may unduly favour those with the money and resources to mount strong campaigns. There can be many different reasons for calling a referendum on a specific issue, or for promoting an initiative. Even in those countries where democratic practices are well entrenched, referendums are sometimes used to postpone or avoid dealing with complex issues, or to gain advantage over political opponents. Initiatives can also be used by powerful interest groups to constrain the powers of the state in harmful ways, or to advantage specific political interests. In the United States particularly, there is a growing literature that is critical of California-style ballot propositions because of such concerns regarding their fairness. On the other hand, direct democratic devices are generally popular with the public in those jurisdictions that use them the most (e.g. California, Switzerland).

Direct democracy in Switzerland

Nadja Braun*

Historical background

The historical roots of direct democracy in Switzerland can be found in pre-modern forms of democracy. There was a living culture of popular assembly democracy and the federative referendum (a referendum that can be triggered by federative entities) dating back to the Middle Ages. Inspiration for direct democracy in Switzerland can also be found in the experience and the ideas of the American and even more of the French revolutions.

The cornerstones of the history of modern direct democracy at the national level are the introduction of the citizens' initiative for a total revision of the constitution and the mandatory constitutional referendum in 1848; of the optional referendum in 1874; and of the citizens' initiative in 1891. After 1891, direct democracy was further extended. The referendum on international treaties was introduced in 1921, and extended in 1977 and 2003. It allows citizens to be involved in decisions on foreign policy. The creation of the so-called resolutive referendum in 1949 restricted the ability of the Federal Assembly to protect decisions from exposure to referendum by declaring them to be 'emergency measures' (in the 1930s the government had used the emergency clause to systematically avoid referendums). The 'double yes' option with a deciding question where there is an initiative and a counter-proposal was introduced in 1987 and extended in 2003.

Direct democracy procedures and legal provisions

Switzerland is a federative state with 26 cantons (individual constituent states) and around 2,740 communes. Swiss voters have the right to cast their votes at the federal, cantonal and local levels. On average, four times a year there are referendums at all three levels.

---

*The opinions expressed in this case study are those of the author and do not reflect any official statement.

The two main pillars of direct democracy in Switzerland are the *citizens' initiative* and the *citizens' demand* (optional/popular referendum).

The legislative framework at the national level

All Swiss citizens, whether living in Switzerland or abroad, who have reached the age of 18 and who are not disqualified on grounds of mental incapacity are entitled to vote in referendums (article 136 of the Swiss federal constitution (FC)). The issues that the people are called to vote on at the federal level are set out in the constitution (articles 138–142 FC). There are no quorum requirements such as a turnout quorum for a referendum to be valid.

The outcome of a referendum – be it an optional or a mandatory referendum – is always binding (articles 142 and 195 FC). A basic distinction is made between mandatory and optional referendums.

A mandatory referendum must be held (article 140 § 1 FC)

- in the event of a total or partial revision of the federal constitution;
- to join a collective security organization (e.g. the United Nations) or a supranational community (e.g. the EU); or
- to introduce urgent federal legislation without the required constitutional basis and which will be in force for longer than a year.

Such a decision requires the approval of both a popular majority and the majority of the cantons. A popular majority means a simple majority of those voting (article 142 § 1 FC). A majority of the cantons is achieved when the popular vote has been in favour of the proposal in a majority of cantons (article 142 § 3 FC). In calculating the majority, the results in six – out of a total of 26 – cantons each count as half a cantonal vote (article 142 § 4 FC).

A referendum is also mandatory (article 140 § 2 FC)

- for citizens' initiatives aimed at a total revision of the federal constitution;
- for citizens' initiatives aimed at a partial revision of the federal constitution which were presented as a general proposal and have been rejected in the Federal Assembly; and
- in order to reach a decision where the Federal Council (the government) and the National Council and the Council of States (the parliament) have disagreed as to whether a total revision of the federal constitution should take place or not.

In the latter three cases, the referendum is decided by a simple majority of the voters.

Swiss citizens who are entitled to vote can propose a partial or total revision of the constitution (articles 138 and 139 FC). Before a citizens' initiative can be officially validated, the signatures of 100,000 citizens who are entitled to vote (corresponding to approximately 2 per cent of the electorate) have to be gathered within 18 months.

A citizens' initiative can be formulated as a general proposal or presented as a fully worked-out text. If the initiative is qualified, a referendum on it is mandatory.

An optional referendum takes place when it is requested within 100 days after the official publication of a statute either by 50,000 citizens (corresponding to approximately 1 per cent of the Swiss electorate) entitled to vote or by eight cantons. The following can be the subject of an optional referendum (article 141 FC):

- federal laws;

- federal laws declared urgent with a validity exceeding one year;

- federal decrees to the extent that the constitution or the law foresee this; and

- international treaties which

  (1) are of unlimited duration and may not be terminated;

  (2) provide for the entry into an international organization
  (e.g. International IDEA); or

  (3) contain important legislative provisions or if their implementation requires provisions in federal laws.

The relevant law, decree or international treaty is approved if the people vote in favour of it (popular majority).

The legislative framework at the cantonal and communal levels

The instruments of initiative and referendum are available to Swiss voters not only at the national (federal) level, but also at the cantonal (regional) and communal (local) levels. Because each canton can choose its own way of allowing citizens to participate, there are extra possibilities: in addition to the constitutional initiative and the legislative referendum, all the cantons except Vaud also have the so-called finance referendum (see the table).

Another important instrument in the cantons is the obligatory legislative referendum, and in the communes the administrative referendum. Some cantons and communes link the referendum question with a popular counter-proposal (the so-called 'constructive referendum'). In the canton of Zurich there is the individual (agenda) initiative. In addition, citizens in several cantons have the right of recall of the administration. In other words, the lower the political level, the more opportunities citizens have to be directly involved in decision making.

The regulatory framework governing direct democracy instruments

In Switzerland, federal elections and federal direct democracy instruments are managed by the executive branch through the Federal Chancellery. However, the Federal Chancellery (national level) does not do this on its own, but jointly with the 26 cantonal electoral management bodies.

The organization of referendum votes

The national polling days are appointed according to the rules laid down in article 10 of the Federal Law on Political Rights (FLP) of 17 December 1976 and article 2a of the Decree on Political Rights (DPR) of 24 May 1978). Federal referendum votes are not held during federal elections. A minimum of four months before polling day, the Federal Council (government) determines which proposals are to be submitted to the vote. The Federal Chancellery provides the cantons with the proposals to be submitted to a vote of the people and the ballot papers (article 11 FLP).

The Federal Council explains each proposal that is put to the vote in a so-called referendum booklet. It has to include the arguments of the committee responsible for the initiative or referendum (article 11 FLP). It is published by the Federal Chancellery in the four official languages and sent to the cantons for distribution to all eligible voters.

Each canton is responsible for the conduct of the vote within its own territory and has its own regulations (article 10 FLP). These regulations sometimes vary considerably. For example, four cantons have one or more centralized electoral registers, while the other 22 cantons have decentralized registers, that is, the communes keep the electoral registers.

The federal law requires that all voters receive the documents required in order to cast a valid vote at a minimum three and at the earliest four weeks prior to the polling day (article 11 FLP). The cantons have to execute this provision but the way they do this is up to them and also depends – among other things – on whether the canton or a commune in that canton decides to organize another referendum vote on the same day.

The management of the polling stations is also organized by the cantons or communes. After the vote, the cantons collect reports on the popular ballots from each polling station, compile the provisional results from the entire canton, and notify the Federal Chancellery of the results. The Federal Chancellery then validates the results and prepares the decision of the Federal Council, which determines the results of the overall vote.

Administering citizens' demands (popular/optional referendums)

The request for a popular referendum must be submitted to the Federal Chancellery before expiry of the referendum period, furnished with the required number of signatures and the certificates of eligibility to vote (article 59a FLP). Certificates of eligibility to vote are issued by cantonal or communal offices (article 59a FLP). These offices certify that the signatories are eligible to vote on federal matters. After expiry of the referendum period (100 days), the Federal Chancellery checks the validity of the signature lists and establishes whether the signature list contains the required number of valid signatures.

Administering citizens' initiatives

Prior to the start of the collection of signatures, the Federal Chancellery checks the signature list and declares in a ruling whether the signature list corresponds to the form prescribed by law (article 69 FLP). This preliminary check by the Federal Chancellery includes checking whether the title of an initiative is misleading, or if it contains commercial advertising or personal publicity or gives rise to confusion; and examining whether the text of the initiative is the same in all the official languages. This usually means that the Chancellery translates the text of the initiative.

The Federal Chancellery does not check the content or wording of the initiative text. Both the title and the text of a citizens' initiative are determined by the proponents of the initiative. However, the proponents do not have an entirely free hand: they must bear in mind certain restrictions on what can be proposed arising from national and international law. The constitution states that, in the case of a popular initiative for a partial revision of that constitution, 'If an initiative does not respect the principle of unity of form, the principle of unity of subject matter, or mandatory rules of international law, the Federal Parliament shall declare the initiative invalid, in whole or in part' (cf. article 139 § 3 FC).

After the preliminary check, the Federal Chancellery publishes the title and text of the initiative, together with the names of the authors (i.e. the members of the initiative committee) in the *Official Federal Gazette* (article 69 FLP). Starting from the day of publication in the *Official Federal Gazette*, the initiative committee has to collect 100,000 signatures and get the certificates of eligibility to vote of the signatures on the signature lists from the cantonal/communal offices within 18 months.

After expiry of the period allowed for the collection of signatures, the Federal Chancellery checks the validity of the signature lists and establishes whether the popular initiative contains the required number of valid signatures. The Federal Chancellery publishes the ruling on the success of the signature lists in the *Official Federal Gazette* together with details of the numbers of valid and invalid signatures for each canton (article 72 FLP).

The financing of the use of direct democracy instruments

In Switzerland, there is no public assistance for campaigners. The initiative or referendum committee is granted space (one page) in the official voters' pamphlet.

There has been a debate in recent years over the financing of referendum campaigns. According to one political scientist, Claude Longchamp, it takes 'around 10 million francs' to organize a professional national citizens' initiative from the initial launch through the actual campaign to tying up all the loose ends after the vote. On the other hand, the example of the 'Sunday Initiative' shows that it can be done with considerably less money: although the group campaigning for 'four car-free Sundays per year' had no more than 50,000 Swiss francs (CHF) with which to campaign, they still managed to get 37.6 per cent of the votes. Even in those cases where wealthy interest groups are involved, there is no evidence that money can directly influence referendum results in Switzerland. Quite the opposite: there are plenty of cases where, despite the spending of large amounts of money, voters went against the majority of the political or financial elites.

The use of direct democracy in Switzerland

How direct democracy procedures have been used and on what issues

The tools of direct democracy are growing in popularity. Since 2000, an average of 10.8 national issues have been voted on per year, compared to 10 in 1990–99 and 6.2 in 1980–89.

Between 1980 and the time of writing (June 2008), a total of 200 constitutional initiatives were started at the national level. Of these 200, 73 did not achieve a sufficient number of valid signatures. Of the 127 initiatives that did achieve the necessary number of valid signatures, 82 were voted on, 29 were withdrawn by the initiative committee shortly before the vote, two were declared invalid by the parliament, and 14 are currently pending at an earlier stage of the process. Over the same period, at the national level, 72 citizen-demanded referendums achieved the necessary number of valid signatures and were voted on.

The issues on which the people are called to vote at the federal level are set out in the constitution (articles 138–142 FC). Except for the invalidity criteria for initiatives, no topics are excluded from a vote – provided the formal conditions are fulfilled.

Coverage of the use of direct democracy instruments by the media

The public broadcasting stations are in a rather special position as regards their reporting of referendum processes: unlike in the private media, the chief editors of the three national radio and television stations make no specific recommendations. Although there is no advertising on public radio, television is partially financed by advertising. However, political advertising is banned. In their dealings with initiatives and referendums, the public broadcast media follow an internally devised code of conduct – the 'handbook of journalism' – which is designed to ensure accuracy, impartiality and fairness.

Voter participation in direct democracy votes, and an analysis of the political dynamic of campaigns related to such votes

Until the end of World War II, at the national level, average voter turnout was around 50 per cent. Between 1960 and the mid-1980s it fell to below 40 per cent, but since the late 1980s it has increased again – up to around 45 per cent. The single most important factor for mobilizing voters is the referendum topic. Accordingly participation varies from one referendum to the next.

Voter education regarding the subject of a referendum is done by means of the referendum booklet. The little red booklet is mailed out to all registered electors, together with the voting slips and the certificate of entitlement to vote. Initiative and referendum committees can draft their own arguments and have them included in the booklet. The government recommends whether the initiative or referendum should be accepted or rejected. The government is not actually allowed to campaign, but it is its duty to give information to the voters. The fact that the four major political parties are represented in the government ensures that the information presented to the voters is balanced.

The experience of Switzerland: lessons learned, problems and controversies regarding the use of direct democracy procedures

The number of signatures required for citizens' initiatives and optional referendums and the collection deadlines have been the subject of political debate for many years. On several occasions the government has proposed raising the signature quorums for initiatives and referendums, and initiative committees have demanded a reduction in the time allowed to the authorities to process initiatives. The proposal to cut the time allowances suffered a clear defeat at the ballot box, and the plan to increase the signature quorums did not even get through the parliament. Although the signature quorum remained the same, it has not become any easier to collect the 100,000 signatures required for a national citizens' initiative. Quite the opposite: it has actually become harder. The trend towards more postal voting has adversely affected the traditional method of collecting signatures outside voting centres.

In terms of the modernization of direct democracy, the government is also looking at the possibility of using the Internet. The first regular referendum at which e-voting was allowed took place on 14 January 2003 in the small community of Anières in the canton of Geneva. Since then several tests were carried out during national referendums in the cantons of Geneva, Neuchâtel and Zurich.

Figure 1. Voter turnout, 1995–2005

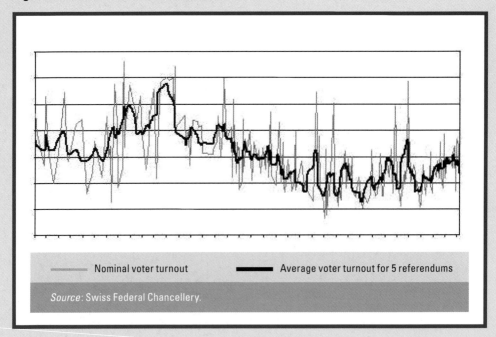

Nominal voter turnout   Average voter turnout for 5 referendums

Source: Swiss Federal Chancellery.

Table 1. Direct democracy instruments in the Swiss cantons as of December 2004

Canton	Constitutional referendum Mandatory	Legislative referendum Mandatory	Legislative referendum Optional	Finance referendum Mandatory	Finance referendum Optional	Administrative referendum Mandatory	Administrative referendum Optional	Initiatives
Zurich	•	•	•		•			•
Bern	•		•		•		•	•
Lucerne	•		•	•	•			•
Uri	•	•		•	•		•	•
Schwyz	•	•	•	•				•
Obwalden	•		•		•			•
Nidwalden	•		•	•	•	•		•
Glarus	•	•		•		•		•
Zug	•		•		•			•
Freiburg	•		•	•	•			•
Solothurn	•	•	•	•	•	•	•	•
Basle (city)	•		•		•		•	•
Basle (county)	•	•	•		•			•
Schaffhausen	•	•	•	•	•	•	•	•
Appenzell Ausserrhoden	•	•	•	•				•
Appenzell Innerrhoden	•	•		•	•			•
Sankt Gallen	•		•	•	•			•
Graubünden	•		•	•	•			•
Aargau	•	•	•		•			•
Thurgau	•		•	•	•			•
Ticino	•		•		•			•
Vaud	•	•	•					•
Valais	•		•		•			•
Neuchâtel	•		•		•			•
Geneva	•		•		•			•
Jura	•		•	•	•			•

Source: Swiss Federal Chancellery.

CASE STUDY

Direct democracy in Venezuela

Miriam Kornblith

Recent experience and the regulatory framework

Hugo Chávez was elected president of Venezuela for the first time in December 1998. His main promise during the electoral campaign had been to convene a Constituent Assembly and enact a new constitution which would allow for the consolidation of a participatory democracy. The constitutional process took place throughout 1999 and unfolded in three electoral phases: the consultative referendum of 25 April 1999 to call an Asamblea Nacional Constitutyente (ANC) or National Constituent Assembly; the election of representatives to the ANC in July 1999; and the consultative referendum of 15 December 1999 to approve the draft constitution drawn up by the ANC. These electoral events took place within the legal framework of the 1961 constitution and the Organic Law on the Suffrage and Political Participation of 1997, which introduced the consultative referendum at the national level.

With the 1999 constitution approved, a series of other events associated with direct democracy took place – the consultative referendum on the renewal of the trade union leadership on 3 December 2000; the failed attempts to initiate a consultative referendum to demand the president's resignation during 2002 and 2003 and a presidential recall referendum (PRR) in 2003; the PRR of 15 August 2004; and, finally, the referendum of 2 December 2007 on reform of the 1999 constitution.

The regulatory framework of direct democracy

In the 1999 constitution, democracy was conceived as 'participatory and protagonistic', in contrast to representative democracy. The constitution established several direct democracy instruments, including consultative referendums, referendums to repeal and approve national and international laws and to amend or reform the constitution, and recall. The recall was given privileged status in the 1999 constitution. The government of Venezuela is defined as democratic, participatory, elective, decentralized, responsible and pluralist, and its mandate can be recalled.

The presidential recall referendum of 15 August 2004

According to the 1999 constitution, when half the term of office of an elected official whose mandate the voters want to recall has elapsed, at least 20 per cent of the registered electors of the corresponding electoral district can demand a recall referendum. When (a) a number of voters that is greater than or equal to those who elected the person in question votes in favour of his or her recall, (b) at least 25 per cent of registered electors participate in the recall referendum, and (c) the votes in favour of the recall outnumber those against it, the official is considered recalled and will be replaced according to the law.

The end of the first half of President Chávez' term of office fell on 19 August 2003. A call for a recall before the fourth year in government should lead to the election of a new leader within 30 days, but if the recall occurs after four full years the vacancy must be filled by the executive vice-president. The Supreme Court of Justice has never clarified whether a president whose mandate has been revoked has the right to stand again as a candidate in order to complete his term in office.

The number of signatures needed to validate a demand for a PRR was 2.4 million, and the number of votes required for an actual recall was 3.8 million. This figure also has to exceed the number of votes in favour of keeping the president in office.

The recall process

The first attempt to recall President Chávez took place on 20 August 2003. Different organizations opposed to the president, united under an umbrella body called the Democratic Coordinator, filed 3.2 million signatures on petitions demanding the activation of the PRR with the Consejo Nacional Electoral (CNE, National Electoral Council), the electoral management body (EMB). The newly appointed CNE was composed of five members. Although it should be an impartial body, it was made up of three members identified with the ruling coalition, and two with the opposition forces (and the ten substitute members with similar affiliations). The CNE evaluated the request for a PRR and rejected it by three votes to two for 'failing to comply with essential formalities'.

On 25 September 2003 the CNE approved the rules to regulate the recall referendum. This regulation shaped the process significantly. It legalized the interference of the CNE in all phases of the recall referendum and the discretionary nature of such interference; established a complex process for checking the petitions; provided for the automation of the process; and introduced a timetable which unnecessarily prolonged the entire process to six months (in practice it took 11 months). The process unrolled in three phases: the collection of petitions; the checking of the petitions and the handling of objections to them; and the convening and carrying out of the PRR.

The collection of signatures

Between 21 and 24 November 2003, signatures were collected to recall the mandate of opposition deputies, and between 28 November and 1 December 2003 signatures were collected to recall government deputies and the president. The CNE took more than a month to organize the process, and the legality and efficiency of its work were much disputed.

On 19 December 2003, the Democratic Coordinator presented the CNE with 3.4 million signatures. This number comfortably exceeded the number needed by nearly 1 million. The responsibility for collecting and processing the forms containing the signatures and individual petitions lay with Súmate, a civil society organization.

The checking of the petitions

According to the regulations, the checking and validation of petitions must be completed within 30 days and starts when the CNE receives them. In practice, however, this was extended by over 100 days, and only on 2 March 2004 did the CNE announce the preliminary results of this phase.

The regulations on the checking of signatures were approved in September and November 2003. When the checking of the petitions started and the initial criteria were applied (albeit in an arbitrary manner), it was clear that there were enough petitions to call the PRR. The pro-government members of the CNE then promoted a procedure to invalidate signatures on a massive scale, fabricating the criterion of *planillas planas* (forms containing similar signatures) – 'signatures in similar writing' or 'aided forms'. By applying retroactively an instruction that was produced only at the end of February 2004, around 1 million signatures were invalidated. This decision generated the greatest controversy of the whole process and caused violent disturbances and protests against the CNE's decision, some resulting in fatalities. The representatives of the observation missions of the Organization of American States (OAS) and of the Carter Center objected to this criterion. This issue caused a major confrontation between the electoral and constitutional chambers of the Supreme Court of Justice, the former opposing the CNE's decision and the latter backing it.

On 2 March 2004 the pro-government majority on the CNE approved the resolution applying the *planillas planas* criterion and others that were equally doubtful, and recognized only 1.8 million of the signatures as valid. However, tremendous pressure from the country and the international community against this decision caused the CNE to agreed to submit the *planillas planas* to 'ratification' and not cancel them, as was the initial intention.

The lack of professionalism and the poor level of security in the checking of signatures were even more obvious given the profusion of databases containing the results of the verification. The first 'final' database, which upheld the resolution of the CNE, was submitted on 10 March, and the fourth 'final' database on 23 April, after which two further databases were generated. Between the first and the fourth database, 956,268 signatures changed status—an inexplicable situation given that according to the first announcement only 78,701 petitions still needed to be checked.

Objections to the petitions

Around 1.1 million voters whose petitions were considered to be *planas* (in similar handwriting) had the 'right' to ratify them, but 375,241 voters whose petitions were rejected without any clear grounds did not have the right to object. The CNE conceded the right to 'change' to those petitioners who supposedly changed their opinion between November 2003 and June 2004. Once again, the international observation missions disputed this decision.

Objections were lodged between 28 May and 1 June 2004. Voters were coerced into withdrawing their signatures (some 91,000 did so) or not ratifying them. Finally, on 9 June 2004, almost six months after the petitions had been presented, the CNE recognized the existence of 2.5 million valid signatures to activate the PRR, and it was called.

The calling and running of the recall

The date chosen for the recall referendum was 15 August, the last available Sunday before the end of the fourth year of the presidential term. The question asked was 'Do you agree with recalling the mandate, conferred by legitimate democratic elections, of Mr Hugo Chávez Frías, as president of the Bolivarian Republic of Venezuela for the current presidential term of office?'. Contrary to conventional practice, the 'No' option was placed first on the ballot paper.

To carry out the automation of the election process, in conditions that were hardly transparent, the CNE contracted the Smartmatic-Bizta-Cantv consortium, which did not have previous election experience. Automated touch-screen voting was introduced for the first time in Venezuela using lottery machines transformed into voting machines. Digital fingerprint-reading machines were incorporated, supposedly to detect cases of multiple voting – something that gave rise to misgivings about the protection of the secrecy of the vote.

The names of the voters who signed the petitions to recall the president and the government deputies were given by the CNE to the pro-government party and were published on the web page of Luis Tascon, a deputy of the ruling party in the National Assembly. The voters included in Tascon's list suffered discrimination, lost their jobs in the public sector, were refused official documentation and were pressed to withdraw their petitions.

Moreover, throughout the first semester of 2004 more than 2 million new voters were included in the electoral registers, many of whom had not followed the legal procedures for obtaining their identification cards and did not fulfil all the necessary criteria. This massive inclusion of new and dubious voters reshaped the composition of the electoral register and created great suspicion about the reliability of the registration lists used for the recall referendum.

The day of the referendum was chaotic. From an organizational point of view, this was the worst electoral event in Venezuela's long experience of elections. There were long queues at the voting centres for many reasons: the massive turnout; inefficient 're-engineering' of the voting centres and polling stations; the introduction of fingerprint-reading machines; deficiencies in the training of polling staff; last-minute mobilization of voters by government officials; and more. Officially, polling stations close at 4 pm, but voting was extended on several successive occasions and some stations stayed open until past midnight.

The strong political polarization and the fact that voters were aware of the importance of their decision and highly motivated accounted for the patience with which they bore the completely unjustifiable conditions in which the voting took place.

The results of the recall

The final official figures were 5.8 million 'No' votes (59 per cent of valid votes) and 4 million 'Yes' votes (41 per cent of valid votes). Turnout was 70 per cent. The results showed the stability of political preferences (for the government in power and the opposition) compared to the previous elections and the continued polarization of opinion. Both sides had mobilized all the resources they could and achieved their best performance since 1998; the combined effects of polarization, the increase in the size of the electoral register and the reduction in the abstention rate generated an absolute and relative increase in the turnout of both sides.

The results of the PRR were controversial. Leaders of the Democratic Coordinator claimed that there had been massive electoral fraud, although the OAS and the Carter Center observation missions endorsed the official results. Perceptions were closely linked to the polarization of society: in October 2004, 96 per cent of those who felt that there had been fraud identified with the opposition, and the 96 per cent who accepted the results identified with the government.

The aftermath of the recall

In December 2007, the electorate voted on a proposal to reform the 1999 constitution and rejected it by 51 per cent of the vote. The proposal aimed at reforming 69 articles of the current constitution. Thirty-two articles were initially presented by the president and the National Assembly added the remaining articles. Among the changes, the legislators proposed to increase the number of signatures and the turnout required for a recall referendum to be called and approved. In the case of the recall, the legislators proposed to increase to 30 per cent the proportion of registered electors needed to demand a recall and to 40 per cent of registered electors the participation threshold required to validate a recall referendum.

Assessment: the opportunities and risks of direct democracy

Contrary to the expectations generated both in and outside the country, the 2004 PRR did not succeed in alleviating the tensions or reducing the degree of polarization in the country, nor did it rebuild confidence in Venezuela's institutions or elections. The activation of the PRR in circumstances which did not guarantee pluralism and transparent decision making eroded the institutional strength and democratic beliefs of the country even further, reinforced the existing polarization, undermined the voting and failed to convince the losers.

Instruments of direct democracy were used again in Venezuela during 2007. Very few voters participated in the processes to recall some governors and mayors. In a tight electoral contest, the voters rejected the attempt to reform the 1999 constitution in order to establish a socialist state and economy, grant indefinite re-election to the president and introduce restrictive conditions on the calling and approval of referendums, among other changes. Although some improvements were achieved in the organization of the electoral processes compared to the 2004 recall referendum, much remains to be done in terms of institutional fairness and equilibrium if the full meaning and potential of direct democracy are to be realized.

CHAPTER 2

CHAPTER 2

When the authorities call a referendum: design and political considerations

36. Referendums may be called either by political authorities or by a number of citizens. This chapter deals with referendums called by the political authorities, whereas chapter 3 deals with referendums called by citizens – generally called initiatives. In this chapter the political authorities are defined, different institutional designs are presented, and various procedural aspects are discussed. Finally, a number of recommendations are offered.

37. Political authorities are defined in this chapter as the executive and legislative institutions of government. At the national level the executive may consist of a president and/or a prime minister and cabinet, and the legislative institutions of the parliament or congress, or whatever the law-making institution representing the people is called. At the regional and local level the political authorities will generally consist of similar institutions – at the executive level a state governor, provincial premier or mayor, and at the legislative level a state or provincial legislature, parliament or council. The decision to call a referendum may rest with one of these, such as the president, and be taken under specific constitutional authority, or it may be a political decision taken by the president or prime minister in consultation with the cabinet, or by a vote of the parliament or legislature. In some jurisdictions, the authority to call a referendum may be specified in a constitution, while in others referendums may be called through legislative acts or executive orders.

38. The political authorities may call referendums either indirectly or directly. They call a referendum indirectly when they choose to make a decision that requires a referendum according to the constitution or ordinary legislation. Such mandatory referendums may be required on specific issues or in specific situations, such as a policy decision which by its nature raises a constitutional question. In such instances, the authorities may of course choose not to deal with the issue or to circumvent the requirement in one way or another. If they do decide to put an issue to a referendum, the authorities control the agenda, but they do not initiate the referendum directly. The authorities call a

referendum directly when they are not obliged to do so according to the constitution or ordinary legislation, but choose to do so for political or other reasons. Such optional referendums might be initiated by the executive, by a majority in the legislature, or in some instances by a minority in the legislature.

39. Mandatory and optional referendums called by the authorities were first introduced during the French Revolution in the 1790s. Napoleon I used referendums to obtain popular approval as he took power, first as consul, and later as consul for life and emperor. During the 1850s, Napoleon III also used referendums to legitimize his assumption of power. In more recent times, the instrument has been used by presidents or other executive authorities for consultative purposes or to obtain popular approval for their policies. Mandatory referendums on constitutional changes were introduced in Switzerland in 1848 and have since been adopted in many countries throughout the world. In recent decades, more countries have begun to use the referendum as either a consultative or constitutional device, and its usage has become more frequent in many jurisdictions. Figure 2.1 illustrates the distribution of mandatory and optional referendums at the national level in various parts of the world today.

Figure 2.1. Countries which have provision for mandatory and optional referendums, by region

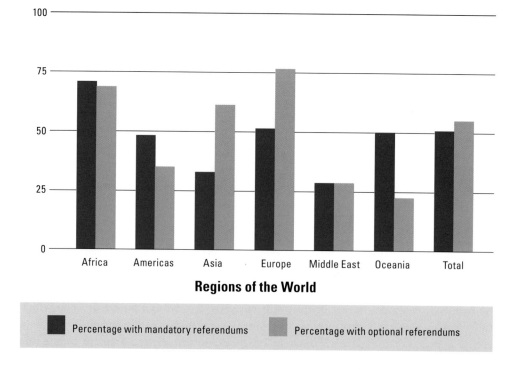

Institutional design

40. A mandatory referendum is a vote of the electorate which is called automatically under particular circumstances as defined in the constitution or ordinary legislation. Such circumstances may arise either through the nature of the issue, for instance an amendment to the constitution, or from the situation in which the decision is adopted, for instance, when the president and the legislative assembly disagree on a specific proposal. Mandatory referendums are quite widespread: about half of all countries have provisions for mandatory referendums of some sort.

41. Mandatory referendums may be required in relation to certain types of predetermined subjects. Typically, these are issues of major political significance, such as constitutional amendments, the adoption of international treaties, the transfer of authority to international or supranational bodies, or other issues concerning national sovereignty or national self-determination. In countries such as Australia, Denmark, Japan, Switzerland, Uruguay and Venezuela, all constitutional amendments have to be approved by referendum, and in countries such as Austria, Iceland, Malta, Peru and Spain this is the case for certain constitutional amendments. In Switzerland certain international treaties have to be approved by a referendum, and in Denmark a transfer of authority to international or supranational bodies requires a referendum unless it is passed by a five-sixths majority in the parliament. In Europe, a number of referendums held on European Union issues have been mandatory because they involve an amendment to a country's constitution, as is the case in the Republic of Ireland.

Box 2.1. Mandatory referendums: the Republic of Ireland's two referendums on the Treaty of Nice

The Treaty of Nice was formally signed by the (then) 15 members of the EU at Nice, France, on 26 February 2001. The aim of the treaty was to determine how power should be shared out within the institutions of the EU after enlargement to 27 member states.

The Republic of Ireland was the only one of the 15 member states in which a referendum on the treaty was mandatory. The referendum was set for 7 June 2001. Because accession to treaties involving any transfer of sovereignty in the Republic of Ireland requires amendment of the constitution, the question put to voters was as follows:

'Do you approve of the proposal to amend the Constitution contained in the undermentioned Bill?

Twenty-fourth Amendment of the Constitution Bill, 2001.

Art. 29 Abs. 4 Lines 7 and 8:

The State may ratify the Treaty of Nice amending the Treaty on European Union, the Treaties establishing the European Communities and certain related Acts signed at Nice on the 26 February, 2001.

The State may exercise the options or discretions provided by or under Articles 1.6, 1.9, 1.11, 1.12, 1.13 and 2.1 of the Treaty referred to in subsection 7 but any such exercise shall be subject to the prior approval of both Houses of the Oireachtas [parliament].'

Unexpectedly, the Irish voters rejected the Nice Treaty by 54 per cent to 46 per cent. Turnout was low, at only 35 per cent. Two other measures – the abolition of the death penalty in the Republic of Ireland and recognition of the International Criminal Court – were also voted on at the same time, and were both approved. The campaign waged against the Nice Treaty had been vigorous, while that in its favour had been more restrained. In part, this was because the government, which supported the Treaty of Nice, was prohibited by Irish electoral laws from actively campaigning for it.

The rejection of the treaty precipitated a political crisis, both in the Republic of Ireland and in the EU more generally. The treaty could not come into force until all the member states had ratified it, and the Republic of Ireland was not in a position to renegotiate it unilaterally. It became clear that a second referendum would be necessary. Ratification of the treaty by other member states made the issue of potential Irish isolation a more central issue in the campaign leading up to the second referendum, which took place on 19 October 2002. Moreover, the campaign waged by the political parties and other groups supporting the 'Yes' side was much stronger than it had been in the first referendum. With a higher turnout (49 per cent), the Nice Treaty was approved in the second referendum by a margin of 63 per cent to 37 per cent.

42. Certain types of issue, such as taxes and public expenditures, are often excluded from being the subject of mandatory referendums. The requirement for, or exclusion of, mandatory referendums on specific issues is usually contained in a jurisdiction's constitution, but may also be specified by ordinary legislation. One example of a constitutional specification of the subjects that are excluded from referendums is found in article 42 of the Danish constitution (see box 2.2). In the absence of such a specification of the types of issue on which a referendum is mandatory, or those which are excluded, the government may from time to time determine, according to its own priorities, what is appropriate for a referendum.

> **Box 2.2. Article 42 of the Danish constitution**
>
> • Finance Bills, Supplementary Appropriation Bills, Provisional Appropriation Bills, Government Loan Bills, Civil Servants (Amendment) Bills, Salaries and Pensions Bills, Naturalization Bills, Expropriation Bills, Taxation (Direct and Indirect) Bills, as well as Bills introduced for the purpose of discharging existing treaty obligations shall not be submitted to decision Referendum.

43. Mandatory referendums may also be required in certain predetermined situations. One example is in a presidential system where, in the event of disagreement between the president and legislature, a referendum may be required to resolve the dispute. Thus, if the president of Iceland rejects a bill that has been passed by the parliament (the Althing), it remains valid but must be submitted to a referendum for approval or rejection as soon as circumstances permit. The law shall become void if it is rejected by the voters, but otherwise remains in force. In Chile, the president of the republic may, if she or he entirely objects to a proposed amendment approved by the Congress, consult the citizens through a referendum, which in the terminology of that country is called a plebiscite. Another example is when decisions on certain issues, such as a transfer of national sovereignty, require a qualified parliamentary majority, and if that is not obtained then a referendum is required; this is the case in Denmark, where a five-sixths majority in parliament is required for a transfer of national sovereignty to international organizations. Otherwise a referendum must take place.

44. Mandatory referendums are usually restricted to what are generally considered very important political issues. Too many referendums may reduce political efficiency and affect political stability. Referendums are costly in terms of money, time and political attention, and the use of such resources needs to be considered carefully. If frequent referendums result in too many changes of policies and rules they may contribute to an unstable political situation where citizens find themselves living in an environment of uncertainty.

45. The second category of referendum is the optional referendum. This involves a vote of the electorate which does not have to be held by law but can be initiated by the executive, by a specified number of members of the legislature, and in some cases by other political actors. The main examples are optional referendums initiated by the executive branch of government, either the president or the prime minister and cabinet. Optional referendums initiated by the executive or legislature may take several forms. In terms of legal regulations, they may either be pre-regulated by constitutional rules or otherwise legally prescribed norms about the use of referendums, or they may be ad hoc, with the particular rules to be followed being specified at the time the referendum is called.

46. Some jurisdictions regulate optional referendums by law, and when this is the case the regulations that apply are usually specified in the constitution or in a referendum law. In Spain, political decisions of special importance may be submitted for a consultative referendum. According to the constitution, the king may call a referendum at the request of the president of the government following authorization by the Congress of Deputies. In France, the president is given a fairly free hand. According to article 11 of the French constitution, the president may submit to a referendum any government bill 'which deals with the organization of the public authorities, or with reforms relating to the economic or social policy of the Nation and to the public services contributing thereto, or which provides for authorization to ratify a treaty that, although not contrary to the constitution, would affect the functioning of the institutions' (see also box 7.1 on the French referendum on the EU Constitutional Treaty). In Russia, the authority given to the president is almost unregulated, as the constitution only stipulates (in article 84) that the president shall 'call a referendum under procedures established by federal constitutional law'. In Austria, according to article 43 of the constitution, a majority of members of the House of Representatives may demand that an enactment of the House of Representatives be submitted to a referendum. It is also possible – as in Argentina – for the constitution to give both the legislative and the executive branch the right to initiate referendums. In some US states, the legislative branch may submit legislation to a referendum in order to circumvent a possible veto by the governor or for other political reasons (see box 2.3).

Box 2.3. Using a referendum to influence elections: Virginia's 2006 proposal to define marriage in the state constitution

In recent years voters in many of the US states have faced the question whether to ban same-sex marriage. The actual question put to voters is whether to define marriage constitutionally as 'a union between one man and one woman', but the effect and clear understanding among voters is to ban same-sex marriage. In Virginia, the voters faced this question in 2006 in what some observers saw as an attempt to draw conservative voters to the polls to aid Republican candidates. Virginia was a critical state for both of the major political parties in 2006 as one of the most closely fought US Senate campaigns in the nation was also on the ballot paper.

In 1997, the Virginia legislature passed a statute declaring any same-sex marriage from another state void in Virginia. In 2004, the legislature passed another statute prohibiting 'civil unions or similar arrangements between members of the same sex, including arrangements created by private contract'. Also during 2004, voters in 13 other states approved bans on same-sex marriage, and there is some evidence that such proposals increased turnout among conservative voters.

Even though the legal status of same-sex marriage in Virginia was not in doubt, the 2006 legislature referred a constitutional amendment to the voters. Some observers saw this as a move by the Republican-controlled state legislature to boost voter turn out among conservative voters in an attempt to influence the US Senate election. The Republican Party controlled the Senate, but the widespread unpopularity of the Iraq War and of President George W. Bush led many to believe that the Democrats could win enough seats in 2006 to take control of the Senate.

The incumbent US Senator in Virginia, George Allen, a Republican, included his support for the marriage amendment in his speeches and contrasted his position with that of his opponent, Democrat Jim Webb, who opposed the amendment. 'We think Senator Allen is on the same side as the majority of Virginians', Allen spokesperson Dick Wadhams told the *Washington Post* on 26 April 2006.

In the end, even though opponents of the measure spent more than three times as much on the campaign than its promoters, the amendment passed by 57 to 43 per cent. Turnout was 53 per cent of registered electors, an increase of 9 per cent over that of a similar off-year election in 2002. If Republicans placed the amendment on the ballot to help ensure Senator Allen's re-election, they failed. Nevertheless, the race was exceedingly close: Webb defeated Senator Allen by 9,329 votes out of 2.4 million votes cast, a difference of less than 0.4 per cent, giving overall control of the US Senate to the Democrats.

47. Optional ad hoc referendums are those that are not regulated in the constitution or in any permanent legislation. In parliamentary systems the decision to hold an ad hoc referendum on a specific issue is generally made by the majority of the legislature by passing a specific law to authorize the holding of a referendum. In Norway, for example, the constitution contains nothing about referendums and the legislative assembly (the Storting) decides not only whether to hold a referendum, but also the details of its implementation. The United Kingdom (UK) has no written constitution, but the Political Parties, Elections and Referendums Act of 2000 sets out the legal framework under which national and/or regional referendums may be held and assigns a number of administrative responsibilities to the Electoral Commission. Nevertheless, parliament must pass a specific law in each instance in order for a referendum to be held. In presidential systems, either the executive may be given a general right to call referendums (as in Azerbaijan and Russia), or the president may act without any specific constitutional authority, as happened in Chile in 1978 when President Augusto Pinochet called a referendum asking the voters to support him.

48. Political authorities might decide to initiate a referendum for several reasons. Referendums are sometimes called by executives to resolve divisions within a governing

party or coalition. Such referendums are motivated by two somewhat different kinds of goal – to use the referendum as a mediation device between competing factions, or to avoid the electoral repercussions of a divisive issue. By announcing a referendum, the executive seeks to depoliticize a specific issue by taking it out of an election campaign. Optional referendums initiated by the executive have been held frequently in Europe on issues such as European integration.

Box 2.4. Referendum by decree of the president of Azerbaijan 'On Conducting a Referendum on Amending the Constitution of the Azerbaijan Republic'

'Taking into consideration of the necessity of amending to the Constitution of the Azerbaijan Republic with new provisions arising from the fact that the Azerbaijan Republic has joined the European Convention on Protection of Human Rights and Fundamental Freedoms, and implementation of courts reforms, and which are related to activities of the Milli Majlis and improvement of the election system of the Azerbaijan Republic, and in accordance with the Constitution of the Azerbaijan Republic, Article 3, Section II, Item 1 and Article 109, Item 19, I hereby decree the following:

1. Draft Referendum Act 'On Amending the Constitution of the Azerbaijan Republic' shall be put on for referendum (the draft is enclosed).

2. The Referendum shall be appointed to August 24, 2002.

3. The Draft Referendum Act of the Azerbaijan Republic 'On Amending the Constitution of the Azerbaijan Republic' shall be published within 48 hours effective the day of signing of this Decree.

4. The Central Election Commission of the Azerbaijan Republic shall ensure conducting of the nationwide voting (referendum) on the date, specified by Item 2 of the present Decree.

5. The Cabinet of Ministers of the Azerbaijan Republic shall be assigned to carry out the necessary measures related to finance of the nationwide voting (referendum).

6. The decree enters into force effective the date of its signing.'

Heydar Aliyev, President of the Azerbaijan Republic
June 22, 2002
Baku

Source: Organization for Security and Co-operation in Europe, Office for Democratic Institutions and Human Rights, <http://www.legislationline.org>.

49. Political authorities have also used the referendum to promote a law that would not have passed through the normal legislative process for various reasons, for example, when a government is unable to mobilize sufficient support for its policies (France, in 1988, on New Caledonia; Denmark, in 1986, on the Single European Act; Bolivia, in 2004, on natural gas reserves); when a government is split on an issue (the UK, in 1975, on membership of the European Community); when there is disagreement between the chambers of the legislature (Belgium, in 1950, on the return from exile of King Leopold III; Sweden, in 1957, on supplementary pension plans); or when the constitution requires a qualified majority or the assent of constituent units in a federal state before a proposal can be adopted (Canada, in 1992, on constitutional reform).

50. Political authorities have sometimes initiated referendums in order to demonstrate popular support for the president or government. In these cases, the vote may be less on the particular issue than on the political leaders themselves, who maintain that chaos may result from a defeat and possible resignation of the president or government. An example in Europe of this kind of vote of confidence occurred in France, where President Charles de Gaulle on several occasions used the referendum as a means to demonstrate public confidence in his leadership. However, such an attempt failed in 1969, leading to his resignation. In Chile, Augusto Pinochet in 1978 called a referendum asking the voters to support him by agreeing to the following ballot text: 'In the face of international aggression against the government of our fatherland, I support President Pinochet in his defence of Chile's dignity, and I once again confirm the legitimacy of the government of the republic in its leadership of the institutional proceedings in this country'. Another and more direct example is Russia where in April 1993 in a referendum the voters were asked questions such as 'Do you express confidence in Boris Yeltsin, president of the Russian Federation?' and 'Do you approve of the socio-economic policies of the president of the Russian Federation and of the government of the Russian Federation since 1992?'.

51. Executives have also initiated referendums in order to demonstrate popular support for a specific political decision. Governments often claim that this is their main or only reason for organizing a referendum, whereas the true motivation may be (and often is) provided by political and tactical considerations. Such political and tactical reasons for initiating referendums have been criticized from a democratic point of view because here the referendum instrument has been used not in order to strengthen popular sovereignty and increase political equality but rather to bypass popular control and maintain or even extend the authority of the executive. Both democratic and authoritarian governments can initiate referendums, which may contribute to the stability and efficiency of the regime. Thus, a large number of referendums held in Latin America have been called by the executive branch, whereas few have been initiated through the collection of signatures (all of these in Uruguay). Some referendums called by the executive in Latin America were attempts to legitimize authoritarian regimes, but such attempts have not always been successful. Whereas the people of Chile in 1978 voted for Pinochet and a continued military regime, in Uruguay in 1980 the people rejected the proposal for

a new constitution put forward by a constituent assembly appointed by the military government.

52. In some jurisdictions referendums serve as way of protecting a legislative minority that may demand a referendum on a decision taken by the legislative majority. In Denmark, one-third of the members of the legislature (the Folketing) may demand a legally binding referendum on a bill passed by the Folketing. In Sweden a pending constitutional amendment must be referred to a legally binding referendum if one-tenth of the members of the legislature (the Riksdag) so request.

53. In terms of the legal consequences, referendums initiated by the political authorities may be consultative or legally binding. The distinction may, however, not be very important. It may be difficult for a democratic government to disregard the result of a referendum even though it is only consultative, as the referendums on the EU Constitutional Treaty in France and the Netherlands in 2005 demonstrate. Moreover, if a government finds it impossible to accept the outcome of a legally binding referendum, it may find ways to circumvent a referendum result, for instance by calling a new referendum on a slightly different question (as happened in the referendums in Denmark in 1992 and 1993 on the Maastricht Treaty and in the Republic of Ireland in 2001 and 2002 on the Nice Treaty). But in some jurisdictions a referendum cannot be repeated within a specified period; for example, in Argentina it cannot be repeated for two years.

54. In Palau, seven referendums were called between 1983 and 1990 on the proposed Compact of Free Association with the United States, which involved access by warships with nuclear capability to Palau waters. In each referendum, there was a simple majority for the compact, but not the 75 per cent vote required for its approval. The failure of this 'keep on holding referendums until you win' strategy led to a constitutional amendment removing the 75 per cent majority requirement and replacing it by a simple majority, following which the compact was approved in an eighth referendum in 1993. However, governments which take this kind of approach may find themselves subject to criticism for manipulation, even when the result is ultimately accepted.

55. It is not always clear for how long the result of a referendum is considered valid and applicable. Swedish voters rejected a proposal to switch from driving on the left-hand side of the road to the right-hand side in a 1955 referendum; in 1963, however, the Swedish parliament passed a law which enacted this change without a further referendum. It may be good practice to address this kind of question in advance in a referendum law rather than resolving it only at a time when a specific issue is under debate.

Procedural aspects

The institutional framework

56. It is important to decide how the referendum fits within the legal system and political culture of the jurisdiction. Referendums can be regulated by a written constitution, by general and permanent legislation or by specific ad hoc laws on a particular popular vote. In Switzerland the federal authorities can only call mandatory referendums on constitutional amendments and certain international treaties. If referendums are regulated by specific laws, the constitution or permanent legislation may specify whether such laws require a specific procedure or follow the ordinary procedure for law-making. If referendums are not directly forbidden by the constitution they may be regulated by specific ad hoc laws passed by ordinary legislative procedures, as is the case in Norway.

57. The advantages of regulating referendums in the constitution or in ordinary legislation are transparency and greater popular control, which contribute to the democratic legitimacy of referendums initiated by the political authorities. If the constitution regulates the issues on which and the circumstances under which referendums are to be held – that is, it provides for mandatory referendums – the citizens have better opportunities to participate effectively in the political process and are less likely to fall victim to deliberate manipulation by the political authorities. Optional referendums, which are unregulated by the constitution or by permanent legislation, tend to give political authorities more opportunities to use referendums for tactical purposes and sometimes to influence the result by deciding the issues to be voted on, the timing of the vote, the wording of the ballot question, the approval quorum, and so on. This is one reason why such optional and ad hoc referendums have often been criticized from a democratic point of view. The disadvantage of regulating referendums in the constitution or in legislation is that this reduces flexibility, particularly if the constitutional regulation is exhaustive and prohibits optional referendums. Thus, a balance has to be found between democratic legitimacy on the one hand and political efficiency and stability on the other. It is not possible to give exhaustive guidelines for achieving this balance, which has to be determined according to the particular circumstances of each jurisdiction.

Political issues

58. Typically, the subjects on which mandatory referendums are to be held are issues of major political significance, such as constitutional reform; the adoption of international treaties; the transfer of national competences and rights to international or supranational organizations; aspects related to national sovereignty such as privatization or nationalization; conflict between government bodies; or the regulation of economic and financial resources such as the imposition of new taxes, rates, public expenditure, and so on. Mandatory referendums may also be required by the constitution on moral issues such as the admissibility of divorce, abortion, euthanasia, the validity of human rights legislation, possible violations of human rights of the past and the present, and so on.

59. Where referendums are optional, the subjects on which they are held may vary. Referendums could be allowed on any issue that is the subject of legislation without restriction. However, some jurisdictions that provide for referendums place restrictions on the issues that can be the subject of referendums. The most common restriction is that taxes and public expenditure commitments cannot be submitted to referendums: such restrictions have been identified in a large number of countries, including some in Western Europe (Greece, Italy); in Central and Eastern Europe (Hungary, Latvia); in Latin America (Chile, Ecuador); and in Africa (Ghana, Lesotho).

60. In the case of a referendum promoted by the political authorities, it may be necessary to determine whether it can be called by any one of the governmental institutions on its own authority or if it requires coordination between different institutions for the procedure to be triggered. If the president or the government according to the constitution is free to call a referendum without the approval of the legislature or other governmental institutions such as a constitutional court – or if no regulation exists – these executive institutions have greater flexibility in making use of the referendum procedure. However, these advantages from the point of view of the political authorities may well be at the expense of democratic legitimacy, as popular support is most often sought when it suits the government.

**Box 2.5. A plebiscite called by a military government:
Thailand's 2007 constitutional referendum**

Since the abolition of absolute monarchy in 1932, Thailand has had a long history of military coups and changes of constitutions. On 19 September 2006 a military junta toppled the democratically elected government of Prime Minister Thaksin Shinawatra. The generals claimed to be acting in defence of King Bhumibol Adulyadej. It was widely claimed that, even though the king did not initiate the coup, no coup could have succeeded without his consent. The leaders of the coup annulled the 1997 constitution and appointed a Constitution Drafting Assembly to write a new constitution in order to eliminate the loopholes that they said had allowed Thaksin to abuse power.

By the end of June 2007 a draft proposal for a new constitution was published by the Constitution Drafting Assembly. The parliamentary system was to remain in place, but critics argued that the new constitution was less democratic than the former because about half of the new Senate was to be appointed by judges and government bodies rather than elected.

The Constitution Drafting Assembly also announced that a national referendum on the proposed constitution would take place on 19 August. Copies of the draft constitution, comprising more than 300 articles, would be ready for the public on 31 July and sent to all Thai families. Thus, a very short period of only 19 days was allowed for the voters to be informed about a lengthy and complex document.

A general election was tentatively scheduled for December, although interim Prime Minister Surayud Chulanont hinted that the poll could take place in November if the public passed the draft constitution. Thus, the military government motivated the voters to turn out and vote, but threats were also indicated: 'If the referendum fails, it will create continuing problems and a chaotic situation', Defence Minister Boonrod Somtad told reporters.

The result of the referendum was an endorsement of the new constitution as 57.8 per cent voted 'Yes' and 42.2 per cent voted 'No'. However, little more than half of the eligible electors (57.6 per cent) participated.

The vote was a typical plebiscite in the derogatory sense, indicating a popular vote where there is no real possibility of free and fair contest over an issue. As Dr Pasuk Pongpaijitr of Chulalongkorn University argued, 'This is not a referendum. A referendum is where you ask the people and there is an alternative – but if you say no to this, you don't know what you get' (BBC News, 17 August 2007).

Timing

61. It may also be necessary to establish when a referendum will take place, thus allowing an adequate period for the campaign. Referendums may have to be held within a certain period of time after they are called. If such a period of time is not established in each particular case, the government may either call the referendum so quickly that a genuine public debate is impossible or prolong the debate for such a long time that the issue becomes submerged among others or public interest is exhausted. A referendum on a new constitution in Thailand, held by the military government in 2007, was widely criticized on a number of procedural grounds, including the length of time allowed for the campaign (see box 2.5). General and permanent rules for the length of referendum campaigns may improve democratic legitimacy, whereas specific ad hoc rules may allow more governmental flexibility and increase efficiency, depending on the level of public knowledge and awareness of the issue(s) placed on the referendum ballot paper.

62. It may be appropriate to consider whether the constitution or general and permanent legislation should stipulate whether referendums can be carried out simultaneously with a national election, regional elections, municipal elections and so on, or if they should be carried out at a different time. From an efficiency point of view, money can be saved

by holding referendums and elections together, and participation may sometimes be improved in circumstances where elections produce a higher turnout. To the extent that the democratic legitimacy of a referendum result often depends on the turnout, this may be desirable. On the other hand, the referendum issue may become submerged during a referendum campaign that coincides with an election, and may not receive sufficient attention. Democratic legitimacy also requires that an issue be sufficiently discussed and debated by the voters, and their attention may be distracted by an election taking place at the same time.

63. Consideration might also be given to the question whether it should be stipulated that referendums on more than one issue can be held at the same time. In some jurisdictions, such as California and Switzerland, several issues are typically decided by the voters on the same day. In the 2003 referendum called by President Álvaro Uribe of Colombia, 19 separate issues were to be decided by the voters. The advantage of this procedure is that the voters are involved more efficiently in the decision making on a wider range of public affairs, which may increase democratic legitimacy and responsiveness. The drawback is that the voters have to inform themselves on a large number of issues which may not be related to each other. Obtaining sufficient information for deciding how to vote on so many issues is both time-consuming and intellectually demanding. Public debate cannot penetrate deeply into all subjects, the campaign tends to be less focused, and the voters may become dependent on the advice given by political parties, interest organizations or ad hoc campaign groups. If votes on several issues at the same time result in less informed decisions, confusion among the voters and a resulting low turnout, the democratic legitimacy of the referendum results is undermined.

The ballot text

64. The alternatives presented to the voters have to be considered carefully. Usually referendums give the voters the possibility to vote for or against a specific proposal. In some cases voters have been given a choice between three alternatives, for example, in Sweden in 1980 on the nuclear power issue. The clearest result is obtained if the voters are asked to choose between two alternatives. If they have to choose between three or more alternatives it may be difficult to interpret the referendum result. However, if a choice between more than two alternatives is really wanted, a vote where the alternatives are rank-ordered could be applied, or the issues could be split up into two or more questions – each of them with two alternatives – as in the Republic of Ireland, where policy on abortion was split up into three separate questions in the 1992 referendum dealing with that issue.

65. Whether referendums are regulated in the constitution or in ordinary legislation or are not regulated at all, an important issue under all circumstances relates to the ballot text – the question put on the ballot paper. The wording of the question can have an important effect on the result and on its legitimacy. In general, the ballot text should be as precise and clear as possible and should have one goal and interpretation only. It should not be vague or capable of different meanings (see box 2.6). It should

be neutrally formulated and avoid expressions with any evident positive or negative overtone. In the abstract, this may seem to be straightforward and self-evident, but in practice it may be less easy to achieve. Malpractices such as double negatives and biased language abound. In some US states disagreements over the language of the ballot text may end up in court.

> **Box 2.6. A controversy of question wording: the text of the ballot paper for the 1980 Quebec referendum**
>
> 'The Government of Quebec has made public its proposal to negotiate a new agreement with the rest of Canada, based on the equality of nations. This agreement would enable Quebec to acquire the exclusive power to make its laws, levy its taxes, and establish relations abroad – in other words, sovereignty – and at the same time, to maintain with Canada an economic association including a common currency. No change in political status resulting from these negotiations will be effected without approval by the people through another referendum. On these terms, do you agree to give the Government of Quebec the mandate to negotiate the proposed agreement between Quebec and Canada?'

66. It may be appropriate to specify who decides the exact formulation of the ballot text. In particular, it is important to consider whether the government shall be responsible for drafting the question, even in cases when the government initiates the referendum and therefore has an interest in designing the question in such a way as to increase the chances of achieving the result it desires (see box 2.6). In some jurisdictions, an electoral management body (EMB) may have oversight of the formulation of the referendum question, so that this responsibility is placed in the hands of a more politically neutral body.

67. The question of appeal should also be addressed. Should there be a possibility of appeal against the way in which the ballot text has been formulated? If this option is adopted, it must be precisely established who can appeal, for instance, a governmental institution different from the one which wrote the ballot text, or a certain number of citizens, and within what period of time. Consideration should also be given to which body shall be called upon to decide upon the matter. In the same way, there should also be a clear regulation about the period of time the body will have to resolve the conflict.

The campaign: organization and regulation

68. Communicating information to the public about the main content of a referendum

question is vital for the legitimacy of the referendum result. Thus, consideration has to be given to whether, and to what extent, rules in the constitution or in a referendum law should regulate campaign activities by limiting the amount of money that can be spent on the campaign, regulating access to the public and private media, and so on. On the one hand, a main principle of good practice in this respect is to ensure a level playing field between those in favour and those opposing the proposal. On the other, a fundamental principle of freedom of expression also has to be respected (see chapter 7).

69. It should be established whether a government that promotes a referendum proposal should limit itself to informing the public about the main aspects of the proposal, or whether it should also be allowed to use public money on advocating for the proposal. In the Republic of Ireland, Supreme Court decisions have held that the government was not allowed to spend public money in support of one side of a referendum campaign and that the public service broadcaster was not allowed to give more air time to one side than to the other in a referendum campaign.

70. If spending limits are imposed on those campaigning for and against the proposal, this may create problems for freedom of expression and the legitimacy of the referendum result. In the Republic of Ireland, under the Referendum Act of 1998, a Referendum Commission was established as an independent statutory body, for each referendum, to oversee the information campaign on proposed amendments to the constitution in order to facilitate debate and discussion on the matter in a manner which was fair to all interests concerned (see box 7.3 in chapter 7). It is a matter of contention whether this provision is conducive to a vibrant public debate or whether it restrains the public debate unnecessarily. Because of this contention, the mandate of the Referendum Commission has been revised on several occasions.

Voting qualifications, mechanisms and rules

71. Regarding the referendum itself, whether mandatory or optional, consideration should be given to how it is to be organized and which authority is to be responsible for ensuring that voting procedures are carried out in accordance with the law. There may be specific regulations stating whether there is a difference between those who can vote in a referendum and those eligible to vote in a national election, for instance with regard to citizenship or the voting age. Similarly, the period of time for the voting and the way(s) in which voting can be done may be specified. The possibilities for postal voting, absentee voting or voting via the Internet, for example, may need to be specified. Regulations may need to be introduced on whether voting in a referendum shall follow the same rules about compulsory or voluntary voting as national elections, and whether rules about compulsory voting shall be strictly administered, as they have been in Belgium and Uruguay. In general, in order to avoid deliberate manipulation by the political authorities, the best practice is to apply the same rules in national elections and referendums.

72. A critical issue to be considered is when a referendum proposal is judged to have passed. In some jurisdictions, it will pass if a simple majority of voters vote 'Yes'. In others, a referendum vote passes only if a specified turnout threshold (turnout quorum) is reached, or a specified number of voters cast a 'Yes' vote (approval quorum). Some jurisdictions require a double majority for a referendum vote to pass, for example, an overall majority among the voters and a majority of the sub-national jurisdictions in a federal country, as is required in Australia and Switzerland. Such general rules about turnout and approval quorums have to be made clear in advance of the referendum. Legitimacy, transparency, fairness and popular acceptance of the referendum results are improved if such quorums are specified in the constitution or in ordinary legislation, and not decided on an ad hoc basis just before each referendum.

73. Although high turnout is often seen as an indicator of the democratic legitimacy of a referendum, specifying a certain turnout quorum may not in itself encourage a high turnout. Experience has shown – for instance in Italy – that those who oppose a proposal may campaign for the electors not to turn out to vote. To encourage political passivity and to undermine the norm of the citizen's duty to vote is not conducive to the development of popular control of political decisions. Important decisions may be stopped without being truly discussed and considered. The risk of a small and active minority dominating a large and passive majority can be handled by other means than turnout quorums, such as opening up genuine opportunities for vigorous information campaigns and political mobilization of the voters by political parties, social movements and ad hoc campaign groups.

74. The result of a referendum may be either legally binding – that is, the government and appropriate authorities are compelled to implement the proposal – or consultative – that is, in legal terms only giving advice to the government or appropriate authorities. It has to be clearly specified either in the constitution or in ordinary legislation what the legal consequences are. If the consequences are not specified prior to a referendum, the political authorities may adapt the legal consequences according to political and tactical considerations. A decision by the authorities not to implement a proposal which commands the support of a majority of citizens runs the risk of undermining the democratic legitimacy of the process. In this context it is important to distinguish between the legal and political consequences.

75. In summary, careful consideration has to be given to how far the rules, norms and principles of good practice are specified in the constitution or in the legislation regulating referendums (see chapter 9 and annex A). A balance has to be found between a large number of specific and detailed regulations that may limit flexibility and transparency, on the one hand, and a complete or almost complete absence of regulations, which may lead to arbitrariness and deliberate manipulation, on the other. In jurisdictions which have greater experience with direct democracy procedures, it is generally possible to specify the rules and procedures to be followed in a constitution or general referendum law, and therefore to provide greater confidence among the citizens that proper

procedures are being followed. Where there is less experience with such procedures, or where a referendum is being held for the first time, the political authorities must make sure that the rules and procedures governing the referendum are not manipulated to favour one side over the other.

Conclusions

76. The referendum is a direct democracy procedure that provides for a vote by the electorate on an issue of public policy. As such it provides the potential for a further development of democracy by granting direct control of public decisions to the people on the basis of political equality. In the hands of the political authorities, however, it involves both dangers and democratic opportunities. Before including the instrument of the referendum called by the political authorities into the constitutional framework of a country or sub-national jurisdiction, a careful evaluation of its probable and possible impacts has to be considered. A referendum may become a weapon in the hands of the political leadership, or may precipitate major divisions in countries where there is little sense of nationhood or where local or regional identities are very strong.

77. Opponents of referendums sometimes argue that if the political authorities – indirectly or directly – have the power to determine when referendums are held, if they can decide what issues they are held on, if they control the campaign and the information provided for the voters, and if they can interpret the referendum result as they like – perhaps calling a new referendum if they do not like the result – referendums become merely a political tool that is used to serve the needs of the governing party rather than the interests of democracy. Furthermore, if the turnout in referendums is substantially lower than that at national elections, the argument that referendums increase the legitimacy of political decisions may not stand up.

78. Opponents of referendums called by the political authorities may also argue that, unless the voters are given a choice between two equally applicable alternatives in a free and fair way, referendums become 'plebiscites' in the derogative sense. In such votes, strong leaders appeal directly to the people for personal support, and more or less explicitly threaten the onset of political chaos if they do not receive the popular support they expect. The referendum held by the military government in Thailand in 2007 was widely criticized on all these grounds.

79. Such objections to referendums initiated by the political authorities, and in particular by the executive branch of government – the president or the government – may be well founded if the political authorities have the exclusive right to call referendums and the citizens are denied all possibilities for demanding referendums or taking initiatives. Chapter 3 considers in more detail the design and political issues that arise when the citizens themselves, rather than only the authorities, can initiate a popular vote.

80. Even though the results of referendums in the hands of the political authorities are sometimes mistrusted, it is possible to improve the democratic quality of such referendums by adhering to principles of good practice. Referendums called by the executive under authoritarian forms of government may stabilize the regime and reduce political pressures on it, but they cannot always be taken as valid expressions of the will of the people and thus often lack democratic legitimacy. The same can hold true, although to a lesser extent, of optional ad hoc referendums initiated by the executive under more democratic forms of government. In order to improve democratic legitimacy it is, in general, recommended to regulate the use of referendums in the constitution or in general and permanent legislation and to avoid ad hoc decisions – in particular in jurisdictions that lack a long democratic tradition and a broad consensus on the democratic rules of the game. The less the experience with referendums and the less mature the democratic culture, the greater the need for regulation in order to avoid misuse or deliberate manipulation of the voters when the political authorities call referendums.

2. When the authorities call a referendum: design and political considerations

CHAPTER 3

CHAPTER 3

When citizens take the initiative: design and political considerations

81. This chapter provides information on two direct democracy procedures in which citizens put forward an initiative – the citizens' initiative and the citizen-demanded referendum, both of which are designed to be concluded with a referendum vote. Table 3.1 shows which countries provide these procedures and their distribution across the regions of the world. The chapter discusses variations of the instruments and issues of design, and presents some data on their use in practice in different countries and regions.

82. These two important variations of direct democracy are based on a process begun 'from below' rather than on decisions taken 'from above'. With a citizens' initiative (also called a 'popular initiative'), a number of citizens present a political proposal (e.g. draft legislation) and register public support by obtaining a required number of signatures, thereby forcing a popular vote (referendum) on the issue. Initiatives can be either direct or indirect. In a direct initiative, the popular vote will take place without any further intervention by the authorities. An indirect initiative involves a procedure whereby the legislative authorities may either adopt the proposal or have the option of presenting an alternative proposal to the popular vote. A citizen-demanded referendum is an optional referendum initiated, or triggered, by a number of citizens referring to existing laws or political or legislative proposals. One version allows repeal of an existing law or parts thereof (the abrogative referendum). The other allows citizens to demand a popular vote on a new piece of legislation that is not yet in force (the rejective referendum). The basic common feature of these instruments is that citizens as non-governmental actors are entitled to act on political or legislative issues by presenting proposals, and can themselves initiate the procedure for a vote of the electorate. These should be distinguished from an agenda initiative, which also allows for proposals to be formally presented to parliament or other governmental authorities but does not lead to a popular vote (see chapter 4).

Distribution and development

83. The number of countries which have initiative instruments is significantly lower than the number that have mandatory referendums or optional referendums called by government authorities. Legal provisions for initiative instruments are available to citizens in 37 countries, mostly in Europe and Latin America (see table 3.1). The citizens' initiative at the national level is legally available in many European countries, several countries in Latin America, and a few in Asia, Oceania and Africa. Provisions for the citizen-demanded referendum are distributed similarly, in smaller numbers, across the regions of the world (see table 3.1). The abrogative referendum is found in Europe only in Italy (since 1970) and in a few countries of Latin America. Some jurisdictions provide both instruments, others only one. However, some countries which have no such instruments at the national level do provide initiative rights at the regional and the local levels – particularly large federal countries such as Brazil, Germany or the United States. In the United States, 24 of the 50 states have provisions for citizens' initiatives. Other jurisdictions offer them at the local level only, for example, Mexico, Panama and many European countries.

Figure 3.1. Distribution of initiative procedures, by region

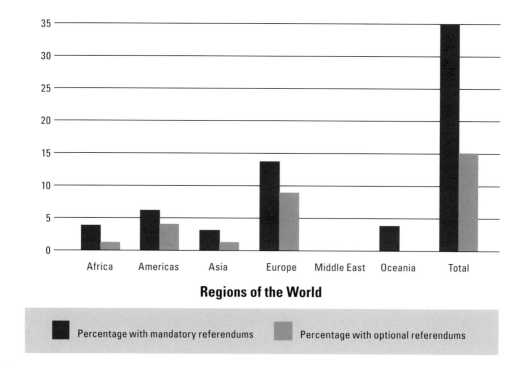

Regions of the World

■ Percentage with mandatory referendums   ■ Percentage with optional referendums

Table 3.1. Countries which have provision for initiative procedures at the national level, by region

	Citizens' initiative		Citizen-demanded referendum
	Ordinary legislation	Constitutional amendment	
Africa (4)			
Cape Verde	•	•	•
Liberia		•	
Togo	•		
Uganda	•	•	
Americas (8)			
Bolivia			•
Colombia	•	•	•
Costa Rica	•	•	
Ecuador	•		•
Nicaragua	•		
Peru			•
Uruguay	•	•	•
Venezuela	•	•	
Asia (3)			
Philippines	•	•	•
Taiwan	•		
Turkmenistan	•		
Europe (18)			
Albania	•		•
Belarus	•	•	
Croatia	•		•
Georgia		•	
Hungary	•	•	•
Italy			•
Latvia	•	•	
Liechtenstein	•	•	•
Lithuania	•	•	
Macedonia, the former Yugoslav Republic of			•
Malta			•
Moldova, Republic of		•	
Russia	•		
Serbia	•		
Slovakia	•	•	

	Citizens' initiative		Citizen-demanded referendum
	Ordinary legislation	Constitutional amendment	
Slovenia			•
Switzerland		•	•
Ukraine	•		
Middle East	N/A	N/A	N/A
Oceania (4)			
Marshall Islands		•	
Micronesia, Federated States of	•	•	
New Zealand	•		
Palau	•	•	

84. The origins of the instruments vary widely. Switzerland was the first country to introduce the citizens' initiative (for a total revision of the constitution) in 1848; this was followed by the introduction of the 'facultative referendum' (citizen-demanded), in 1874, and the citizens' initiative to propose amendments to the constitution, in 1891 (see the case study on Switzerland following chapter 1). As in many US states after the 1890s, these instruments were intended to curb the misuse of representative institutions by powerful business interests. In other countries the instruments have been adopted in periods after dictatorial regimes, as in Italy or Germany (in the *länder* – the regional states) since 1945, as an expression of popular sovereignty and to support the re-establishment of democracy. Similarly, in the 1990s, initiative rights were introduced during the post-communist transition period in the majority of the countries of Eastern Europe and in some of the successor states of the Soviet Union. The above reasons also hold for some countries in Latin America after periods of dictatorial regimes. Some countries have provided initiative rights in their constitutions but have no laws to regulate their implementation: Guatemala and Paraguay are examples. Uruguay, which uses such instruments extensively, seems to be exceptional in Latin America (see the case study following chapter 7).

Institutional design

85. Initiative instruments are designed to provide additional channels of political expression and participation beyond those that are available through representative institutions alone, emphasizing citizens' ability to articulate their opinions and the openness of the democratic system. Initiative procedures should, therefore, reflect the principles of democratic equality, fairness and transparency. Using initiative instruments generally implies criticism of the performance of a governing majority or of a representative institution such as a parliament or legislature. Thus, there will often be some tensions between major actors in the governmental system and the proponents of citizens' initiatives or citizen-demanded referendums, which often include opposition

parties, interest organizations or civil society groups. Such tensions may be reflected in the design of the regulations governing the initiative instruments, and in their practical application.

86. The citizens' initiative provides a procedure whereby political issues can be put on the agenda, a public debate can be encouraged, and issues can be finally decided by a popular vote. Such a proactive process can open the agenda to a broader range of issues and groups, working against the tendencies towards 'closure' of the political agenda that are found in many representative systems (e.g. two-party systems). One important design question may be whether initiative rights can be used primarily by strong parties or organized interest groups, or whether they also provide access points for smaller and less powerful groups, or for newly emerging groups and social movements. Highly restrictive regulations may be biased towards strong organizations or parties.

87. The citizen-demanded referendum can take two different forms. In Italy the abrogative referendum (see box 3.1) applies the initiative procedures only to repealing existing laws or parts thereof. It has some similarity to the citizens' initiative, but it provides for existing legislation to be repealed and does not allow explicit proposals to be put forward for a new law to replace the one being challenged. The second form, the rejective referendum, offers a procedure for citizens to stop new legislation before it comes into force and is therefore more a reaction to the activities of a parliament or legislature. This instrument can serve a function of political control to ensure that the representative law-making body does not violate the interests or convictions of sections of the citizens and social groups. Thus, majorities in the representative bodies can be questioned by appealing to a (supposed) popular majority, or by articulating the interests and values of large minorities which have a chance to find support in the popular referendum. Referendums, if called successfully by citizens, will mostly apply to rather controversial legislation and may lead to conflict resolution by a majority vote.

Box 3.1. The abrogrative referendum in Italy

Although the post-fascist constitution of 1948 (article 75) established the right to citizen-initiated referendums, a law to implement the procedure only came into force in 1970. The initiative procedure most often used in Italy, called the *referendum abrogativo*, allows citizens to propose the repeal (abrogation) of an existing law or parts thereof. No procedure for a citizens' initiative to propose a new law exists. Other direct democracy procedures (e.g. a constitutional referendum or agenda initiative) are of minor importance in practice.

To start a citizen-demanded *referendum abrogativo*, the signatures of 500,000 registered electors (*c.* 1 per cent of registered electors), or of five regional councils, are required. Tax and budget matters, amnesties and pardons, the ratification of international treaties, and amendments to the constitution cannot be submitted to a referendum. The law to be abrogated must have been in force for at least one year. Proposals have to be submitted between 1 January and 30 September of each year, and signatures can be collected within a period of three months. The Constitutional Court will check the constitutionality of the proposal. All the referendum proposals of the year are put to the vote on a single voting Sunday between 1 April and 15 June of the following year. The referendum vote will be valid if, in addition to a majority of the votes cast, a majority of registered electors have voted (turnout quorum).

The first *referendum abrogativo* took place in 1974, when a proposal to abolish the law of civil divorce was rejected by the voters. Since then, more than 60 votes (up to 2006) have taken place on a broad range of subjects. In June 1985, a proposal to eliminate the inflation adjustment of wages *(scala mobile)* was rejected. In June 1991, the voters agreed in a referendum to the abolition of the List proportional representation (PR) voting system – an outcome which led to the reform of the Italian party system. In June 1995, 12 propositions were on the ballot paper (turnout was c. 57 per cent), including the status of trade unions and several issues of television policy. Seven of these propositions attracted turnouts of only c. 30 per cent. In April 1999, a proposal to completely abolish the proportional element in the electoral system achieved a turnout of only 49.6 per cent and was thus invalid, despite a vote in favour of 91.5 per cent. In June 2005, four proposals on restricting research on human embryos, in vitro fertilization and related issues attracted a turnout of only c. 26 per cent. Since 1995, no referendum vote has been successful in abrogating a law, in part because of the turnout quorum.

88. If elected representatives anticipate that they will be used, the existence of initiative or referendum procedures may influence political decision making indirectly by inducing political leaders to act in a more responsive way to the concerns of citizens, thereby strengthening the legitimacy of political decisions. However, it can also have the effect of causing prominent political figures in the party system to become leading actors in this procedure as well as in electoral politics.

Subject restrictions

89. In many countries the range of subjects that are open to initiative procedures is restricted. Three common groups of restrictions can be discerned: (a) restrictions referring to constitutional amendments; (b) those concerning issues of the integrity of the state, matters of war and peace, the transfer of state jurisdiction to supranational and international bodies, and international treaties; and (c) various limitations relating to ordinary legislation and other political decisions. Subject limitations which are too

narrowly defined may, however, destroy any potential for using these instruments.

90. Citizens' initiatives on constitutional amendments are most often found in countries in which mandatory or optional referendums on constitutional amendments called by the authorities are also available. These instruments most strongly reflect the idea that popular sovereignty may be expressed in a vote of the people. Countries which exclude an initiative on constitutional amendment may be motivated by the desire to protect the stability of the constitution against the contingencies of popular activities; yet the democratic principle of popular sovereignty would suggest that citizens' initiatives on constitutional amendments should be allowed. Constitutional amendments are formally open to citizens' initiatives in more than half of the countries which have provisions for initiative instruments (i.e. 20 out of 37 countries, see table 3.2).

Table 3.2. Countries which have provision for citizens' initiatives for constitutional amendments at the national level, by region

Region of the world	
Africa	Cape Verde, Liberia, Uganda
Americas	Colombia, Costa Rica, Ecuador, Uruguay, Venezuela
Asia	Philippines
Europe	Belarus, Georgia, Hungary, Latvia, Liechtenstein, Lithuania, Republic of Moldova, Slovakia, Switzerland
Oceania	Marshall Islands, Federated States of Micronesia, Palau

91. Even if initiatives on constitutional amendments are allowed, the subject matter may still be restricted. One example of this is Slovakia, where constitutional initiatives affecting 'basic rights and liberties' are excluded. In favour of this it may be argued that the fundamental guarantees contained in a democratic constitution should not be at the disposal of a majority or even a super majority in a vote. Sometimes the basic structures of governmental institutions are also excluded from initiatives. The Russian Federation has one very particular restriction whereby only initiatives referring to the structure of the federation are allowed.

92. In some countries, including Switzerland, a completely opposite concept of restrictions is to be found: the citizens' initiative is allowed only for constitutional amendments and not for proposals for legislation (although in Switzerland the citizen-demanded referendum can be used for all legislation except finance laws). In Panama, an initiative can only be used (by a minimum of 20 per cent of registered electors) to authorize the election of a constitutional assembly. Uruguay provides for the citizens' initiative for both constitutional amendments and proposals for legislation. In federal

countries which have initiative procedures only at the state or regional level, these normally include initiative rights for constitutional amendments, for example, in many states of the USA and most of the German *länder*.

93. Issues of the integrity of the state or a transfer of state jurisdiction to supranational or international bodies are often subject to a mandatory or optional referendum called by the authorities, but are rarely cases for a citizens' initiative. Sometimes these subjects are treated as constitutional issues and the rules for constitutional amendments therefore apply. In addition, questions of war and peace or of military service are sometimes excluded from initiatives (e.g. in Latvia). For similar reasons, only in a few cases can international treaties be the subject of a citizen-demanded referendum, and almost never of a citizens' initiative. International treaty negotiations seem very often to be excluded from initiative procedures, as regulated, for example, in Italy, Latvia and the former Yugoslav Republic of Macedonia. Switzerland, however, requires mandatory referendums for very important treaties. Sometimes the territorial integrity of the state is insulated against popular votes whereas in other cases it can be put to a mandatory or even an optional referendum vote.

94. In a few countries, initiative instruments on ordinary legislation are restricted in a general way to the 'most significant issues concerning the life of the state and the people' (Lithuania) or 'important issues of public interest' (Slovakia). Other matters that are excluded from being the subject of initiative instruments are pardons (Italy) or issues related to elections (the former Yugoslav Republic of Macedonia). When restrictive clauses are not clearly defined, such as 'important issues' (Slovakia), they may be open not only to legal interpretation but also to political manipulation by the authorities in charge of approving initiative proposals. All restrictions should be clearly specified and give a transparent and unequivocal framework. In many countries budget, tax and public expenditure issues are excluded from initiative mechanisms (e.g. Hungary, Italy, Latvia, Slovakia and several Latin American countries). Financial matters, particularly taxes, are often regarded as being too complex for an initiative instrument or as likely to attract fiscally irresponsible campaigns. However, since public finances are a fundamental factor of political life, this exclusion can lead to a substantial restriction of the areas to which initiative instruments can be applied. If any kind of costs of specific legislative measures were excluded, the limits of initiatives would become quite unclear, and legal challenges would easily be provoked.

Procedural aspects

95. A few basic features shape the procedural framework within which citizens or political groups can initiate a decision-making process for new proposals or to demand a referendum on legislation. Three kinds of requirements are important for the procedures: (a) a specific number of signatures of registered electors is required to demonstrate political support for a proposal or demand by a significant proportion of the citizenry; (b) the period of time allowed for collecting signatures; and (c) the specific conditions under which the result of the vote is declared to be legally valid (such as

quorums). Substantial variations in these requirements can be observed in different jurisdictions.

- The *number of signatures required* may be expressed as a percentage of the electorate (registered electors) (e.g. 10 per cent in Latvia), or as a share of the votes cast in a previous election (e.g. in California 5 per cent of the number of votes cast for governor is required for a proposal for legislation, and 8 per cent for a constitutional amendment), or as a fixed number of signatures, for example, 500,000 for an abrogative referendum in Italy (in this case the proportion relative to the total number of registered electors is around 1 per cent; see box 3.1 above). The thresholds show a wide range from about 1 or 2 per cent of the electorate (in Switzerland) up to 10 or even 25 per cent (in Uruguay).

- Some countries require a specific *geographical distribution of signatures*, for example, a minimum number in half or more of the administrative subdivisions of the country, as in some of the successor states of the Soviet Union (Belarus, Georgia, Russia, Ukraine).

- The *period of time* allowed to collect supporting signatures may range from a few weeks (e.g. two weeks in Bavaria, Germany) to 18 months (Switzerland, constitutional initiative).

- For the final referendum vote, only in some cases is a simple majority of votes cast sufficient (e.g. in Switzerland in the 'facultative [rejective] referendum'). More often various versions of double majorities with additional *validity requirements* are applied. An *approval quorum* specifies that the votes cast in favour of a proposal must meet a specific proportion of registered electors (or a fixed number), for example, 50 per cent of registered electors in constitutional amendment votes in Latvia and Lithuania, or 25 per cent in Hungary (since 1997). A *turnout quorum* means that, in addition to a majority vote, a specific participation rate must be met, for example, 50 per cent of the whole electorate must have participated in the vote (as in Italy). Again, both versions can be combined with geographical distribution requirements.

96. For constitutional amendments several countries have set higher requirements for qualifying initiatives and defining valid referendums than apply for initiatives that concern ordinary legislation. Constitutions, as the source of the basic rules and values of the political system, are often expected to be more stable and to enjoy broader legitimacy and acceptance than ordinary legislation (there are often special requirements before a legislature can amend the constitution). There is, however, the exceptional case of Uruguay, where the signatures of 10 per cent of the electorate are required for a citizens' initiative for a constitutional amendment, but 25 per cent is required for (rejective) referendums on legislation.

97. Countries vary in these basic requirements and also in the combination of these features. Some countries (e.g. Switzerland) combine a low signature threshold with low requirements for a valid vote. In other countries, high signature requirements (25 or even

33 per cent) can be coupled with a high validity requirement (as in Belarus). Between such extremes, other more moderate or mixed versions of these requirements can be found. Switzerland represents the classic case of low requirements. For a constitutional initiative only 100,000 signatures or about 2 per cent of registered electors are required, and for demanding a rejective referendum the requirements are even lower (50,000 signatures, or about 1 per cent of registered electors, and a simple majority in the referendum vote). Italy combines a low threshold of signature support (c. 1 per cent) for an abrogative referendum with the high turnout requirement of 50 per cent of registered electors for a valid popular vote. Lithuania represents a high requirement profile in both criteria (see table 3.3).

Table 3.3. The requirements for a citizens' initiative to be held: some examples

Signature requirement	Validity requirement	
	Low	High
Low	Switzerland (constitutional initiative) 100,000 signatures (c. 2% of registered electors) Simple majority of voters and a majority of the 26 cantons	Italy (abrogative referendum) 500,000 signatures (c. 1% of registered electors) 50% turnout of registered voters
High	Hesse (Germany) Signatures of 20% of registered electors Simple majority of referendum votes	Lithuania 300,000 signatures (c. 11.5% of registered electors) 50% turnout of registered electors plus 33% approval of registered electors

98. Low or moderate signature requirements give citizens easier access to the decision-making agenda and support the principles of an open democracy and political equality. High signature requirements are likely to limit or even prohibit the practical use of initiative instruments. They may be motivated by the need to avoid abuse of the mechanism, but at the same time they can undermine the whole idea of initiative rights. In countries with signature thresholds of more than 15 per cent of registered electors, almost no initiatives will qualify to go forward to a vote. In particular, high signature thresholds will provide preferential access to initiative rights for very strong political organizations (parties and large interest groups) and transform initiative rights into instruments of power for larger groups or organizations.

99. As to the time factor, most countries that employ citizens' initiatives allow for reasonable periods, such as some months, for signatures to be collected and, after an initiative has formally qualified, for the referendum vote to be held. These time periods are also important to allow for information to be distributed, opinions on the issue disseminated and a process of public deliberation started. Time needs to be allowed for

immediate, possibly emotional reactions to give way to rational debate. This has not been realized, so far, by some of the German *länder*, such as Baden-Württemberg or Hesse, which allow only as little as two weeks after official registration of an initiative for signature collecting.

100. Defining the criteria for the validity of the voting result raises questions similar to those that apply in the cases of mandatory or optional referendums. If a jurisdiction has mandatory referendums, optional referendums called by the authorities and referendums initiated by citizens, the level of votes required should surely be defined in a consistent way for all three types. A simple majority of votes cast would reflect issue preferences in the clearest way. A high approval quorum (perhaps combined with a double majority) would stress the legitimacy of the referendum decision, or the need to take into account other political or territorial considerations. However, the existence of an approval quorum can exaggerate the effect of abstentions, since they have the same effect as 'No' votes. The consequence can be that opponents of an initiative need only to recommend abstaining from the vote in order to get a negative referendum result, and it may be easier to convince potential voters not to bother than to convince them to vote a certain way. It may often follow that high approval quorums discourage the use of initiative instruments. Turnout quorums produce even more such consequences: opponents of a referendum proposal must actively avoid negative votes being cast because they would help to reach the quorum. Turnout quorums tend to work against the basic idea of initiatives and referendums, which is to encourage citizen participation, and they are not generally recommended as a criterion for determining the validity of a referendum. On the other hand, there is often a concern that a proposal that is endorsed by less than a majority of the electorate may call the legitimacy of the result into question.

Interaction between the initiators and government bodies

101. Initiative instruments are institutionally linked with other governmental actors in the political system. Institutional and political tension and competition are often involved, and there are various reciprocal influences and interactions. Governmental actors should interact with the initiators in fairness and good faith and not use their procedural role for political manoeuvring and manipulation of the process. The procedural rules should make sure that the functions of citizen initiatives cannot be counteracted by the elected representatives, otherwise the basic ideas of keeping democracy open and under popular control might be lost.

102. One function of governmental (institutional) actors may be the formal administration of the procedure, including verifying the legality or constitutionality of the citizens' initiative. It is important that clear and transparent rules and specific administrative responsibilities are assigned to the proper authorities – for example, a president's office, government agencies, the central administration of the legislature or an EMB (which may or may not be a government body). Regulations should make sure that the controlling authorities act in a way that is as politically neutral as possible and not allow these functions to become combined with a political interest.

103. Checking the constitutionality of an initiative proposal is of special importance. Sometimes this is within the competence of an administrative authority with the right to appeal to a court, especially the constitutional court; in some countries (e.g. Italy) this function lies directly with the constitutional court. Some jurisdictions do not provide this check of constitutionality at an early stage of the procedure but only at the end. For example, in several US states, judicial review of a proposal occurs only after the popular vote. There may, however, be advantages in having the question of constitutionality settled after the initiative is registered and before the collection of signatures begins or, at the latest, before the referendum vote is called. Otherwise the debate on the issue may become mixed up with constitutional questions and, if a positive vote is declared unconstitutional, the citizens may become frustrated or the entire process may be de-legitimized as a consequence. Questions may be raised, however, if the regulations are ill-defined and/or a constitutional court is acting as a quasi-political institution. Under such circumstances, an early check of constitutionality or legality might be transformed into inadequate or politically motivated limitations on initiative activities.

104. In the design of a citizens' initiative, two types of procedure can be distinguished. In a 'direct initiative' (as in many US states), after the initiative has been registered and qualified, no formal interaction with the legislature takes place before the popular vote is called. In the 'indirect initiative' version (as in some European countries), a qualifying initiative will be referred to the legislature, which then has two options – either to adopt the (legislative) proposal and thereby avoid a referendum, or to refuse approval and allow the referendum to take place. In some countries the legislature can also put its own alternative proposal to a referendum vote (e.g. Switzerland, the German *länder*, and Uruguay in the case of the constitutional initiative). Since initiative procedures operate within the institutional environment of representative democracy, there are good reasons for having an interactive process between the various actors. If a legislature can formally consider and debate an initiative, and can adopt it or opt for an alternative proposal to be put to the popular vote, the political process may be enriched by more complex deliberations and greater public involvement in the issues to be decided. A choice between clear alternatives in the popular vote may also be more rewarding for the citizens.

105. There are circumstances under which minor modifications may transform the initiative procedure into the form of an agenda initiative (see chapter 4). For instance, if the required number of signatures is not reached for an initiative proposal but the parliament or legislature can decide freely whether it wants to call a referendum or not, then a hybrid type of institution has been created. The combination of an initiative started by citizens and decisions made by a parliament or legislature based on such action may have the potential to combine elements of both direct and representative democracy.

The practice of initiative procedures

106. The extent of the use of initiative procedures varies significantly between countries

(see table 3.4) and seems to be influenced by several factors. Only four countries use these instruments of direct democracy frequently: Italy, Liechtenstein, Switzerland and Uruguay. For their low restriction profiles and long tradition, Liechtenstein and Switzerland are the most famous cases. In Italy, the many initiatives for an abrogative referendum may also have been invited by relatively low signature requirements. In addition, the party system in Italy has a long history of polarization, and the transformation process of the early 1990s worked as a second factor in promoting the use of the abrogative referendum. Uruguay also has a significant number of initiatives and votes on constitutional amendments for which signature support of 10 per cent of the electorate is required. Rejective referendums and legislative initiatives, however, need 25 per cent signature support, which makes it more difficult to use these instruments. A general conclusion may be that under low-requirement conditions 'cultures' of frequent use may develop which can establish initiative instruments as an integral part of the political system.

Table 3.4. Usage of citizens' initiatives and citizen-demanded referendums at the national level (frequency of votes, up to 2006): some examples

Region of the world	Frequent votes	Occasional votes	No votes
Africa			Cape Verde, Liberia, Togo, Uganda
Americas	Uruguay	Bolivia, Colombia, Ecuador, Venezuela	Costa Rica, Nicaragua, Peru
Asia			Philippines, Taiwan, Turkmenistan
Europe	Italy, Liechtenstein, Switzerland	Hungary, Latvia, Lithuania, the former Yugoslav Republic of Macedonia, Slovakia, Slovenia	Albania, Belarus, Croatia, Georgia, Malta, Republic of Moldova, Russian Federation, Serbia, Ukraine
Oceania		Federated States of Micronesia , New Zealand	Marshall Islands, Palau

107. In contrast, in a number of countries where initiative rights exist formally, no votes have taken place. This applies to the Russian Federation and other successor states of the Soviet Union, such as Belarus, Georgia, Republic of Moldova and Ukraine. Highly restrictive requirements such as subject restrictions and procedural thresholds, as well as a non-participative political culture, particularly in the context or the tradition of an authoritarian political system, mean that initiative procedures are hardly used and are regarded as eccentric features of the political system in these countries. In other polities, if the system of representative institutions is fragile or unstable, this may create an unlikely context for initiative rights to be practised. Other, very different, factors may also lead to a situation in which they are little used in practice and in fact there is little

need to resort to initiative procedures. If a party system is open enough for new issues and change to occur, for example, or in a consociational democracy where all the major minority interests have an integrated position in political decision making, initiative instruments may be less likely to be used even when the legal procedures exist. Malta may be an example of this type of polity.

108. A considerable number of countries show infrequent use of initiative procedures, even though they exist in law. In the Central and East European countries (e.g. Hungary, Latvia, Lithuania, the former Yugoslav Republic of Macedonia, Slovakia, Slovenia) initiatives have focused mostly around issues of transformation from communist rule. For instance, in Hungary, four out of six referendum votes took place in the critical transitional year of 1989. In some countries in Latin America there has been only minimal use of initiative rights because the structural conditions for exercising those rights have not been supportive. The instability of the political system (Bolivia), the shaky general condition of the state (Colombia) or the context of the 'Bolivarian Revolution' (under President Hugo Chávez in Venezuela) mean that the initiative mechanism is not likely to develop. New Zealand introduced a new law providing for non-binding citizen-initiated referendums in 1993 (see box 3.2).

Box 3.2. New Zealand's citizens-initiated referendum

In 1993, New Zealand introduced provisions for citizens' initiatives. Any citizen or group who wishes to do so may submit a proposed question to the clerk of the House of Representatives. The question is then advertised, and comments on its wording are invited. Within three months of its submission, the clerk will determine the final wording of the question. The proposer then has 12 months within which to obtain signatures in support. For the proposal to qualify for the ballot, the signatures of at least 10 per cent of registered electors must be obtained. Upon submission of the required number of signatures, the clerk conducts a random check of the signatures to determine their validity. When these qualifications have been met, the question is submitted to parliament, and the governor general sets a date for the referendum to be held.

In the ten years following passage of the Citizens Initiated Referenda Act in 1993, 40 proposals were submitted to the clerk. They dealt with a wide range of issues such as the prevention of cruelty to animals, a reduction in the size of parliament, minimum sentences in criminal trials, guaranteed access to health care and education, welfare benefits, conservation and euthanasia. Only three of these obtained the number of signatures required to be put forward for a vote.

The results of the vote on a proposal are not binding. parliament alone determines whether it wishes to act on a proposal, regardless of the number of votes obtained in the referendum. Two of the three questions submitted to a vote since implementation of the act – a proposal to reduce the size of parliament and a proposal to impose harsher sentences for violent crimes – received overwhelming public support but were not acted on by parliament.

The non-binding character of New Zealand's initiative process has been much criticized, and was itself the subject of an initiative proposal put forward in 2003. The high signature requirement has also acted to prevent many proposals from going forward to a vote. Taken together, the difficulty of qualifying a proposal for the ballot and the uncertainty of parliamentary action even if it passes have reduced public enthusiasm for the initiative process in New Zealand, and fewer proposals have been submitted to the clerk in recent years. However, New Zealand's citizens' initiative law remains an experiment in the use of direct democracy, and future reforms to the process are likely to be considered based on the experience with the current law.

109. A very different picture can be found in federal countries which provide initiative instruments at the state or regional level. Much activity can be observed in many of the 24 states of the USA that have initiative provisions, particularly Arizona, California, Colorado, North Dakota and Oregon (see the case study following chapter 4). A typical example of the process found in many of the US states may be seen in the example of California's Proposition 71 to facilitate stem cell research, which was approved by the voters in the 2004 election (see box 3.3). In Germany, where all the *länder* have such instruments, a number of initiatives, some resulting in referendum votes, have been launched by citizens (particularly in Bavaria, Brandenburg, Hamburg and Schleswig-Holstein).

Box 3.3. A US state initiative: California Proposition 71

Official title and summary (prepared by the state attorney general)

Stem Cell Research. Funding. Bonds – Initiative Constitutional Amendment and Statute

- Establishes the California Institute for Regenerative Medicine to regulate stem cell research and provide funding, through grants and loans, for such research and research facilities.

- Establishes the constitutional right to conduct stem cell research; prohibits the institute's funding of human reproductive cloning research.

- Establishes an oversight committee to govern the institute.

- Provides a General Fund loan of up to 3 million USD for the institute's initial administration/implementation costs.

- Authorizes the issuance of general obligation bonds to finance Institute activities up to 3 billion USD subject to an annual limit of 350 million USD.

- Appropriates monies from the General Fund to pay for bonds.

California Proposition 71 was one of 17 state measures that appeared on the California ballot paper at the time of the November 2004 US presidential election. Twelve of these measures, including the stem cell research proposal, were citizens' initiatives and the other five were items put on the ballot paper by the state legislature. Proposition 71 was initiated by the Coalition for Stem Cell Research and Cures, which became the registered committee supporting the proposal. The initiative was developed in part in response to a 2001 federal regulation prohibiting federal funds from being used on research that involves newly derived embryonic stem-cell lines. Private funds, however, were exempt from these federal restrictions, and the individual states were also free to make their own decisions regarding funding biomedical research, which might include stem cells. However, the issue was very contentious. Five other groups registered officially with the California secretary of state as committees in opposition to Proposition 71 and campaigned actively against it.

As is the practice in California, the legislative analyst provided a neutral summary and explanation of the proposal, which was included in the 2004 *Voter Information Booklet*. The individuals and committees supporting the proposition were also allowed to include their own statement in the booklet, as were the opponents of Proposition 71. The measure passed by a vote of 59 per cent to 41 per cent, with approximately 49 per cent of eligible California electors voting on Proposition 71. Following its passage, it then became the responsibility of the state to implement the proposal.

110. Many jurisdictions which have initiative instruments at the national or regional level also provide such procedures at the local level (e.g. Germany, Italy, some of the US states). Very often, restrictions and requirements are similar to those that apply at the national or regional levels. In addition, many other countries that do not have instruments of this type at the national level provide initiative channels at the local level

(e.g. Belgium, the Czech Republic, Mexico, Norway, Poland, Spain, Sweden). The scale of initiative activity varies significantly between countries, according to restrictions on subjects, profiles of procedural restrictions, and political cultures.

Box 3.4. Citizens' initiatives at the local level: Germany

The Federal Republic of Germany, in contrast to the Weimar Republic (1919–33), did not include initiatives and referendums at the national level in the constitution of 1949. However, the regional states (*länder*), founded after 1945, introduced initiative procedures, as did the re-established *länder* of East Germany after 1990. During the 1990s all the *länder* also introduced initiative rights at the local level. The associated regulations vary significantly between the *länder* for the state and the local level.

In *Bavaria*, at the state level, for a citizens' initiative proposing a law or a constitutional amendment, the signatures of 10 per cent of registered electors are required to be collected within a period of two weeks. Parliament can consider the proposal and put forward a counter-proposal to the referendum vote. The referendum vote is valid with a simple majority of the votes cast (plus, since 1999, a turnout of 25 per cent of registered electors for a constitutional amendment). Between 1946 and 2005, 38 initiatives (out of 172 in all Germany) were submitted in Bavaria. Of these, 16 were registered for collecting signatures, five (out of 13 in all of Germany) led to a referendum vote, and two (out of seven in all Germany) were successful at the referendum vote. Subjects have included schools, radio regulation, waste management, the introduction of local referendums and the abolition of the non-elected Senate.

At the local level, initiative and referendum procedures were introduced in 1995 by a citizens' initiative at the state level. For an initiative, the signatures of 10 per cent of registered electors are required, decreasing to 3 per cent in large cities. A valid vote requires a double majority including the approval of 20 per cent of registered electors, decreasing to 10 per cent in large cities. Up to the end of 2005, some 1,200 initiatives (out of about 3,000 in all of Germany) were submitted, leading to 538 referendum votes, and a valid and successful result in 305 cases. In addition, local councils started 217 referendums with a successful vote in 103 cases.

In *Hesse* at the state level, the signatures of 3 per cent of registered electors are required in order for an initiative to be submitted, and 20 per cent for it to qualify as a citizens' initiative. This requirement has not been met in any instance since 1946. In 1993, local initiative rights were introduced, with a requirement for the signatures of 10 per cent of registered electors. For a valid referendum vote a double majority including 25 per cent of registered electors is needed. Up to the end of 2005, in 426 municipalities, 240 citizens' initiatives had been submitted, of which 79 were declared inadmissible. Of the resulting 90 referendum votes, 45 ended in a success for the initiators. Referendum votes are binding for three years. The subjects have included city planning, public facilities for childcare and sports, investment projects, environmental issues and road plans. Taxes, budget matters and the structure of the local administration cannot be the subject of an initiative.

Table 3.5. Countries with provision for initiative procedures at the regional or local level, by region

Region	Regional level	Local level
Americas	Brazil, Colombia, Ecuador, Peru, United States	Bolivia, Brazil, Canada, Colombia, Ecuador, Mexico, Peru, United States
Asia		Philippines, Taiwan, Turkmenistan
Europe	Germany, Italy, Sweden, Switzerland	Austria, Croatia, Czech Republic, Finland, Germany, Hungary, Italy, the former Yugoslav Republic of Macedonia, Norway, Poland, Slovenia, Sweden, Switzerland

Conclusions

111. Citizens' initiatives and citizen-demanded referendums as instruments of direct democracy can contribute to the quality of democracy by providing supplementary channels of political articulation and control with a focus on political issues rather than on candidates or parties. Apart from the final referendum vote, the initiative process itself is often regarded as supportive of democracy, since proponents have the opportunity to put forward ideas, attract political input and political support 'from below', and induce the participation of citizens in the legislative process. To perform these functions, initiative and referendum procedures should be designed according to the principles of political equality, transparency and fairness.

112. Empirical data show that initiative instruments are available in significantly fewer countries than those with mandatory or optional referendums called by the political authorities (compare figure 2.1 in chapter 2 with table 3.1). In Europe, for instance, the proportion is less than one-third, and in Africa and Asia, where there are very few initiative instruments in existence, the difference is even more striking. It seems that referendum procedures and votes controlled by the political authorities have a stronger

institutional basis than those which can be initiated by citizens. While there may be good arguments for the instrument of the referendum, an enhanced role for initiative processes may also deserve stronger support. There is a good case for arguing that citizens' initiatives and citizen-demanded referendums have strong democratic qualities since they originate from citizens' activities 'from below'. Thus, initiative procedures may be an option for enhancing the quality of democracy in many countries.

113. Restrictions on the subjects included in initiative procedures should be consistent with the rules for optional referendums called by the authorities, and not put particularly excessive limits on initiative procedures. If restrictions are deemed to be necessary, they should be fairly specific and formulated in clear and transparent terms in order to avoid political manoeuvring by the authorities to outlaw initiatives which may be politically unpopular with them.

114. If initiative instruments are generally available in a jurisdiction, constitutional amendments may also be included. Since in a democracy the citizens are considered to be the owners of the constitution, there are good reasons for allowing citizens to initiate amendments on constitutional matters. To secure the stability, coherence and broad legitimacy of a constitution, rather than ruling out citizens' initiatives, special requirements for the validity of a constitutional referendum vote could be established.

115. For designing initiative procedures, the main issues are the requirements for qualifying an initiative for the referendum and the criteria for a valid referendum vote. Signature requirements will determine the access citizens have to initiative procedures. Lower thresholds are more user-friendly and attract more active participation by citizens. This trend is seen in countries which have signature requirements not higher than 5 per cent of registered electors. In countries requiring the signatures of more than 10 to 15 per cent of the electorate, hardly any initiative activity can be observed, suggesting that a lower signature requirement may be preferred if public participation is to be encouraged. Adequate design for the validity requirement of the popular vote is a more complex choice. The normal requirement of a majority of votes cast is quite often supplemented by criteria of qualified majorities or double majorities which are supposed to ensure the broader legitimacy of the referendum vote. However, they can also have some problematic side effects. Turnout quorums tend to attract abstention campaigns which undermine debate and participation. Approval quorums with majorities qualified by high percentages of votes or double majorities can impose requirements that can hardly ever be reached, and therefore may discourage use of the instrument. If the approval of a certain percentage of all registered electors is required, this means in effect that all undecided and non-participating citizens are treated as equivalent to 'No' voters. This may also invite campaigns to recommend abstention from voting.

116. The procedures of direct democracy serve as a supplement to, not a substitute for, representative democracy. The quality of an initiative procedure may be improved by cooperative interactions with governmental institutions, particularly with legislatures. In most US states, however, the procedure of a 'direct initiative' does not include any

formal interaction with a state legislature. A debate in the legislature and the option of presenting an alternative proposal to the initiative can offer clearer and more qualified alternatives to the referendum vote of the citizens.

117. The result of a referendum initiated by citizens should be legally binding rather than purely consultative. In the case of a citizen-demanded rejective referendum on new legislation, this should be self-evident since the very meaning of the procedure is to stop the new law from coming into force. In the case of a citizens' initiative, it is fairly unusual for the result to be non-binding, although this is the case in a few jurisdictions (e.g. New Zealand under the law adopted in 1993). This may also be counterproductive since citizens can become frustrated if their referendum vote is not taken seriously. As a procedure without a binding referendum vote, the agenda initiative provides an alternative process (see chapter 4). For a legally binding vote the regulations should specify clearly whether the referendum decision is only legally sustained for a certain period of time (as with local referendums in some German *länder*), and whether after that period it can be replaced by a decision of the legislature, or only by a new referendum vote.

CHAPTER 4

CHAPTER 4

Agenda initiatives: when citizens can get a proposal on the legislative agenda

118. Within the family of direct democracy instruments, the agenda initiative plays a specific role. It is the only popular right that does not necessarily lead to a referendum vote. It places an issue on the political agenda and requires a specified authority – typically the legislature – to consider and/or act on a proposal. This action may sometimes include the possibility that the legislative body will put the issue to a referendum vote. Agenda initiatives are subject to certain regulations, covering, for example, the number of signatures required, the time allowed for gathering the signatures, and restrictions on the kinds of issue that can be the subject of an agenda initiative.

119. It is important to distinguish the agenda initiative procedure from petitions, which have little formal structure and can be as simple as a letter from a constituent to a legislator or official. These are weakly regulated and exist almost everywhere in the world. The agenda initiative is a stronger instrument.

120. Sometimes agenda initiative procedures can overlap with those of petitions or with citizens' initiatives requiring a referendum vote. This is the case when just one person is eligible to put an issue on the political agenda or when agenda initiatives request a legislative body to trigger a referendum vote on a certain issue. As a specific direct democracy procedure 'in between' petitions and citizens' initiatives, agenda initiatives are sometimes called by other names, such as 'people's motions', 'submission rights' or 'popular legislative initiatives'.

Table 4.1. Agenda initiatives: the instrument 'in between'

Procedure	Definition	Example
Petition	A procedure which allows one or several citizens to present a proposal to the authorities	In 2005 a group of concerned Thai citizens gathered signatures in order to protest against the national film censorship practice.
Agenda initiative	A direct democracy procedure which enables citizens to submit a proposal which must be considered by the legislature but is not necessarily put to a vote of the electorate	In 2002 in Argentina almost 400,000 citizens signed a proposal to end special pension funds for state officials and legislators.
Citizens' initiative	A direct democracy procedure that allows citizens to initiate a vote of the electorate on a proposal outlined by those citizens. The proposal may be for a new law, for an amendment to the constitution, or to repeal or amend an existing law.	A California citizens' initiative, which gathered more than 500,000 signatures, led to a 2008 state-wide referendum on a high-speed railway system.

Table 4.2. The agenda initiative: an instrument with many names

Country	Name in the language of the country	Name in English
Austria	*Volksbegehren*	Popular demand
Argentina	*Iniciativa popular indirecta*	Indirect popular initiative
Benin	*Pétition citoyenne*	Citizens' petition
Italy	*Initiativa delle Leggi*	Law initiative
Netherlands	*Volksinitiatief*	Popular initiative
Norway	*Innbyggerinitiativ*	Inhabitant initiative
Switzerland	*Volksmotion, motion populaire, mozione populare*	Popular motion

121. An agenda initiative procedure can be described as the right of a group of voters, meeting predetermined requirements, to initiate a process for the revision of a law, the introduction of a new law, or an amendment to the constitution. However, the legislative body retains full decision-making power. This is crucial for differentiating the agenda initiative mechanism from that of citizens' initiatives: it means that the power-sharing aspect which is characteristic of all direct democracy instruments is limited here to agenda setting.

122. This chapter examines the existence and development of agenda initiative procedures around the world and considers issues related to their design and regulation. It also offers an overview of the use of agenda initiatives in practice, and identifies elements that need to be considered carefully when an agenda initiative procedure is designed, administered and used.

123. Historically, agenda initiative procedures surfaced for the first time in the constitutions of European countries after World War I. This group of countries included Austria, Latvia and Spain. After World War II, a second wave of introductions followed in Latin America (including Guatemala, Uruguay and Venezuela). Since 1989 agenda initiative procedures have been established in several jurisdictions around the world, including countries in South East Asia (the Philippines, Thailand), West Africa (Ghana, Niger) and Eastern Europe (Hungary, Poland, Slovenia).

The distribution of agenda initiative procedures

124. National-level agenda initiative procedures are also found at the sub-national (first tier/local) levels of many countries (e.g. Germany). At the transnational level, the EU has included an agenda initiative provision in the Treaty of Lisbon. While many countries in Europe and Latin America provide for an agenda initiative procedure, the mechanism is less well known in Africa, Asia and Oceania.

Table 4.3. Agenda initiative procedures, by region

Region of the world/country	National level	Only sub-national level
Africa		
Benin	•	
Burkina Faso	•	
Cape Verde	•	
Congo, Democratic Republic of the	•	
Liberia	•	
Niger	•	
Togo	•	
Uganda	•	
Total for Africa	8	
Americas		
Argentina	•	
Bolivia	•	
Brazil	•	
Colombia	•	
Costa Rica	•	

Region of the world/country	National level	Only sub-national level
Ecuador	•	
Guatemala	•	
Honduras	•	
Mexico		•
Nicaragua	•	
Paraguay	•	
Peru	•	
Uruguay	•	
Venezuela	•	
Total for Americas	13	1
Asia		
Kyrgyzstan	•	
Philippines	•	
Thailand	•	
Turkmenistan		•
Total for Asia	3	1
Europe		
Albania	•	
Andorra	•	
Austria	•	
Belarus	•	
Finland		•
Georgia	•	•
Germany		•
Hungary	•	
Italy	•	
Latvia	•	
Liechtenstein	•	
Lithuania	•	
Macedonia, the former Yugoslav Republic of	•	
Moldova, Republic of	•	
Montenegro	•	•
Netherlands	•	
Norway		•
Poland	•	
Portugal	•	
Romania	•	
San Marino	•	
Serbia	•	

Region of the world/country	National level	Only sub-national level
Slovakia	•	
Slovenia	•	
Spain	•	
Sweden		•
Switzerland		•
Total for Europe	22	7

Design and regulation

125. Design and regulation are critical to the efficient functioning of direct democracy procedures. Agenda initiatives have many similarities with other direct democracy procedures such as citizen-demand referendums, citizens' initiatives and recall. Very high signature requirements, for instance, will limit the possibility of a qualifying agenda initiative being brought forward, as will very short time periods allowed for the collection of signatures. However, as an instrument for agenda setting, the agenda initiative tool may be used fairly frequently, and with large numbers of signatures being gathered, as the Austrian experience shows (see box 4.1).

Box 4.1. Austria: the most intensive practitioner of the agenda initiative

In Austria a binding referendum cannot be initiated by gathering signatures, but the agenda initiative has been used frequently and successfully. Since 1964 more than 30 nationwide agenda initiatives have been launched. This step requires 8,000 signatures in support, which is the equivalent of 0.1 per cent of the electorate. For an initiative to qualify to be dealt with in the national parliament there is a second, more demanding, target of 100,000 signatures, which must be gathered within just eight days in state offices. Almost all these 30 initiatives reached this target. An agenda initiative can also be launched by just eight members of the national parliament, or by 12 members from at least three state parliaments.

One reason for the frequent and successful use of the agenda initiative may be the fact that the first three agenda initiatives in the 1960s were all accepted and implemented by parliament. Those initiatives covered issues such as the introduction of the 40-hour working week and school reform. But the most successful was the first, in 1964, when the state broadcasting company was reformed based on an agenda initiative supported by no less than one-fifth of the electorate. Another factor is that the agenda initiative is often seen by opposition political parties as a way to get publicity and to educate and motivate their voters.

An example from 2006 illustrates the role of the agenda initiative in Austrian politics. During one week in March, over 250,000 Austrians went to the offices of their local municipalities to sign an agenda initiative to the national parliament requesting a referendum on any future EU membership deal for Turkey. This initiative – by the right-wing Freedom Party – led to an announcement by the prime minister that a referendum will be held to let the people decide as soon as Turkish membership is formally placed on the EU agenda.

126. An important feature when assessing the procedural aspects of agenda initiatives is the number of signatures in support required at the national level. The available data present a picture of considerable variation regarding these requirements: for example, in Uruguay a legislative agenda initiative requires the signatures of not less than 25 per cent of the electorate, while the threshold in Georgia is less than 1 per cent. Many countries also have different requirements for legislative and constitutional agenda initiatives. In Kyrgyzstan one needs to gather 30,000 signatures for a proposal for legislation while a proposal for an amendment to the constitution requires ten times as many. In a third group of countries (e.g. Costa Rica), however, where signature requirements are concerned there is no difference between agenda initiatives to amend a law and agenda initiatives to amend the constitution.

Table 4.4. Examples of variations in signature requirements for agenda initiatives

Country	No. of registered electors	Agenda initiative for ordinary legislation		Agenda initiative for an amendment to the constitution	
		No.	% of registered electors	No.	% of registered electors
Ecuador	8,154,424	20,386	0.25	81,544	1
Georgia	3,143,851	30,000	0.95	200,000	6.36
Kyrgyzstan	2,537,247	30,000	1.18	300,000	11.8
Lithuania	2,719,608	50,000	1.84	300,000	11.03
Romania	17,699,727	100,000	0.56	500,000	2.82
Venezuela	12,048,000	12,048	0.10	1,807,200	15

127. Beyond signature requirements, there are several additional important design and regulation issues, such as: (a) issues which may be excluded from being the subject of an agenda initiative; (b) the specified timeframe and venues linked to the signature gathering; (c) how legislative bodies may deal with an agenda initiative; (d) possible

support by the authorities for agenda initiative committees, and; (e) the legal status of agenda initiative committees vis-à-vis the legislative body.

128. Jurisdictions differ with regard to the types of issues citizens can raise through procedures of direct democracy, just as they differ with regard to the types of issue elected legislative bodies can decide. This also applies to the 'soft' agenda initiative mechanism ('soft' because of its lack of decision-making power). Issues that cannot be the subject of an agenda initiative may include amendments to the constitution (as in Austria, Brazil, Cape Verde, Thailand), the adoption of international treaties (Austria, Mali, Peru), taxes and public expenditure commitments (Albania, Burkina Faso, Uruguay) or issues of devolution (Niger). Issues that are excluded from the agenda initiative procedure are therefore sometimes of great public interest, and are often politically controversial. Such exclusions may therefore weaken the agenda initiative instrument.

129. Where and how signatures can be gathered is also of considerable importance. They may be gathered freely and in any location, or in person only (excluding e-signatures) and in specified venues. Another important aspect is the time allowed for the gathering of the required number of signatures. Here again there are substantial variations around the world. For example, in Austria the required 100,000 signatures must be gathered within eight days at official bureaux, while Lithuanians are offered three months for the collection of 50,000 signatures for legislative agenda initiatives. There are, however, many countries where there are no fixed time schedules at all for the collection of signatures. Additionally, in comparison to citizens' initiatives, the requirements with respect to citizenship status may be less stringent when it comes to agenda initiatives. While only registered citizens may be eligible to sign a citizens' initiative, registered non-nationals may be entitled to sign an agenda initiative (as in Finland, Norway, Sweden).

130. In contrast to the special requirements, hurdles and restrictions outlined above, a dedicated initiative infrastructure may be provided to support the conduct of an agenda initiative procedure. A 'dedicated initiative infrastructure' means, for instance, providing public services for an agenda initiative committee during the various steps involved in the initiative process (as described in detail in chapter 6). Initially this may include checks of the language of the proposed text, translation assistance, and procedural advice (e.g. in Niger, the Philippines, Switzerland). At a later stage, the agenda initiative infrastructure may include some practical and financial support as well as the right for initiative committees to present their case in the legislative body themselves (as in Norway and Sweden at the local level).

Box 4.2. Poland: the agenda initiative as a test ground for reform

In Poland, an agenda initiative procedure was introduced with the national constitution in 1997. Legislation to regulate the procedure followed in 1999. All issues can be addressed through such a citizen-triggered initiative except finance laws and constitutional amendments. All proposals must be put forward in a fully formulated way, including an explanatory statement on the social, economic and financial effects of the proposal. All this must be done without any official assistance and is done by a 'legislative initiative committee'. Such a committee can be founded by a group of 15 registered citizens, who sign a written statement on membership of the committee together with personal data.

The name of the committee must reflect the subject of the proposed legislation. Only one proposal can be made at a time. To enable the initiative to be registered with the authorities, at least 1,000 signatures are required. When the proposal reaches this threshold, a specified official of the national parliament, the marshal of the Sejm (the lower house), will check the legality of the agenda initiative. If the answer is negative, the initiative committee has 14 days to correct the faults or to appeal to the Supreme Court. If the proposal is accepted, the committee should publish the initiative with all relevant information in a national newspaper – at its own expense. From then on, the committee has three months to gather at least 100,000 signatures. There are further limitations on how and where these signatures can be collected. If this second milestone is not met within three months, the committee is dissolved. If the proponents are successful, the marshal of the Sejm will forward the agenda initiative to the National Electoral Commission for the signature lists to be validated and verified. If approved, the bill is then sent to the national parliament for further debate.

Since 1999 almost 60 nationwide agenda initiatives have been launched. In 50 cases, the authorities rejected the proposal on formal legal grounds. Within 14 days, the committees responsible for about 40 initiatives managed to correct the faults and launch the initiative. Of the 45 agenda initiatives that reached the stage of signature collecting, 23 achieved the 100,000 signature target. Three of these were disallowed by the authorities leaving 20 agenda initiatives the subject of legislative processes in the parliament. None was completely rejected, and many were implemented in an amended form. Polish agenda initiatives have included proposals to improve the country's teacher training programmes, to establish a Foundation of National Education, to ban the promotion of violence in the mass media, to strengthen the laws on environmental protection, and to offer financial support to single-parent families.

131. The legal status of an agenda initiative committee is important, as it is this group that may be heard by the legislative body or may follow up (politically and juridically) the fate of an agenda initiative which has gathered enough signatures to qualify.

Box 4.3. Argentina: agenda initiatives as crisis management tools

In Argentina, when the economic crisis reached its peak in the early 2000s, the newly introduced agenda initiative was used more often than in any other country. Since 1996 Argentine legislation has provided the basic rules of this direct democracy mechanism: the signatures of 1.5 per cent of the electorate – about 400,000 registered electors – are required to bring a legislative proposal forward to the national parliament. As Argentina is a federal state, the 1.5 per cent threshold is additionally required in at least six out of the 24 states. However, according to the law, some issues cannot be forwarded by the citizens on to the legislative agenda. These include constitutional reforms, international treaties and the penal code.

While several dozen nationwide agenda initiatives have been launched since 1996, just two of them gathered the 1.5 per cent signatures required for them to be – at least partly – implemented by the parliament. In 2002 more than 400,000 signatures were delivered to the Electoral Commission proposing an end to special pensions for government officials and elected officials. In the same year another agenda initiative got as far as the parliament, demanding special funds for starving children and their families, who were suffering badly during the economic crisis of the time. The latter initiative was even signed by the president and was implemented by the parliament. Several other prominent attempts did not reach the signature threshold, including an agenda initiative to reform the electoral system and a citizen proposal to increase transparency and accountability in the political process.

In sum, the agenda initiative mechanism in Argentina has proved to be a powerful tool for agenda setting, while the elected parliament has retained its full decision-making powers. Moreover, its use during the economic crisis has shown that the instrument can be used as a political crisis management tool.

Conclusions

132. Any discussion of the use of agenda initiatives in practice should ideally be accompanied by an assessment of those that have been launched and have qualified to go forward. However, only limited data are available as yet to provide a basis for a more comprehensive overview of their use at the national, regional and local levels

worldwide. In fact, as the world survey on direct democracy (annex A) shows, it is often somewhat unclear whether a participatory instrument called an 'initiative' is a petition, an agenda initiative or a citizens' initiative. In Italy, between 1978 and 2002, there were 320 agenda initiative attempts, of which approximately one-third managed to get the required 50,000 signatures. One agenda initiative even made it indirectly to the ballot box – in 1988, when more than 110,000 signatures were gathered to ask the European Parliament to launch an EU constitution-making process. This non-binding demand was subsequently put to a consultative referendum by the Italian parliament and, in 1989, 88 per cent of the voters supported the proposal (turnout was 86 per cent). Other countries which have used agenda initiatives in a comprehensive way include Hungary (more than 150 attempts at the national level), Spain, Poland and Argentina (see box 4.3). In Sweden, local and regional agenda initiative rights were introduced in 1994, following up a recommendation by the Council of Europe in the same year. More than 150 local and regional agenda initiatives have been submitted to legislative bodies, but fewer than 15 have become the subject of a referendum process or have been implemented.

Box 4.4. The European Union: towards the first transnational agenda initiative mechanism

In the 2007 Lisbon Treaty and in the proposed European Constitutional Treaty of 2005, the European heads of state and government introduced an article on participative democracy, which includes the provision for an agenda initiative right (called the citizens' initiative). Article I-8b.4 reads: 'Not less than one million citizens who are nationals of a significant number of Member States may take the initiative of inviting the Commission, within the framework of its powers, to submit any appropriate proposal on matters where citizens consider that a legal act of the Union is required for the purpose of implementing the Treaties'. On ratification, an implementation law will have to decide important questions such as the range of issues which can be addressed, the forms of signature gathering across the EU member states, and the time limits allowed for the process. The idea of the first transnational procedure with direct democracy elements has inspired at least 20 committees across Europe to launch a 'European agenda initiative'.

A brief assessment of these 20 pilot initiatives shows that the new instrument is being used by many groups from different sections of society, including politicians, human rights groups, economic foundations and broad alliances of non-governmental groups. However, as the concept of the European citizens' initiative is still new, and as the culture and practice of initiatives are as yet only weakly developed in many European countries, several initiatives are still calling their attempt to gather 1 million signatures a 'petition'. Furthermore, the fact that the implementation regulation does not yet exist means that all kinds of ways of collecting signatures are being used, including the simple and hardly verifiable registration of names online. At the same time, it is clear that the Internet offers a unique transnational platform for launching and conducting such initiatives. Interestingly, most of the initiatives so far launched understand the need to publish their information in as many European languages as possible.

This early but dynamic development of transnational direct democracy practice offers many practical opportunities, both for academics and for political practitioners, to test and assess the first steps towards transnational direct democracy. One question will be what a democratic infrastructure beyond the raw tool of the initiative could look like, including some kind of European 'agenda management board' to assist, test and follow up European citizens' agenda initiatives, as well as implementing a comprehensive voter education programme across the region.

Source: Kaufmann, Bruno et al., *The Initiative and Referendum Institute Europe Guidebook to Direct Democracy in Switzerland and Beyond,* 2009 edn (Marburg/Brussels: IRI Europe, 2008)

133. As a direct democracy mechanism the agenda initiative offers a functional means for citizens and legislators to share power. However, the special value of being able to put an issue on the agenda of a legislative body is linked to the collective effort of gathering signatures in support of a certain idea. For this reason the signature-gathering period is significant for the democratic success of an agenda initiative. This leads us to the conclusion that the collecting of signatures should not be limited to certain official offices, and that the period available for gathering the required number of signatures should be neither too short (e.g. a few days or weeks) nor too long (more than a year or even unlimited). As with citizens' initiatives, extended lists of excluded issues are not helpful as these often include the most interesting and controversial issues. As a simple rule, the agenda initiative should cover the same range of issues as the targeted legislative body is able to deal with.

134. As the agenda initiative is a fundamentally 'limited' direct democracy procedure, the public infrastructure provided for initiators and supporters is even more important to the democratic success of the procedure. This public infrastructure may include structured forms of presentations and deliberations between initiators and legislators as well as comprehensive forms of official assistance during the whole agenda initiative process. An examination of national and sub-national practice shows clearly that more frequent use of the mechanism is linked in several ways to the success of the instrument. When agenda initiative procedures fail to achieve their goals, citizens are inclined to try to find other ways of gaining influence in the legislative process.

Direct democracy in Oregon

Paddy McGuire

Historical background

The roots of direct democracy in the US state of Oregon can be traced back to the progressive movement in the late 1800s. William U'Ren, who briefly served in the Oregon legislature, was almost single-handedly responsible for the introduction of the right of Oregonians to write their own laws through the citizens' initiative, repeal acts of the legislature through the abrogative referendum, and remove elected officials through the recall, all of which were adopted in Oregon at the end of the 19th century.

The growth of direct democracy was a reaction to the view among the electorate that the railway industry, through its lobbyists and legislators beholden to it, controlled the actions of the state legislature. The railways held great political power in the early days of European settlement of the American West. To encourage quick settlement across the continent, in the 1860s the US Congress had granted vast tracts of unoccupied land (this was just after the removal from that land of the American Indians to reservations) to construct railways across the nation. In Oregon, those land grants to the railways meant that the companies owned much of the timber that would be the cornerstone of the state economy for the next 120 years.

U'Ren was elected to the legislature in 1896 as a member of the People's Party. Neither of the major parties had a majority in the 1897 legislature, and U'Ren controlled the swing votes that could allow either the Democrats or the Republicans to organize a majority. In what was known as the 'Holdup of '97', U'Ren withheld support from either side until the Republicans finally agreed to refer to the voters a constitutional amendment granting the right of citizens' initiative and rejective referendum to the citizens. The amendment was put to the voters in 1902 and was adopted by a vote of 62,024 to 5,668.

The Oregon constitution contains the following provision: 'The people reserve to themselves the initiative power, which is to propose laws and amendments to the Constitution and enact or reject them at an election independently of the Legislative Assembly'.

In quick succession following the enactment of the initiative, the people used their new power to enact a number of political reforms – the direct primary election, in 1904; the direct election of United States senators (state legislatures elected members of the United States Senate in the early days of the Republic), and the instruments of initiative and referendum at the local level, in 1906; recall of public officials, in 1908; the presidential primary election, in 1910; and women's suffrage, in 1912.

Interestingly, one of U'Ren's primary motivations for pushing the initiative system was that he advocated funding state government by a 'single tax' on the appreciation of real property values. He knew that the legislature would not approve the single tax but thought that the voters would. In 1908, the voters got their chance when U'Ren sponsored an initiative to enact the single tax. It was defeated, and he was subsequently defeated in 1914 when he stood for governor on a single tax platform. He left the political scene shortly thereafter.

Procedures and legal provisions

The citizens' initiative

The 1902 amendment to the constitution gave the people the right to amend both the constitution and state statutes.

Petition organizers have up to 23 months to complete all the steps necessary to qualify an initiative for the ballot. To begin the process, one must gather at least 1,000 valid signatures on a petition containing the text of the proposed law. When that proposal is filed with the EMB, the state attorney general has 60 days to write a ballot title. The title is a statement of up to 25 words that explains the impact of the measure. Anyone may appeal against the attorney general's ballot title to the State Supreme Court. Typically, the first five or six months of the 23-month window are taken up with the procedural processes needed to move forward.

Once a ballot title is finalized, the circulators may begin gathering signatures. The proposal may be to amend the constitution or to adopt a statute, the only structural difference being that to amend the constitution the proponents must gather valid signatures equal to 8 per cent of the number of people who voted in the most recent election for governor (in 2007–11 that threshold is 110,358), while a statutory change requires 6 per cent (82,769 during the same period).

The deadline for turning in signatures is 120 days before the biennial general election (the only election at which citizens' initiatives can be voted on). Once the signatures are turned in, the EMB has 30 days to check their validity. The EMB takes a statistical sample of the signatures and 5 per cent of the signatures are actually verified. One invalid signature among the sample results in the invalidation of 20 total signatures and one duplicate results in the invalidation of 400 signatures.

Initiatives that qualify are sequentially numbered based on the date on which they were submitted for verification and are voted on in the general election in November of each even-numbered year. Since 1902, 340 initiatives have appeared on the ballot paper and 118 of them (35 per cent) have passed.

The rejective referendum

The 1902 constitutional amendment also granted to the people the right to reject new enactments of the legislature. Under this mechanism, petitioners must gather signatures equal to 4 per cent of the number of persons who voted in the previous election for governor (55,179 during 2007–11) within 90 days of the end of the session of the legislature that enacted the law.

The governor, who has 30 days to sign or veto a law from the date when it is enacted by the legislature, can frustrate this action substantially. Thus, when it is clear that there may be an attempt to organize a referendum on new legislation, the legislature can wait until its last day to enact it and the governor can wait the full 30 days to sign it, effectively using up one-third of the time available to petitioners to take the matter to the voters. Since 1902, 62 rejective referendums have been put to the voters and 21 (33 per cent) have succeeded in repealing the law concerned.

Recall

One of the first citizens' initiatives passed by Oregon voters was the right to recall public officers. Oregon was the first of the US states to do so, in 1908, and followed only the City of Los Angeles, which adopted the recall in 1903. A citizen may begin the recall process by filing a notice with the Electoral Management Body (EMB) and then has 90 days to gather valid signatures equal to 15 per cent of the votes cast in that district for all candidates for governor in the most recent election. Once the signatures are verified, the EMB has 45 days to call a special election to vote on the recall. The recall has only been used very rarely at the state level in Oregon. In 1988, a state senator accused of malfeasance was recalled. The recall is used with some regularity in smaller municipalities where it is easier to reach the 15 per cent threshold. Available evidence suggests that recalls are successful less than 50 per cent of the time.

Referendums

Oregon also has constitutional provisions for both mandatory and optional referendums. An amendment to the constitution adopted by the legislature triggers an automatic popular vote to accept or reject it. The legislature may also refer other matters directly to the people and generally does so for one of two reasons.

First, statutes must be adopted by a majority of both houses of the legislature and signed by the governor. If the governor vetoes the legislation, the legislature may override that veto and enact the statute directly by a two-thirds majority of each house. Veto overrides rarely happen. However, if the legislature refers the legislation to the people through an optional referendum, the governor has no opportunity to exercise the veto. Thus, a narrow legislative majority (more than 50 per cent but less than 66 per cent) may lead to the calculation that there is a better chance of getting the people to approve a piece of legislation than the governor, and the legislature may use the referendum mechanism in order to bypass the governor.

Second, the legislature may choose to refer a matter to a referendum because the subject is important enough to warrant it or because there is a belief that there will be a rejective referendum anyway. A referral gives the legislature greater control of the process. Of the 407 matters referred to the people by the legislature since 1902, 233 (57 per cent) have passed.

Campaigns both for office and for direct democracy instruments are privately financed in Oregon (as in most other US states), but there are strict reporting requirements, giving the public access to information on who is financing campaigns. There are no restrictions on who may contribute to a political campaign or how much they may spend. Thus corporations and labour unions alike often spend large amounts of money to support or oppose questions on the ballot paper. The press regularly reports on who is contributing to campaigns so that this discussion is a regular part of the election dialogue. In early 2007, the Oregon secretary of state introduced a new web-based system, called OreStar, to give citizens access to campaign finance information.

The use of direct democracy in Oregon

The 'Oregon System', as it has come to be known in the US, was envisaged as a way to take power away from the railway companies and other moneyed interests and return it to the people. In fact one of the very first initiatives in Oregon that was adopted in 1904 prohibited legislators from accepting free railway passes – a direct attempt to rein in the influence of the railways. The last 20 years have seen a shift towards the initiative process being used in many cases by moneyed interests which see the system as an easier (and perhaps cheaper) way to get what they want from the legislature. Oregon has seen initiatives in recent years regarding medical malpractice (essentially a battle between the insurance industry and trial lawyers), a ban on triple-tractor trailer trucks (a battle between truckers and the railways) and even allowing 'licensed denturists' to distribute dentures (opposed by dentists).

This is not to say that the system has been completely taken over by vested interests. Oregonians have also used the system to adopt a number of measures that would probably never have come out of the legislature – the legalization of physician-assisted suicide and the use of marijuana for medical treatment, regular increases in the minimum wage, a requirement that marriage be between one man and one woman, mandating that all voting be by post, and tough sentencing requirements for those convicted of violent crimes.

The Oregon experience

Direct democracy is a central part of the political scene in Oregon. Some bemoan the fact that the ease with which the electorate can amend the constitution has led to a founding document that is littered with the minutiae of tax policy. Few, however, suggest a fundamental change in the mechanisms that have allowed the citizens direct control of a significant part of the process of enacting legislation.

The public has been very resistant to any significant changes to the system. In 1996, the legislature referred to the people a constitutional amendment that would have required a portion of petition signatures on a citizens' initiative to be collected in each congressional district. As a practical matter, it is much easier to gather signatures in urban than in rural areas. The proposed amendment would have made it more difficult to qualify an initiative, and it was defeated by a 56 per cent to 44 per cent vote. In 2000, the legislature referred a constitutional amendment that would have increased the number of signatures required to place a citizens' initiative to amend the constitution on the ballot paper. It too was defeated, by 59 per cent to 41 per cent.

However, citizens have also been reluctant to limit the power of the legislature with regard to the initiative process. In 1996, there was a citizens' initiative that would have limited the ability of the legislature to change statutes passed by the voters. This proposal was defeated by 51 per cent to 49 per cent. In 2000, voters defeated an initiative that would have prohibited the legislature from 'making the initiative process harder', by 62 per cent to 38 per cent.

The only significant change to the initiative process that voters have approved in recent years was a 2002 citizens' initiative to amend the constitution to prohibit signature gatherers being paid by the number of signatures. This initiative came on the heels of widespread press reports of fraud and abuse in signature gathering and was approved by voters overwhelmingly, by 75 per cent to 25 per cent. Oregon voters thus appear satisfied with the balance currently being struck between their rights to amend the constitution and state statutes and the power of the legislature to do the same.

Direct democracy in the Republic of Hungary

Krisztina Medve

Historical background

The modern instruments of direct democracy in Hungary are the achievements of the democratic political transition in 1989. The first law on referendums and popular initiatives was Act no. XVII of 1989. This law was exceptionally liberal and surpassed the corresponding provisions of many of the West European parliamentary democracies. The political transition led to a reassessment of the value of the mechanisms of direct democracy as authentic legitimating institutions. The 1989 act was adopted before the new, democratic constitution (Act no. XX of 1989), and this gave rise to a number of conceptual difficulties. The act confused the different types of referendums and initiatives; and it failed properly to determine what kinds of questions could be the subject of the mechanisms of direct democracy, which made it impossible to establish whether the initiatives were compatible with the constitution. According to Act no. XVII, the collection of 100,000 signatures (with no time limit) was enough to launch a national referendum on nearly any question that fell within the competence of the parliament. In practice, this liberal regulation led to chaos: the parliament failed to handle the cases properly and often turned to the Constitutional Court, alluding to problems of interpretation of the constitution.

In 1995 the Constitutional Court called on the parliament to resolve this controversial situation and adopt a new act which would be in conformity with the constitution. The present regulation of *referendums* and *popular initiatives* was adopted in 1997, when a thorough revision and modification of the constitution took place.

The rules for *local* referendums and initiatives are established in Act no. LXV of 1990 on local government, which provides a framework regulation to be further refined by the local governments themselves in local government decrees.

The *recall* is unknown in Hungarian law.

The legal framework and institutional structure

The regulation of national referendums and popular initiatives can be found in three different legal acts: the 1989 constitution of the republic; Act no. III of 1998; and Act C of 1997 (the electoral code).

The constitution stipulates that citizens shall take part in conducting the affairs of the country primarily through their elected representatives. However, the people may also take part directly in either deciding or influencing issues of overriding public interest. Hungarian law provides for two forms of this – the referendum and the popular initiative. The constitution covers the main substantive aspects of the direct democracy instruments at the national level, namely the types of referendum, the conditions for ordering a referendum or handling an initiative, and the right to vote on them.

According to the constitution, there are two main types of national referendum – mandatory and optional. In both cases, the calling of a referendum is the exclusive competence of the parliament, while the date of the referendum is appointed by the president of the republic.

- *Mandatory referendums* (i.e. citizens' initiatives for the introduction or repeal of legislation). The parliament must call a referendum at the initiative of a minimum of 200,000 voters, whether or not it itself approves of the idea of issuing the writ of referendum.

- *Optional referendums.* Under the circumstances provided for by the law, parliament shall consider issuing a writ of referendum but is not obliged to do so. An optional national referendum may be held at the initiative of:

(a) the voters (if the initiative is supported by more than 100,000 but fewer than 200,000 voters);

(b) the president of the republic;

(c) the government; or

(d) at least one-third of the elected members of parliament.

As for the outcome of the referendum, the constitution distinguishes two different types of referendum – binding and indicative. The results of mandatory referendums are always binding. The results of optional referendums may be binding or indicative, depending on the decision of the parliament when it calls the referendum. The results of a referendum called with regard to a law already enacted by the parliament but not yet signed by the president of the republic (a rejective referendum) is binding.

There are certain subjects on which referendums may not be called as they fall within the exclusive competence of the parliament:

(a) the contents of acts on the budget, on the execution of the budget, on types of central taxes and stamp duties, on customs duties, and on the regulation of local taxes;

(b) obligations arising out of international agreements in force, or the contents of the acts containing these obligations;

(c) the provisions of the constitution regarding referendums and popular initiatives;

(d) any issues of personnel and organizational change (the transformation or dissolution of official bodies) that fall under the authority of the parliament;

(e) the dissolution of the parliament;

(f) the government programme;

(g) the declaration of a state of war or a state of emergency;

(h) the deployment of the armed forces abroad or within the country;

(i) the dissolution of the delegates' assembly of the local government; and

(j) a declaration of amnesty.

There is a threshold for the validity of the referendum vote: a nationwide referendum shall be valid if (a) more than half of the voters casting valid votes and (b) at least one-quarter of all registered electors give the same answer to the referendum question. In the event of the ballot paper containing more than one referendum question, the referendum result must be established separately for each question.

The right to vote in national referendums is identical to the right to vote in parliamentary elections.

The agenda initiative is regulated by the constitution as follows. An agenda initiative may be submitted by at least 50,000 voters. It may be directed at putting a certain question that falls within the parliament's competence onto its agenda. The parliament is obliged to discuss the question contained in the initiative.

The regulatory framework

The regulatory framework is based on Act no. III of 1998 and the electoral code of 1997.

The role of the National Electoral Committee

Attestation of the question and the signature-collecting sheet

A specimen of the signature-collecting sheets shall be submitted to the National Electoral Committee (NEC) for attestation before the collection of signatures begins.

The specific question put to a referendum shall be worded in such a way that it can be answered unambiguously, and shall be in compliance with the requirements enshrined in the constitution.

The NEC shall refuse to attest the signature-collecting sheet if:

(a) the question does not fall within the competence of the parliament;

(b) the question is one on which a national referendum may not be held;

(c) the wording of the question does not comply with the requirements set out in the law; or

(d) the signature-collecting sheet does not comply with the requirements stipulated in the Act on Electoral Procedure.

In the case of an agenda initiative, the initiative shall accurately and unambiguously contain the question proposed to be discussed by the parliament. The NEC will refuse to attest the signature-collecting sheet if criteria (a), (b) or (d) are not met. The NEC's decision with regard to the signature-collecting sheet or the particular question must be published within eight days in the official *gazette*.

Signatures may be collected over a period of four months in the case of a national referendum, and of two months in the case of an agenda initiative, from the attestation of the signature-collecting sheet. After the signature-collecting period expires, the signature sheets shall be submitted to the NEC, which shall arrange for the signatures to be checked.

The role of the parliament

In the case of a national referendum, the parliament decides on the citizens' initiative aimed at the ordering of a referendum. Its resolution must specify whether the referendum is binding or non-binding and the specific question put to the referendum, and shall give orders pertaining to the budget of the referendum.

In the case of an agenda initiative, the speaker of the parliament must announce it on the next session day following the receipt of the information from the head of the NEC. The parliament is obliged to put the initiative on the agenda and discuss it. The initiative must be decided within three months after the announcement.

The role of the Constitutional Court

Appeals against any decision of the NEC regarding the attestation of the signature-collecting sheet, or the particular question, may be lodged with the NEC (addressed to the Constitutional Court) within 15 days of the resolution being published.

Appeals against a decision of the parliament either to order a referendum, or not to order a referendum which would be mandatory may be lodged with the NEC within eight days of the resolution being published, addressed to the Constitutional Court.

The Constitutional Court shall either confirm or annul the resolution of the NEC or the parliament.

The role of the president of the republic

The president of the republic shall call the referendum within 15 days after the term for redress has elapsed without any result, or, in the event of redress, after it has been adjudged. The referendum shall be called for a date within 90 days after the parliamentary resolution ordering it has been published, or, in the event of redress, after it has been adjudged.

The national referendum process is managed by the election offices and 'guarded' by the election committees.

Regarding the reservations and appeals submitted against the decisions of the election committees (except for the decisions of the NEC concerning the attestation of the question and the signature-collecting sheet), the responsible bodies are the competent election committees and the courts (county or capital court, Supreme Court).

The financing of the use of direct democracy instruments

The funds for the conduct of referendums are granted out of the state budget to the amount established by the parliament and allocated to the organization appointed by the minister of the interior. Under the electoral code the determination of the rules of financial conduct is within the competence of the minister.

Voter participation and the dynamic of campaigns related to referendums

Voter participation is generally lower for referendums than it is for parliamentary elections, but it is a significant factor, as the validity of the referendum vote depends on whether more than one-quarter of all registered electors give the same answer to the referendum question. Voter turnout is strongly influenced by the way in which and the efficiency with which the campaign is run and by the non-partisan information received from the state organs concerning the voting process and deadlines. Usually turnout is around 40 per cent.

The dynamic of the campaign depends on who the initiators are and on the issue involved. When the referendum is initiated by the government, it is inevitably in an advantageous position where both access to the media and public appearances are concerned; however, public funding of referendum campaigns is prohibited. The general rules for campaigns embodied in the electoral code apply to referendums.

Media coverage

The general rules established by the electoral code apply to referendum campaigns. Regarding broadcasters' participation in an election campaign, the provisions of the law on radio and television broadcasting apply. Apart from parliamentary, local government and lower-level elections, television and radio broadcasters may only transmit political advertisements in connection with a referendum that has already been called. Access to the media depends heavily on the financial resources of the campaigning organizations.

No special obligations apply to public service broadcasters in referendums concerning the allocation of broadcast time between the campaigning organizations. The electoral code contains special rules for legal redress concerning the media campaign.

Voter education

Non-partisan information for the voters is provided by the National Election Office (part of the Ministry of the Interior) and by the election offices at different levels (regional, local etc.). This information is purely technical and addresses the issues regarding the referendum system and practical details about the election procedure (notices, brochures, guidelines etc.).

The success of a referendum initiative depends on an efficient election campaign as the key element in the forming of public opinion by the initiating organizations.

The funding of campaigns

There is no public funding for referendum campaigns. The rules on the functioning and financing of political parties apply for the parties participating in referendum campaigns. Whether, if a referendum is initiated by that government, it is 'fair' or 'legal' for that government to use the advantages of incumbency when campaigning is an interesting question.

Opportunities and constraints – strengths and weaknesses

Why are the instruments of direct democracy hardly used in Hungary? The answer lies in the weaknesses of the direct democracy system. It is not a neglected instrument, as the number of unsuccessful initiatives shows great activity on the part of the electorate – on average 20–30 initiatives a year since 2003 (see table 1). However, the strict regulations governing the initiatives and the wording of the questions often present obstacles and hamper or prevent the realization of such initiatives. In general, the main problems are:

- the difficulty of collecting the required number of signatures (200,000 for a national referendum, and 50,000 for an agenda initiative); and

- difficulty in wording the question (forbidden issues have to be avoided; questions must not be ambiguous; and it is forbidden to hold a referendum on the modification of the constitution or in matters that would force the parliament to act as a constitutional convention – for example, in the referendum initiative for the abolition of compulsory military service in 2001).

In the case of agenda initiatives, the parliament is only obliged to put the question on its agenda if the number of valid signatures collected is at least 50,000. Between 1989 and 1999, 20 agenda initiatives were unsuccessful because of this requirement.

The Constitutional Court plays a significant role in relation to the direct democracy procedures and constantly forms and establishes practice through its resolutions. The majority of the cases arise in connection with the prohibited referendum issues. The referendum initiative of the Fidesz party in 2006 also encountered this problem, as a number of the questions proposed concerned the 'government programme' which is prohibited as the subject of a referendum.

The number of signatures to be collected ensures that only serious and important issues are decided in a nationwide referendum or affect the work of the parliament. The requirement that at least one-quarter of all registered electors in Hungary have to give an identical answer to the question put to a referendum means that it is highly unlikely that a referendum would lead to a result that is not in the public interest.

The prohibited referendum issues also protect the exclusive competence of the parliament established by the constitution and ensure that those questions that need a particular approach or affect the constitution remain the competence of the supreme legislative body of the republic.

Table 1. National referendums in Hungary to date

(1) The 'four-aye' referendum, 6 November 1989

Question no.	Question	Result	No. of valid votes	No. of invalid votes	No. of 'Yes' votes	No. of 'No' votes
1	Should the president of the republic be elected after the parliamentary elections?	The vote was conclusive	4,283,642	242,630	2,145,023	2,138,619
2	Should party organizations leave the workplace?	The vote was conclusive	4,297,131	229,412	4,088,383	208,474
3	Should the MSzMP* account for the assets in its ownership or its custody?	The vote was conclusive	4,300,400	225,872	4,101,413	198,987
4	Should the Workers' Guard be dissolved?	The vote was conclusive	4,271,528	254,744	4,054,977	216,551

* MSzMP: the Hungarian Socialist Workers' Party, which was the then-governing communist party.

(2) The national referendum of 29 July 1990 on the direct election of the president of the republic

Question no.	Question	Result	No. of valid votes	No. of invalid votes	No. of 'Yes' votes	No. of 'No' votes
1	Do you think the president of the republic should be directly elected?	The vote was inconclusive	1,078,899	9,069	926,823	152,076

(3) National referendum of 16 November 1997 on the issue of joining NATO

Question no.	Question	Result	No. of valid votes	No. of invalid votes	No. of 'Yes' votes	No. of 'No' votes
1	Do you agree that the Republic of Hungary should join NATO in order to ensure the protection of the country?	The vote was conclusive	3,919,114	44,961	3,344,131	574,983

(4) National referendum of 12 April 2003 on the issue of joining the European Union

Question no.	Question	Result	No. of valid votes	No. of invalid votes	No. of 'Yes' votes	No. of 'No' votes
1	Do you agree that the Republic of Hungary should become a member of the European Union?	The vote was conclusive	3,648,717	17,998	3,056,027	592,690

CHAPTER 5

CHAPTER 5

When citizens can recall elected officials

Definitions

135. The recall is a direct democracy procedure that allows the appropriate authority and/or a specified number of citizens to demand a vote for the electorate on whether an elected holder of public office should be removed from that office before the end of his or her term. This definition implies that the recall must fulfil a set of requirements, which distinguish this procedure from others aimed at terminating an elected official's period in office, such as impeachment. To be considered an instrument of direct democracy, the process of legally interrupting the period in office of an elected official must involve the initiative and/or the vote of the electorate. When the initiative and the decision to do this come exclusively from the legally established authorities, such as the legislative or the judicial branch, and do not require the voters' involvement at any phase of the process, the procedure is more properly called impeachment.

136. In contrast, a recall requires citizens' intervention, whether it be to support or to reject through a vote in a referendum a decision taken by an authoritative body (as in Austria, Iceland, Palau, Romania), or as the initiators of the request which may then be processed and approved by an authoritative body (as in Uganda). These could be considered mixed recalls. The procedure is most participatory when both the initiative and the approval of the recall require the direct intervention of the citizens, first as the initiators of the request and second by expressing their support for or rejection of the initiative by casting their votes in a referendum (see tables 5.1 and 5.2). We define this procedure as a full recall. Some countries provide for a mixed recall for the highest executive officials and a full recall for members of national legislative bodies, as is the case in Palau.

137. The subjects of the recall are elected officials working at the local, regional or national levels. However, some countries provide for the possibility of removing appointed officials from office through procedures that involve citizens' participation

(Peru and many US states). In Peru, officials appointed by the central and regional governments at the regional, state, provincial and municipal levels, except for military chiefs in areas in a state of emergency, can be removed if 50 per cent of the electorate of the corresponding electoral district request their removal. The Peruvian constitution and legislation distinguish between recall and removal, and apply the first to elected officials and the latter to appointed officials. A recall procedure is more coherent with a presidential system of government (with a directly elected executive official) than with a parliamentary system of government. A recall of individual legislators seems to be more in line with an electoral system of single-member constituencies rather than with a system of proportional representation.

138. In contrast to impeachment, the initiators do not need to support the demand on legal grounds in order to begin the process of recall. It is a political instrument through which the electorate in a particular electoral jurisdiction can express their dissatisfaction with a specific official. When a justification is required, the acceptable charges can often cover a wide range, for example, corruption, incompetence, criminality and so on. In Ecuador, a recall can be activated at any point of an official's term in office. Even though the recall does not generally require a legal justification, the procedures for calling for a recall can be complex and have to be followed in order to activate the instrument and to proceed to the voting phase, as well as to provide for the selection of a replacement for the recalled official.

Provisions and usage

139. Among the procedures of direct democracy, the recall is the least widespread, and consequently the least applied. Only a few countries have included the recall, either the mixed or the full types, in their constitutional and legal systems (see table 5.2). The broadest application of the recall is found in Venezuela, where the full recall applies to all elected officials, including the president. The attempted recall of the president of Venezuela in 2004, which was initiated by 2.4 million Venezuelan citizens, remains one of the most prominent examples of the use of the recall mechanism at the highest level. In that instance, 40.6 per cent of the voters supported the recall, and the president remained in office (see the case study following chapter 1).

140. The pioneering countries in the conception and implementation of the recall at the local and state levels were Switzerland at the end of the 19th century and the USA around the late 19th to the early 20th century. Throughout the 1990s, Latin America became the region of the world where the recall increased its presence, in the new constitutions enacted, following a growing trend to combine representative democracy with participatory democracy. Some of these new constitutions have included the recall mostly for local and regional authorities, and commonly less for national elected officials. As in the rest of the world, other forms of direct democracy have a greater presence in Latin American constitutions than the recall.

141. The constitutions of some countries (e.g. Ecuador, Ethiopia, Peru, Taiwan) contain generic statements about the possibility of revoking the mandate of elected officials as a right of the people in those countries. However, in each case the specific design of the recall, the legal rules, and the level of and opportunity for the citizen's involvement differ significantly. In Venezuela, recalling elected officials is a substantive feature of the form of government, as government is defined in the constitution as 'democratic, participatory, elective, decentralized, alternative, responsible, pluralistic, *and with revocable mandates*'. The Peruvian constitution calls the right to revoke and remove officials a 'fundamental right of the person'. The constitution of Taiwan establishes that 'A person duly elected may be recalled by his constituency in accordance with law'; however, this only involves citizen participation to endorse, through a referendum, a petition initiated by the legislative body. The Cuban constitution contains a similar statement inspired by the 'principles of socialist democracy', according to which 'those elected must render an account of their work and may be recalled at any time'. However, the mechanisms for revoking the mandate are not defined. The constitution of Ecuador also establishes that the people will enjoy, among other political rights, 'the right to revoke the mandate conferred to elected officials'. Similarly, the Ethiopian constitution states that 'The people may recall any one of their representatives whenever they lose confidence in him. Particulars shall be determined by law'.

Table 5.1. Recall in the USA: recall provisions at the state level*

State	Year adopted	Positions	Signature requirements
Alaska	1959	All but judicial officers	25% of votes cast**
Arizona	1912	All	25% of votes cast
California	1911	All	State-wide officers: 12% of votes cast, 1% from each of 5 counties. Others: 20% votes of cast
Colorado	1912	All	25% of votes cast
Georgia	1978	All	15% of eligible electors,*** and 1/5 from each congressional district
Idaho	1933	All but judicial officers	20% of eligible electors
Kansas	1914	All but judicial officers	40% of votes cast
Louisiana	1914	All but judicial officers	If over 1,000 eligible electors – 33% of eligible electors; if fewer – 40% of eligible electors
Michigan	1913	All but judicial officers	25% of votes cast
Minnesota		Executive, legislators, judicial officers	25% of votes cast
Montana	1976	All	State-wide officers – 10% of eligible electors; district officers –15% of eligible electors

State	Year adopted	Positions	Signature requirements
Nevada	1912	All	25% of votes cast
New Jersey		All	25% of registered voters in the electoral district of the official subject to recall
North Dakota	1929	All	25% of votes cast
Oregon	1908	All	15% of total votes cast in officers' districts for all candidates for governor in last election
Rhode Island		Governor, lieutenant-governor, secretary of state, treasurer, attorney general	15% of votes cast for the office in the last general election
Washington	1912	All but judicial officers	State-wide officers: 25% of votes cast; others: 35% of votes cast
Wisconsin	1926	All	State-wide officers: 25% of votes cast; others: 25% of votes cast for president in the last election

* States may not recall their members of Congress regardless of the state law.
** Votes cast for office in previous election.
*** Eligible electors in previous election.

142. Recall provisions also exist in many of the US states (see table 5.1), although they are used less often than the other forms of direct democracy, such as citizens' initiatives or legislative referendums. In all, 18 US states have provisions for recall at the state level, and 36 have provisions for the recall of local officials. (States may not recall their members of Congress regardless of the state law.) The use of the recall is more extensive at the local level than at the state level. About three-quarters of recall elections in the USA take place at the city council or school board level. Recall attempts at the state level have generally been unsuccessful. Prior to California's 2003 recall of Governor Gray Davis (see box 5.1), the only successful recall of a state governor took place in North Dakota in 1921, when voters removed the governor from office (as well as the attorney general and the commissioner of agriculture). California voters have initiated 32 gubernatorial recall attempts since 1911, but the 2003 recall was the first to ever to reach the ballot in that state. Few recall attempts get so far, because signature requirements are generally set quite high – typically at 25 per cent or more of the votes cast for a particular office in the last election (see table 5.1). An important issue in the US recall model has been the method of selecting a replacement for the recalled official. In most states, a special election must be held subsequent to the recall to select a replacement, although the rules and procedures for such special elections vary. In a few states there are provisions by which a successor to the recalled official may be appointed. In the 2003 California recall, the governor was removed from office by a vote of 55 per cent, and his replacement (Arnold Schwarzenegger) was elected to serve the balance of his term at the same time. Five other states have similar laws providing

for the simultaneous election for a replacement of the official removed from office in the recall.

Box 5.1. The California recall of 2003

The 2003 recall in California of Governor Gray Davis and simultaneous election of actor Arnold Schwarzenegger provided Americans with a view of a very powerful yet little-used tool of direct democracy – the recall. Governor Davis, a Democrat, faced a plethora of problems. In his five years in office (he had been re-elected in November 2002, defeating his Republican opponent by 47 per cent to 42 per cent), California's financial situation had turned from boom to bust. Davis inherited a 9 billion USD budget surplus, which in five years had turned into a 38 billion USD deficit. He and the Democratic legislature had to raise college fees, close health clinics and triple the automobile licence fee. Electricity shortages gripped the state, resulting in rolling blackouts, and the cost of electricity soared. The voters had had enough.

The recall effort gathered steam when Republican Congressman Darrell Issa, a car alarm millionaire, contributed 1.6 million USD of his own money to pay people to gather signatures on petitions to recall Governor Davis. The army of paid signature gatherers gave discontented voters an outlet for their anger: they were able quickly to gather more than the necessary 900,000 valid signatures to force the vote. California law requires signatures numbering at least 12 per cent of the number of those who voted in the last election to qualify a recall.

Under a unique provision of California law, there would be only one election to decide whether to recall the governor and also to name his replacement should voters recall him. The election would only require a plurality to win. To qualify as a replacement candidate, one could either file signatures or pay a 3,500 USD filing fee. One hundred and thirty-five Californians filed to run for governor.

During the (by US standards) short campaign, two candidates emerged from the field – Republican Schwarzenegger and Davis' Lieutenant-Governor Cruz Bustamante, a Democrat. There were numerous court challenges to the election, causing it to be put on hold by the US Court of Appeals for the Ninth Circuit and then finally allowed to proceed by the same court.

In the end, a very decisive majority of 55 per cent voted to recall Governor Davis. Turnout was high at 61 per cent of registered electors. Schwarzenegger received 49 per cent of the vote, compared with 32 per cent for Bustamante. Interestingly, because of the high interest and turnout in the recall election, Schwarzenegger received 650,000 more votes in his election than Governor Davis had received when he was re-elected 11 months earlier.

143. From a conceptual point of view, the procedure of the recall is associated with the idea that representatives must remain accountable to the people who elected them. Thus the voters should be able to choose to terminate their mandate before the end of their term if the representatives are falling short of the citizens' expectations. The adoption of the recall in several US states at the beginning of the 20th century was associated with the so-called 'progressive era'. The movement to adopt recall and other instruments of direct democracy was triggered by the objective of displacing elected officials who were perceived as too closely connected to powerful economic interests (see, e.g., the case study on Oregon following chapter 4). Elected officials seemed to be more responsive to the interests and pressures of economic groups than to those of the electorate. The recall was conceived as a mechanism to induce representatives to be more sensitive to the electorate's demands.

144. From the critics' perspective, the recall is considered a highly polarizing mechanism that triggers serious confrontation and disrupts the normal work of elected officials during their mandate. It is also viewed as a mechanism that creates incentives for opposition groups to attempt to displace elected officials. The supporters of the recall consider that the procedure encourages close oversight of elected officials on the part of the citizens, and creates effective mechanisms of vertical accountability that establish a close relationship between the electorate and their representatives. However, the recall is still considered highly controversial, and international experience with its application is still very limited, particularly at the national level. This explains why it is the least common among the instruments of direct democracy.

Types of recall

145. There are two main types of recall according to the level of involvement of the citizens in the process:

(a) full recall – recalls that require citizens' involvement both at the phase of initiation and at the approval or rejection of the recall; and

(b) mixed recall – recalls that require citizens' involvement either in initiating the process or, at the approval stage, through a popular vote.

Both kinds of recall can be used at the national, regional and local levels, and both types can be used for either officials of the executive branch or elected members of the legislature.

Table 5.2. Countries with provisions for recall, by type of recall

Recalls initiated and approved by citizens – national level	
Country or state	**Officials**
Belarus	Deputies
Ecuador	President, governors of autonomous regions, deputies, mayors, *prefectos*
Ethiopia	Members of the Chamber of Representatives
Kiribati	Members of the Maneaba ni Maungatabu
Kyrgyzstan	Deputy of Legislative Assembly or Assembly of People's Representatives
Liechtenstein	Entire legislature
Micronesia, Federated States of (Chuuk, Pohnpei, Yap)	Governor, lieutenant-governor, senators, representatives
Micronesia, Federated States of (Kosrae)	Governor, lieutenant-governor, justice of the State Court, senators
Nigeria	Members of Senate or House of Representatives
Palau	Members of the Olbiil Era Kelalau
Venezuela	All elected officials, including the president
Recalls initiated and approved by citizens – regional and local level	
Country or state	**Officials**
Argentina	Local elected officials
Colombia	State governors, mayors
Cuba	Delegates to municipal assemblies
Germany (*länder* – Baden-Württemberg, Bavaria, Berlin, Brandenburg, Bremen, Rhineland-Palatinate)	Entire legislature
Peru	Mayors, *regidores*, regional elected authorities, elected *magistrados*
Taiwan	Local and regional legislators, municipal city councillors, municipal city and county mayors, county (city) councilmen and township (city) chiefs
USA (18 states)	Local and state officials
Recalls initiated by authorities, approved by citizens	
Country*	**Officials (authority)**
Austria	President (Federal Assembly)
Germany	Mayors (local councils)
Iceland	President (members of the Althing)
Palau	President and vice-president (members of state legislatures)
Romania	President or vice-president (Chamber of Deputies and Senate)

Serbia	President (National Assembly)
Taiwan	President and vice-president (members of the Legislative Yuan)
Turkmenistan	President (Peoples' Chamber)
Recalls initiated by citizens, approved by authorities	
Country	**Officials (authority)**
Uganda	Members of parliament (Electoral Commission)

* Bolivia also has a law which applies to the current administration. It provides for a mixed recall, called by authorities and decided by the electorate. It is not known whether it will apply in future.

146. *Full recalls.* These are found at the national level for the executive and/or legislative branch (see table 5.2). At the regional, state and local levels, the full recall is found in a number of US states and in some provinces in Argentina. The full recall has also been adopted in countries such as Colombia for state governors and mayors, and in Peru for mayors, members of municipal councils and regional authorities. The recall is generally conceived and used to remove individual elected officials before the end of their full term in office, but in a few cases, for example Liechtenstein and the German *länder* of Berlin and Baden-Württemberg, it can be applied to the entire parliament (see box 5.2).

Box 5.2. Recall of a state legislature in Berlin

According to the constitution of the city-state of Berlin (article 63), a recall of the complete legislature can be initiated by 20 per cent of the registered electors. For a valid referendum vote a turnout of 50 per cent of registered electors and a majority of the voters participating are required.

During a political crisis in January 1981 the Christian Democratic opposition started a citizens' initiative to recall the legislature (Abgeordnetenhaus). Within a few days, 300,000 signatures – more than the quorum required – had been collected. In March, the parliament decided to call an early election in May 1981, without waiting for the referendum vote. Since the goal of the initiative had been reached the petition was withdrawn.

In other German *länder* the requirements for a valid referendum vote are higher (e.g. 50 per cent plus one of registered electors). There, the recall procedure has not been used.

147. *Mixed recalls.* In some countries (e.g. Austria, Iceland, Taiwan) the mixed recall initiated by the authorities is used to remove higher elected officials such as the president and vice-president from office before the end of their term. In the countries that provide for this form of recall, the need for the people's endorsement of the authorities' decision contributes to citizen participation, but also turns such an important decision into a more difficult process. In the case of Uganda, where it is applied to remove members of parliament (MPs), the process is reversed. At least two-thirds of the registered electors of an electoral district can promote a recall against an MP and present the petition to the speaker. If the Electoral Commission judges the request to be valid, the representative is removed from office. One well-known case of the use of the mixed recall is the attempt by the Romanian parliament to remove President Traian Basescu from office (see box 5.3).

Box 5.3. Recall in Romania: a vote for the president

On 19 April 2007, by a vote of 322 to 108, members of the Romanian parliament decided to remove President Traian Basescu. The resolution to remove him was backed by the members of the Socialist Party, the Greater Romania Party, the Conservative Party, the Democratic Union of Hungarians in Romania, and the ruling National Liberal Party; there were ten abstentions. Basescu's years in office had been marked by harsh confrontation with the parliament and his former ally, Prime Minister Calin Popescu-Tariceanu.

According to the Romanian constitution, if the president has committed grave violations of the provisions of the constitution, s/he may be suspended from office by the Chamber of Deputies and the Senate, in joint session, by a majority vote of both, and after consultation with the Constitutional Court. After examination of the allegations filed by the parliament, which included abuse of power, interfering with the law and protecting private economic interests, among others, the Constitutional Court ruled that Basescu had not committed serious acts against the constitution, but allowed the parliament to make its own decision regarding his removal. The president was suspended from office and Nicolae Vacariou, the speaker of the Senate, was appointed interim president.

The constitution establishes that, if the proposal for suspension from office is approved, a referendum shall be held within 30 days in order to remove the president from office. On 24 April 2007, the parliament set the date for the referendum, which took place on 19 May 2007. This was the first time in Romania's history that such a referendum was held. The question printed on the ballot paper was 'Do you agree with the removal of the president of Romania, Mr Traian Basescu, from office?'. The results favoured President Basescu, who returned to office. The 'No' side obtained 75 per cent of the vote (6.1 million votes), the 'Yes' side 25 per cent of the vote (2 million votes), and turnout was 44 per cent. Throughout the process, opinion polls showed that the likelihood of his being removed was very low, not because he was popular (although he had strong popular support), but because the electoral law establishes that at least 50 per cent of the registered electors have to participate in the referendum in order for it to be valid. Basescu had been elected in a run-off election on December 2004 and had obtained 5.1 million votes. In the referendum his support increased by almost 1 million votes.

148. As with electoral systems and the other instruments of direct democracy, the recall can vary widely in terms of different legal and structural aspects, all of which may have an impact on the ability of the recall mechanism to serve its purpose. At least three main categories of issues have to be taken into account in deciding to include a recall in a specific institutional arrangement, and in the process of designing this instrument – the legal framework, the signature requirements and the approval quorum that determines whether the vote has been passed.

The legal framework

149. The recall can be enshrined in the constitution or in specific electoral laws and regulations. In the case of unitary countries, the right of recall may be established in the national constitution or in legislative acts. In federal states, such as Argentina, the Russian Federation and the USA, the recall is established in the individual state constitutions. The electoral laws define the different aspects of the recall. In some countries, the recall is provided for in detail in the constitution, as in the case of Venezuela, but in most cases it is only broadly defined in the national constitutions and the electoral laws specify the procedural aspects. In the case of mixed or full recalls that are used to remove high-ranking officials such as the president and vice-president or the equivalent, the conditions of the recall are established in the constitution.

150. One of the most important aspects of the legal framework is defining to which elected officials recall may be applied. Theoretically, once the right to recall elected officials is enshrined, it could be applied to any elected official. In practice, except in the case of Venezuela, the use of the recall is restricted to a number of elected officials, usually of local authorities. The decision to include national or sub-national, lower-ranking or higher-ranking elected officials stems from political and institutional considerations, and the decision may depend on a judgement as to the advantages and disadvantages of the mechanism: in general, the higher the rank of the elected official, the greater the impact of a recall could be, in terms of political polarization and disruption of government and public affairs. This consideration has played an important role in preventing the more widespread use of the recall, especially in the case of the highest-ranking positions.

151. The different types of recall require different administrative procedures during the several phases of the recall. The main phases are: (a) initiating a recall; (b) processing and validating the initiative; (c) campaigning against/for the recall; (d) submitting the recall petition to a vote; and (e) replacing the recalled official. In the case of full recalls at the national level, the requirements that define who can demand a recall vary from country to country and according to the officers subject to the recall.

Table 5.3. Countries with provisions for full recall: officials subject to and initiatives to promote the recall

Country or state	Elected official subject to recall	Initiative
Belarus	Deputies	Not less than 20% of the citizens eligible to vote and resident in the corresponding area
Ecuador	President, governors of autonomous regions, mayors, *prefectos* and deputies	At least 15% of the registered electors for the president and governors of autonomous regions and at least 10% of the registered electors in the electoral district for others
Kiribati	Member of the Maneaba ni Maungatabu	A majority of those who were registered as electors at the time of the last election of that member
Micronesia, Federated States of (Chuuk)	Governor or lieutenant-governor	Registered electors equal in number to at least 15% of those who voted in the last general election
	Senator or representative	Registered electors from the official's district or region equal in number to at least 20% of those who voted in the last general election in the district or region
Micronesia, Federated States of (Kosrae)	Governor, lieutenant-governor, a justice of the State Court, senator	At least 25% of the persons qualified to vote for the office occupied by the official, except that recall of a justice of the State Court requires the same number of signatures as state-wide elective office in Kosrae
Micronesia, Federated States of (Pohnpei)	Governor and lieutenant-governor	35% of the registered electors of Pohnpei
	Member of legislature	35% of the registered electors of the electoral district
Micronesia, Federated States of (Yap)	Governor, lieutenant-governor and members of the legislature	At least 25% of the persons qualified to vote for the office occupied by the official
Nigeria	Member of the Senate or of the House of Representatives	More than one-half of the persons registered to vote in that member's electoral district

Country or state	Elected official subject to recall	Initiative
Palau	Member of the Olbiil Era Kelalau	Not less than 25% of the number of persons who voted in the most recent election
Venezuela	All elected officials, including the president	At least 20% of the electors registered in the relevant electoral district

152. Some countries have more difficult requirements in terms of the number of voters required to sign the initiative (see table 5.3). A very demanding case is that of Nigeria, where the initiative has to be signed by more than 50 per cent of the registered electors in the electoral district concerned. An important distinction is whether the petition is signed by any registered elector within the electoral district of the official, or only by voters who participated in the last election at which the official was selected. This requirement increases the difficulties of promoting a recall.

153. In the case of mixed recalls, the authorities that can initiate the process are shown in table 5.4. In the cases of mixed recalls for presidents and vice-presidents, the decision adopted by the authorized bodies according to the established procedures has to be approved or rejected by the electorate through the vote in a recall referendum. In order to avoid promoting irresponsible and groundless recall processes, the decision has to be taken by strong majorities in the legislative bodies and has to be approved by the electorate. In the cases of Austria, Iceland and Serbia, if the recall is rejected by the voters at the recall referendum, the chamber of the legislature that promoted the recall shall be dissolved. The stringent high thresholds of the vote required in the legislative chambers, combined with the submission of the decision to recall the president or vice-president to a referendum and the possibility of dissolution of a legislative chamber, are intended to prevent irresponsible use of the recall by the authorities.

Table 5.4. Countries with provisions for mixed recall: officials subject to recall and initiatives to promote the recall

Country or state	Official subject to recall	Initiative
Austria	Federal president	The House of Representatives vote requires the presence of at least one-half of the members and a majority of two-thirds of the votes cast.
Iceland	President	Three quarters of the members of the Althing
Palau	President or vice-president	Resolution adopted by not less than two-thirds of the members of the state legislatures in not less than three-quarters of the states

Country or state	Official subject to recall	Initiative
Romania	President	Chamber of Deputies and the Senate, in joint session, by a majority vote of deputies and senators, and after consultation with the Constitutional Court
Serbia	President	Two-thirds of the total number of representatives
Taiwan	President or vice-president	Initiated a quarter of all members of the Legislative Yuan, and also passed by two-thirds of all members
Turkmenistan	President	The People's Council may express its lack of confidence in the president.

154. The requirements of the recall referendum and for approval of a recall vote also vary. In terms of the timing of a call for a recall referendum, there are also variations and a number of possibilities for extending the period that elapses from the moment the drive to initiate a recall begins until the point at which it is effectively carried out. The period of signature collection and validation can vary and extend the process significantly, as in the case of the attempt to recall the president of Venezuela in 2004 (see the case study following chapter 1).

155. Table 5.5 shows that there are different criteria to define when a recall is approved or rejected. These involve defining who can vote in the referendum; the percentage or absolute number of electors who are required to participate; and the percentage or absolute number of votes required in favour or against the recall. In some cases the only requirement is that the absolute number of voters in favour of the recall exceeds the number of those who oppose it. Other cases require a turnout quorum that ranges from a simple majority (Belarus) to 25 per cent (Venezuela) of registered electors if the referendum is to be valid. Additionally, there can be requirements for approval, for example, a simple majority of voters, or a predetermined absolute number of voters, as is the case in Venezuela, where the recall is approved if the number of voters in favour is equal to or greater than the number of those who elected the official. An example of a very demanding case is that of the state of Pohnpei in the Federated States of Micronesia, where 60 per cent of the registered electors have to approve the recall, which means that at least 60 per cent of the registered electors have to participate in the recall in order to validate it.

Table 5.5. Countries with provisions for full recall: timing and rules for the approval of a recall referendum

Country or state	Timing of recall referendum	Rules for approval
Belarus		The referendum shall be held if more than one-half of the citizens who are entitled to vote support the referendum petition. The decision shall be considered as adopted by the referendum if it is supported by more than one-half of the total number of votes cast.
Ecuador	15 days after verification that the requirements have been fulfilled, the recall is called for, and it takes place 60 days afterwards.	
Kiribati		A majority of those entitled to vote in the referendum (i.e. registered as an elector at the time of the last election of the member named in the recall petition, in the electoral district from which that person was last elected)
Micronesia, Federated States of (Chuuk)	The sufficiency of the signatures on a recall petition shall be validated by the Election Commission within 30 days after receipt of the petition. Upon validation of the petition a recall election shall be held within 60 days after receipt of the petition.	A simple majority of the votes cast on a question
Micronesia, Federated States of (Kosrae)	Not later than 60 calendar days after the filing of the recall petition	A simple majority of the persons voting in the election
Micronesia, Federated States of (Pohnpei)	To recall the governor or lieutenant-governor, within 30 days of the determination of the validity of the petition	The affirmative vote of 60% of registered electors
	To recall a member of the legislature, within 30 days of the determination of the validity of the petition	The affirmative vote of 51% of the registered electors of the electoral district
Micronesia, Federated States of (Yap)	Not later than 60 calendar days after the filling of the recall petition	A simple majority of those voting
Nigeria	Within 90 days of the date of receipt of the petition	A simple majority of the votes of the persons registered to vote in that member's electoral district
Palau	No later than 60 calendar days after the filling of the recall petition	A simple majority of the voters

Country or state	Timing of recall referendum	Rules for approval
Venezuela	Within 97 days of approval of the report stating the validity of the petition	A number of voters equal to or greater than the number of those who elected the official vote in favour of the revocation, provided that a number of voters equal to or greater than 25% of the total number of registered electors have voted in the recall election, and the number of votes for the revocation is higher than the number of votes against it

Conclusions

156. The relatively limited international diffusion and use of the recall suggests that this procedure is quite problematic both in itself and in its interaction with the important principles and institutions of representative democracy. In order to ensure that the recall can contribute to improving the means of participation and citizen oversight of elected officials in a democratic setting, the rights of both the citizens and the elected officials have to be guaranteed. To achieve this balance, the rights of all citizens – those in favour of and those against removing the official concerned – as well the rights of the official involved in the process have to be protected. The recall, like other direct democracy procedures, has to balance the principles of participation and effective governance. Achieving that balance is difficult, and failure to achieve it may lead to extreme consequences. On the one hand, if recall is very easy to initiate, this may lead to the trivialization of the recall. On the other hand, tough requirements may make it ineffective as citizens may feel discouraged from using it because of the difficulty of meeting the legal requirements needed to remove a public official through a vote. Finally, in addition to the liberality or the difficulty of the requirements, the assessment of the strength or weakness of the institutional setting may have a strong impact on the willingness and the citizens' ability to use the recall to increase oversight of elected officials.

157. The recall interacts with other institutions and rules of representative and of direct democracy. The decision to introduce it in a particular institutional setting must consider its possible impact in that setting. Conversely, the rules and institutional setting can affect the recall instrument itself. For example, if the presidential term is long – as in the case of Venezuela, where it is six years – the recall would seem to be more necessary than it is in political systems where the presidential term is shorter. Additionally, because of its potential to create polarization and disruption in the regular business of government, it may be preferable to introduce this procedure at the local level, where its impact may generate less negative consequences, rather than at the national level. This may explain why so few countries have adopted the recall to remove elected officials in the national-level executive and legislature.

CHAPTER 6

CHAPTER 6

How citizens get involved – step by step

158. Within the set of direct democracy instruments, registered electors play an important role both as agenda setters and as decision makers. Under some procedures, citizens are able to trigger certain procedures, and even final decisions, by gathering a specified number of valid signatures. This chapter deals with the procedural aspects of such citizen-triggered direct democracy activities. It set outs the major steps in a citizen-initiated process and offers insights into the various processes found throughout the world today.

159. There are four distinct categories of citizen-initiated procedures available. Three of these – citizens' initiatives, citizen-demanded referendums and agenda initiatives – are introduced in chapters 3 and 4. These three procedures deal with substantive issues. A fourth procedure – recall – deals with elected representatives and is introduced in chapter 5. Citizen-triggered procedures do not offer fast tracks or short cuts towards a ballot vote. Most of these mechanisms 'from below' involve some interaction with the authorities and thus offer opportunities to make representative democracy more representative. In contrast, some direct democracy procedures 'from above' have shortcomings that could amount to manipulation of the electoral process.

160. Often citizen-triggered procedures involve many years of political work by both citizens and the authorities in order to prepare, initiate, conduct, verify, conclude and implement a process (see box 6.1). This is especially true for the various initiative mechanisms, which symbolize the right of a minority first to put an issue on the political agenda and then – in the case of citizens' initiatives – to have a ballot question answered by the electorate in a way that is binding on the political authorities. In this way initiatives offer a possibility for citizens to press a political accelerator. Citizen-demanded referendums and recall processes, on the other hand, enable citizens to control, brake or stop a certain issue put forward or decided by elected officials, or – in the case of recall – even the office-holders themselves.

Box 6.1. Switzerland: a lengthy debate, the initiative on Equal Rights for the Disabled

In May 2003, the Swiss electorate of just over 5 million was able to vote in the federal referendum on the popular initiative entitled Equal Rights for the Disabled, which proposed the addition of a new article to the federal constitution: 'The law guarantees equal rights for disabled people. It provides for measures for removing and compensating for existing disadvantages. Access to buildings and other facilities and the use of institutions and services intended for the general public will be guaranteed, as long as the costs are within reasonable limits' (article 8, §4). Between August 1998 and June 1999, more than 120,000 signatures were collected by no fewer than 35 organizations for the disabled. In the four years between the official submission of the initiative and the deciding referendum, the proposal was debated by the Swiss government (the Federal Council) and by both chambers of the federal parliament (the Federal Assembly). It was rejected by both, mainly on economic grounds. In its recommendation that the voters also reject the initiative proposal (which was included in the referendum booklet sent to all registered electors before the vote), the government argued that 'A right of direct access to buildings would have significant financial consequences for both the public and private spheres'. The government also pointed out that a new law on the disabled, which was adopted almost unanimously by the Federal Assembly in December 2003, and which came into force on 1 January 2004, addressed many of these issues.

The Equal Rights for the Disabled initiative had little chance of success in the referendum vote on 18 May 2003. On a turnout of exactly 50 per cent, 62 per cent of the voters (1.4 million) voted against the proposal and 38 per cent (almost 900,000) voted in favour. Free access for the disabled to all areas of public life, for which the initiative had campaigned, was approved in only three of the 26 cantons – Geneva (by 59 per cent), Jura (by 55 per cent) and Ticino (by 54 per cent). For the initiative to have been accepted, a majority of the cantons would also have had to vote in favour as well as a simple majority of the total electorate, as is prescribed in Switzerland for all constitutional amendments. However, the example of the 'Disabled Initiative' shows that popular initiatives are not just put to the vote from one day to the next. Rather, they are part of a long-term process which may take up to a decade to complete. At the beginning there is usually an idea for radical change – in this case, redressing the inequality of opportunity of people with disabilities. At the end of such a long initiative process, the result is often a referendum defeat for the proposal (fewer than one out of ten initiatives in Switzerland are accepted). Yet in many cases the parliament goes some way to meeting the initiative's aims with either a direct (where both proposals are voted on at the same time) or an indirect (as in the case of the initiative on the disabled) counter-proposal.

Source: Kaufmann, Bruno et al., *The Initiative and Referendum Institute Europe Guidebook to Direct Democracy in Switzerland and Beyond*, 2009 edn (Marburg/Brussels: IRI Europe, 2008)

161. It is possible to identify a series of common features of citizen-initiated direct democracy procedures, beginning with the availability of those procedures and their initial use by citizens. Interaction with official bodies often continues until the moment when an initiative, demand or recall is qualified for the ballot or, in the case of the agenda initiative, for consideration by the legislature. The story often does not end with a decision by the electorate or by the legislature, but may be followed by legal (e.g. appeal) or political (e.g. implementation) battles. This chapter deals with all these procedures, offers an overview of the various steps and the administrative issues involved in each of them, and creates a worldwide typology of the processes that qualify an initiative to go further to the ballot.

162. Direct democracy procedures are available in many jurisdictions throughout the world. They can vary in a number of ways, including the specific exclusion of certain types of issues, the number of signatures required and the predefined time frames for completing the various steps within the initiative/referendum/recall process. They can also be supported by certain opportunity structures provided by the authorities, such as assistance in drafting an initiative text, free access to public premises and infrastructure, or more proactive measures such as financial reimbursements for each signature or free air time and/or advertisements in the press provided to qualified initiative committees. This chapter looks into a range of possible interactions between initiators and governmental institutions, including judicial, legislative and executive bodies.

163. There also exist various hybrid processes by which an issue can be put to the ballot. In the US state of Alaska, for example, the state constitution provides that once every ten years citizens are automatically asked whether they wish to call a convention to revise the state's constitution. In two Canadian provinces (British Columbia and Ontario), a Citizens' Assembly was convened to first debate the issue of electoral reform and then recommend a proposal which would be put to a referendum vote (on Ontario, see box 6.2). Under this arrangement, the government organized and funded the assembly, but the formulation of a proposal and the decision to hold a referendum rested entirely with the Citizens' Assembly, not with the government. The 'citizens' assembly' model has also been used in the Netherlands (known as the *burgerforum*). In Australia, a proposal to replace the British monarch as Australia's head of state was first referred to a 'peoples' convention' before it was submitted to a binding referendum vote in 1999. In the UK, a 'citizens' jury' was recently held in Bristol to recommend proposals for reform in education and children's services, and there is increasing interest in this model in other jurisdictions. While these structures are different from those of an initiative process, they seek to retain many of the aspects of citizen involvement in the development of public policy that are commonly associated with citizens' initiatives or agenda initiatives.

Box 6.2. A hybrid process: Ontario's referendum on electoral reform

Reform of the electoral system has been widely discussed and debated in Canada in recent years. Because the parliament or legislature is not generally considered the most appropriate forum for a debate on political institutions, the government of the province of Ontario convened a 'Citizens' Assembly' to consider various proposals and ultimately to make a recommendation to be put to a referendum. The Citizens' Assembly consisted of 103 men and women whose names were selected at random from the electoral register, with provision for an equal representation of men and women and an appropriate distribution of age groups. One representative was selected by random draw from each of the 103 constituencies in the province. This unique model of deliberative democracy was similar to a process employed in the province of British Columbia two years earlier, and has also been used in the Netherlands.

The Citizens' Assembly met on alternate weekends in Toronto for eight months. It was chaired by a retired judge, and a prominent professor of political science served as its academic director. The first four months of its work involved what was called the 'education phase', in which members of the assembly studied the issue of electoral reform, read materials prepared by the research staff, and listened to lectures and panel discussions conducted by scholars, practitioners and other knowledgeable parties. The second phase of the assembly's work, the deliberation phase, consisted of discussion and debate among its members, as well as public hearings at which the general public and other interested parties were invited to present their views. At the conclusion of the process, the assembly voted by 94 votes to 8 to recommend that Ontario change to a Mixed Member Proportional (MMP) electoral system. This recommendation was sent to the government, and a referendum was scheduled to coincide with the provincial election held on 10 October 2007.

The question presented to voters was a choice between the Citizens' Assembly's recommendation of MMP and the existing First Past The Post (FPTP) electoral system. The referendum campaign suffered from a lack of information among the voters, in part because it was overshadowed by the election, but also because the Citizens' Assembly had received relatively little publicity over the course of its deliberations. The major political parties generally opposed the MMP proposal, and much of the press and the media lined up against it. There was no public financing of the campaigns, but the government allocated a sum of 6.5 million Canadian dollars for 'public education'. The public education campaign, however, was mandated to be strictly neutral, and therefore did relatively little to inform the public on the substance of the issue.

In the referendum, the MMP proposal was overwhelmingly defeated by 63 to 37 per cent. Although the referendum did not result in a change in Ontario's electoral system, the Citizens' Assembly process proved to be a unique and valuable mechanism for putting an issue on the electoral agenda and providing a forum in which ordinary citizens could debate a complex issue. Although the process itself is unique, it combines some elements of both the citizens' initiative and the agenda initiative models, while at the same time providing a forum in which more intensive deliberation of an issue by citizens can take place, and leaving the final decision to the voters.

164. While in many jurisdictions only a few of the procedures described below are of relevance, in some others there are additional intermediate steps linked to judicial reviews or checks. Often these are spelled out in a constitution or in an initiative and referendum law. The example from Lithuania (see box 6.3) suggests one way in which the process might be managed. However, the key steps identified in this Handbook offer a fairly comprehensive overview, guideline and checklist for designers, administrators, users and observers to assess the time and resources (both human and financial) that will be needed and the complexity of either active or passive involvement in such a process. Table 6.1 presents a summary of these steps.

Box 6.3. Managing the initiative and referendum process in Lithuania

The rules and procedures for conducting national referendums in Lithuania may be found in two legislative acts – the constitution of the Republic of Lithuania (articles 9, 69, 71, 148, 151–154) and the Referendum Law adopted in 2002.

Both mandatory and consultative referendums take place under identical rules, as a result of either a citizens' initiative or a proposal put forward by the Seimas (parliament). Initiatives may be proposed by (a) no less than one-quarter of the members of the Seimas or (b) at least 300,000 citizens who have the right to vote.

The Central Electoral Commission (CEC) administers referendums according to the 2002 Referendum Law. The CEC

- registers the group (a minimum of 15 persons) and issues signature collection forms to the group;

- verifies and determines whether 300,000 citizens' signatures have been properly collected;

- appoints city and regional referendum commissions;

- determines the official stamps and forms, the referendum ballot paper, and other documents to be used in the referendum;

- manages the state funds allotted for the referendum; and

- organizes the voting in and publishes the final results of the referendum.

A group may submit an application to the CEC. Their application must indicate the referendum type and the preliminary or final text of the resolution, and also designate a coordinator(s) for the group. The CEC must register the initiative group within a 15-day period and within the next five working days provide them with the forms for collecting the signatures of citizens.

A period of three months is allowed for signature collection, starting from the day the CEC issues the citizen signature sheets. The CEC must verify the signatures that have been collected within 15 days after the collection of signatures is over, and if the documents contain non-essential deficiencies or if the number of signatures falls only slightly short of the number required (up to 0.5 per cent), an additional 15-day period is given to allow the promoters of the initiative to correct these deficiencies. The CEC may refuse to register the initiative for a referendum if (a) the required number of citizens' signatures has not been collected or (b) the voluntary principle in collecting signatures has been violated. The initiative group can appeal against the CEC's decision to the Administrative Court of Lithuania within a period of one month.

The CEC officially publishes the results of the referendum in the *State Gazette* not later than within four days after the referendum vote. In addition, the CEC is obliged to present to the president of the republic the text of the resolution adopted by referendum not later than the day following the official publication of the final referendum results.

Steps, actors and events involved in direct democracy procedures

165. *Knowledge.* Before an issue can become part of a direct democracy procedure, it is essential that information about the instrument is publicly available. Certainly the frequent use of initiatives, demands or recalls is the best way to make the availability of these procedures well known. In jurisdictions where such instruments have only recently been introduced or where they are seldom used, they can be part of a dedicated

democratic infrastructure, for example, information available on the Internet, printed materials, educational efforts and media coverage. In many countries, electoral processes (including direct democracy instruments, if available) are a major subject of civic education efforts in both elementary and secondary schools.

166. *Idea*. The starting point of all citizen-initiated direct democracy procedures – the 'idea' – is especially important. Citizen-triggered procedures only come into practice when there is a group of people or an organization that wants to address a certain problem and formulate a proposal. This may be a totally new and radical idea, a very pragmatic and feasible reform, or just the determination to control the legislature by blocking one of its (old or new) decisions. This non-official phase often includes a good many meetings and discussion of strategies for promoting the idea. In New Zealand, one person may begin the process of registering an initiative under New Zealand's Citizens Initiated Referenda Act, but just as often the process may involve an organization or a group formed for the purpose (see box 6.4).

> **Box 6.4. Steps for registering an initiative under New Zealand's Citizens Initiated Referenda Act**
>
> The Citizens Initiated Referenda Act of 1993 allows any person in New Zealand to file an initiative asking that a national referendum be held on an issue. To start the process, a citizen presents a written proposal to the clerk of the House of Representatives, accompanied by a 500 New Zealand dollar fee. The clerk advertises the proposed question, and the public then has at least 28 days to make written comments to the clerk. The clerk then has three months to determine the final wording of the question.
>
> Once the wording is determined, the clerk approves the form to be used to collect signatures. A period of 12 months is allowed in which to collect signatures. The initiative must have the signatures of at least 10 per cent of all eligible electors. When the required number of signatures has been delivered to the clerk, a two-month period is then allowed for checking the signatures and for the submission of additional signatures if needed. Following certification by the clerk, the proposal is first presented to the House of Representatives. The governor general has a month from the time the initiative is presented to the House to set a date for a referendum. The chief electoral officer will announce the final results of the referendum, and the government may or may not decide to act on the outcome, which is non-binding.
>
> *Examples*
>
> • On 30 June 1997, Margaret Robertson presented an initiative to the clerk

proposing that the size of the New Zealand parliament be reduced from 120 members to 99. Signature collection began on 21 August 1997 and the required number of signatures was obtained and certified within the prescribed one-year period of time. The initiative was presented to the House of Representatives on 17 February 1999 and the referendum date was set for 27 November 1999. The proposal received the support of 81.5 per cent of those voting in the referendum. Turnout was 85%. Parliament declined to act on the proposal.

- On 6 May 1999, Julie Waring presented an initiative to the clerk proposing that 'the Government be required to reduce the number of unemployed to below one percent of the labour force'. Signature collection began on 12 August 1999 and the proposal lapsed when the required number of signatures was not obtained before the deadline of 12 August 2000.

- On 21 July 2004, the NZflag.com Trust presented an initiative to the clerk proposing that 'the design of the New Zealand Flag should be changed'. Signature collection began on 13 October 2004. The initiative was withdrawn by the proposers on 1 August 2005.

167. *Organization.* The first persons to draft, deposit, sign and register an initiative/demand/recall document are the proponents. In order for a proposal to be registered, most jurisdictions require the establishment of a designated committee, which has to fulfil certain conditions. This is important because this group of individuals or organization will be the legal body responsible for dealing with the authorities and other actors during the subsequent steps. For example, in California just one proponent can write a first draft of an initiative proposal.

168. *Draft.* With the first written version of a text – the initial proposal – the initiative/demand/recall idea is transformed into a direct democracy instrument. One of the preconditions for registering a citizen-triggered proposal in most jurisdictions is the formulation of a legal or constitutional text. It is of course possible that at this early stage of the process the final text will already have been agreed. However, some jurisdictions provide official assistance with this task, including support for translations in multilingual polities. There is nevertheless always a danger of mistrust developing between the authorities and the initiative committee.

169. *Title.* A title must be found which will identify the proposal and will also convey a political message. In addition to the proposed legal or constitutional text, the title serves an important function in communicating its purpose. Because of its importance, the determination of the title is generally subject to certain regulations. There are different rules on who may be eligible to decide the actual title – for example,

the proponents of the initiative or the agency responsible for the administration of the process, or (in a few rare instances) even the legislature. Additionally, certain mistakes such as inconsistency with the content or the use of commercial or inflammatory statements may disqualify a proposed title. It is also important at this early stage in the process to take into consideration that the title chosen may be of importance for the later ballot question. For this reason, as the recommendations of the UK Electoral Commission show (see box 6.5), careful consideration of the title and the eventual wording of the ballot question are important. Although the advice provided is directed to the formulation of the ballot text for referendum questions in the UK, the points raised by the UK Electoral Commission are also useful for the initiative process, and have application in any jurisdiction that employs direct democracy procedures.

Box 6.5. The UK Electoral Commission's 'question assessment guidelines'

Under the Political Parties, Elections and Referendums Act 2000, The Electoral Commission has a statutory obligation to comment on the intelligibility of UK, national and regional referendum questions. In assessing intelligibility, the Commission will have regard to the question's effectiveness in presenting the options clearly, simply and neutrally. The Commission has developed these guidelines to facilitate the assessment of referendum questions and to try to achieve an acceptable level of intelligibility. We intend to keep them under review in order to ensure they remain relevant and applicable.

Guideline one: The question should prompt an immediate response. It should be clear what decision the voter is being asked to make. Voters should not have to work out, or try to interpret the question; the voter's preferred answer should be immediately identifiable. Voters should not have to re-read the question several times to understand its content. The question should be written in a way that encourages each reader to interpret it in the same way. To achieve this, clear and unambiguous language should be used. The response options should be phrased in terms that are consistent with those used in the question. For example, if the question contains the words 'agree' and 'disagree' the possible answers should also be 'agree' and 'disagree'.

Guideline two: Words and phrases used in the question should not have positive or negative connotations. Certain words or phrases may encourage support for one particular outcome. For example, words such as 'new' and 'approve' may in some instances imply that something is a positive concept. Equally, negative words and phrases should be avoided. For example, 'abolish', 'old' and 'reject' may in some instances imply that something is a negative concept. Attempts should be made to find unbiased descriptive words to replace such terms. Consideration should be given to perceptions that voters may have about the subject matter and potential negative or positive connotations associated with particular words.

Guideline three: Words and phrases used in the question should not be intentionally leading.

The question should not be phrased so as to guide the voter towards one particular outcome.

Guideline four: Words and phrases used in the question should not be loaded. The question should be balanced and should not contain words or phrases which prompt one particular answer. Words and phrases that are, or could be perceived as, false or misleading should be avoided.

Guideline five: The question should not contain 'jargon'. Words, phrases and acronyms that are only commonly used and understood by specialist groups should be avoided.

Guideline six: The language used in the question should be consistent. If certain words or concepts are referred to once in a question or preamble, their use should be consistent throughout the entire text.

Guideline seven: Words and phrases used in the question should reflect the language used and understood by the voter. Consideration should be given to the language used during any informal campaigning that may have taken place prior to the referendum period commencing, providing this could not be perceived as potentially influencing the outcome.

Guideline eight: The question should not provide more information than is necessary to answer the question meaningfully. The question should not contain unnecessary detail about the options or subject matter.

The question should focus on the main issue(s), rather than less important consequences or implications. Policy alternatives that are not directly related to the referendum question should not be mentioned, as they will only make it less clear what the voter is being asked to do.

Guideline nine: The question should not be longer than necessary. The question should be sensitive to the level of public awareness surrounding the referendum issue. If there is limited public awareness of the subject, it may be appropriate to include more detail about the choices. Where the referendum issue is a complex one or an unfamiliar one, it may be appropriate to use a preamble to explain the context and/or provide additional information to the voter, rather than have a long question.

Guideline ten: The question should be well structured. The text of any question should be carefully structured and easy for the voter to read. Questions should present the issues and key words in a logical and rational sequence.

This may involve the use of several short sentences and/or a preamble. Reverse wording or "double negatives" should be avoided as they can make it difficult for the voter to understand the question.

Source: UK Electoral Commission, Question Assessment Guidelines [no date], <http://www.electoralcommission.org.uk/templates/search/document.cfm/8644>, reproduced by kind permission.

170. *Registration.* The legal process officially starts with the presentation of an initiative/demand/recall for publication. With the first steps completed, it should now be possible to register the plan to trigger a citizen-initiated procedure. The process of filing the proposal generally also involves the formal registration of the responsible committee, thereby assigning it certain duties and rights. Such a step brings new responsibilities, including political ones. A registered committee may, later in the process, be able to withdraw an initiative.

171. *Legality check.* The legality and/or constitutionality of a proposal by a designated authority is often determined at this stage, although it may also be done earlier or later in the process of qualifying a citizens' initiative (demand/recall) for the ballot. An early legality and/or constitutionality check implies both risks and opportunities. If the authorities are challenged, they may use an early legality check to stop a citizen procedure, even on weak grounds, before it even takes off. However it is also important not to allow a process which involves many people to advance further if, at the end, the proposal turns out to be invalid on legal or constitutional grounds. This determination may occur after registration of the initiative, after publication when the signatures are already collected, after the submission but before the vote, or, as in most US states, after the vote itself if an initiative has been passed.

172. *Launch.* After the publication of a proposal, initial registration and legality checks, it is time for the citizens to sign up and convince others to do so, typically within a certain time limit. This is the beginning of the public phase of the initiative process. Signature gathering officially begins after publication of the proposal in an official journal. At this stage it is very important to understand the rules on signature gathering (see the next step). The need to understand and follow established legal

procedures is illustrated in the example from the US state of Oregon (box 6.6). Oregon sets out its rules in an official *Initiative and Referendum Manual.*

Box 6.6. Initiative and referendum manuals and guidelines: the example of the US state of Oregon

Many US states provide official information and assistance to prospective initiative committees. Publications such as a state initiative and referendum manual can provide a full range of basic information, practical advice and even model initiative signature-gathering sheets for download. They often provide guidance on how to register an initiative, which constitutional requirements must be met, and where and how an initiative can be circulated, as well explaining how a citizen initiative can be withdrawn.

But, even though such manuals and guidelines are openly available, many initiative groups do not follow the rules, and this has raised concerns at the responsible governmental agency. A press release by the Oregon secretary of state, Bill Bradbury, on 24 July 2006 featured the following statement: 'Chief petitioners and the companies they pay to gather signatures for initiative campaigns have again done a poor job of training circulators on how to follow state law, and have failed to check their own work for compliance with state law. "We're seeing the same individuals from the same campaigns make big mistakes over and over again", said Bradbury. "There is just no excuse for chief petitioners and businesses dedicated to signature gathering to operate this sloppily. In any other business sector this would be gross negligence." Bradbury has repeatedly asked the legislature to require mandatory training for signature gatherers, and plans to ask again in the next legislative session. The Election Division's initial review of petition signature sheets revealed that paid signature gathering firms have again failed to read the regulations published in the State Initiative and Referendum Manual and failed to train their employees in the basics of signature gathering. In some petitions, thousands of signatures were disqualified because circulators failed to follow simple rules relating to signing and dating their petition sheets' (http://www.sos.state.or.us/executive/pressreleases/2006/0724.html>). As a result of the problems identified, in 2007 the Oregon legislature tightened restrictions on signature gathers.

---

173. *Signature collection.* Signing by hand has been and still is the most common method of formally supporting a proposal. However, there are electronic and digital methods available as well. All available and allowed methods of gathering signatures may be used in this phase to bring the numbers of supporting citizens up to the required number. While some jurisdictions only allow signatures by hand – and in some cases only collected at specified places – others also provide the possibility of

electronic signature gathering. In some countries it is explicitly forbidden to use paid signature gatherers for this work. While a citizens' initiative in Switzerland needs to gather 100,000 signatures (*c.* 2 per cent of the electorate) within 18 months, a citizen-demanded referendum to bring a legislative act to the decisive referendum requires 50,000 signatures within 100 days of the publication of the new law. Other jurisdictions may have considerably shorter time requirements. For example, in the German state of Bavaria, an initiative committee has just 14 days to gather the signatures of at least 10 per cent of the electorate. An additional hurdle is the restriction that these signatures can only be gathered within designated official premises. In contrast, in Switzerland, signatures can be gathered freely. Initiative committees often have their own strategies for gathering signatures (see box 6.7 for an example from a US state). It is also common in many of the US states to use paid signature gatherers, particularly when an initiative is sponsored by a well-funded organization or group.

Box 6.7. 'Smile and have fun!': an initiative committee in the US state of Ohio

'The Natural Law Party of Ohio needs 55,000 signatures to be on the ballot in the primary elections.

1) **The person (circulator) collecting signatures**

    A) Must be an Ohio registered voter.

    B) Cannot sign his/her own petition.

    C) Must be sure that each petition sheet contains only names from the same county.

    D) Can collect anywhere in Ohio.

    E) May turn in either full or partially filled petitions.

    F) Must complete and sign the Circulator Statement at the end of petition.

2) **People signing the petition must**

    A) Sign in ink

    B) Be a currently registered voter in Ohio (and may be of any political party).

    C) **SIGN** with the same signature used when registering; then if the signature is not readable, print the person's name above or to the side of the signature.

    D) Use the same address as used when they registered to vote (if they have moved and want to use their new address, they must first fill out a new voter registration card).

...

HELPFUL HINTS FOR SIGNATURE GATHERING

Don't mind a no, keep on going

1. Family, friends, neighbors are the easiest to get. Tour your neighborhood.

2. Collect signatures in busy places such as in front of stores, parking lots, parks, malls, libraries and college campuses.

3. Use clipboards or cardboard backers to support the petition. Take plenty of pens.

4. Have more fun by going with someone. You can sign each other's petition because you can't sign your own.

5. Smile and have fun.

6. You will be the one that will make this happen. It is a tremendous job, can't be done with only a few. Bless you and Good Luck.'

Source: http://www.ohionlp.org/Files/Directions_SignatureGathering.html>.

174. *Submission*. After gathering the required number of signatures, the proponents/ registered committee will deposit the collected signatures with the proper authorities. This is called the submission of an initiative/demand/recall. Submitting a sufficient number of signatures is a major step in each citizen-triggered procedure as it signals the point at which the issue of the few becomes an issue of the many. At this moment, the initiative committee should be quite sure that the required threshold of signatures and all additional possible requirements have been met. This can be a problem if the time provided for the gathering of signatures is very short or if it has been difficult to collect the required number of signatures within the time provided.

175. *Validation*. The authorities then check that the submission is valid in order to ensure that the proposal and its qualifying process have conformed to all existing rules and regulations. Also at this stage the signatures submitted will have to be validated, generally by checking them against the official electoral register. Different methods of validation are used, depending on the structure of the particular polity and the methods used for identification. In some jurisdictions a sampling procedure

is used to validate signatures, while in others every signature must be checked. An important factor for the validity check is the method of voter registration. Different methods of validation may be required depending on whether the electoral register is updated continuously or set up anew at each election.

176. *Verification.* When the authorities have carried out the validity check and have established that the required number of valid signatures have been obtained, the proposal can be verified. Successful verification concludes the first phase of the qualification process. In the remaining steps, more actors will become involved. For the initiative committee, this means a new and even more challenging role, as it will have to interact with the authorities, the media and critics of the proposal in a more serious way than before verification. A verified initiative sometimes also qualifies for additional support and services provided by the authorities. While most citizens' initiatives (and agenda initiatives) will be considered by a legislature (to adopt them, for counter-proposals to be made or for the proposal to be debated), verified citizen-demanded and optional referendums as well as recalls will now, depending on the jurisdiction, qualify for the ballot. How much time is allowed for counter-proposals to be considered, or for an administration to prepare for and decide on the voting day, is in most jurisdictions written into the legal or regulatory acts that govern such procedures.

177. *Interaction.* It is possible that a legislature or parliament may itself decide to adopt the proposal, or it may offer its own alternative proposal on the issue. In the latter case, the possibility is opened up for the registered initiative committee to withdraw its proposal. The role of the legislature may be crucial in the remainder of the process, as it may offer its own proposal which may either meet the central aspects of the citizens' proposal, or form the basis for a counter-proposal. In some jurisdictions, such an alternative proposal can also be made even after the initial registration of an initiative. For all these options specific time limits may apply.

178. *Certification.* It is now up to the specified authority to determine that the citizen-triggered initiative/referendum/recall proposal has qualified to go forward to the ballot. Following the additional stage of possible counter-proposals and expressions of opinion under the 'interaction' step, it is finally time for a decision to be made at the ballot box. If an additional alternative proposal has been put forward, some jurisdictions qualify both proposals (that of the citizens and that of the legislature or other eligible authority) for the ballot (as in Switzerland), while others allow only the alternative proposal to be voted on (as in some German *länder*).

179. *Campaign.* At this stage the initiative becomes an electoral issue involving many different actors and sectors within the polity. This step is critical to ensuring that the public is well informed about the issue. The final campaign may offer many additional challenges to both sides in the decision-making process. In order to complete this step in accordance with global democratic standards, a growing number of countries have implemented campaign regulations regarding finances and media coverage.

Such regulations may also include more supportive aspects of campaigns, such as financial subsidies or free air time (see chapter 7). Germany provides reimbursements for verified signatures in a few states. In the state of Saxony, for example, the initiative committee gets approximately 0.05 euros (EUR) for each signature regardless of the final success or failure of the signature-gathering process. Some of the German states also have reimbursement schemes based on the number of votes cast in a referendum: in Schleswig-Holstein, the most northern state of Germany, each 'Yes' vote for a citizen-triggered proposal pays 0.28 EUR in subsidy.

180. *Voting.* Generally, voting on the proposal will follow the same rules and procedures as voting in elections. It may be possible to vote in advance, or by post before the actual voting day and up to the point when the polling stations close on voting day. During the voting phase, specific rules may apply for the various actors. These rules can include a prohibition on publishing opinion polls or even a prohibition on all campaigning activities for a specified period (typically the final 24 or 48 hours of the campaign period). However, both sides in the decision-making process may discover that many voters make up their minds well ahead of the final day, making last-minute campaign efforts more or less ineffective.

181. *Appeal.* While free and fair majority decisions must be respected, irregularities often have to be addressed and in some circumstances may be the subject of an appeal procedure. For an initiative committee, the publication of the ballot results may mean the end of its efforts or the beginning of new ones. This may include the right to restart an initiative on the same issue or a similar issue on the spot. In some jurisdictions, there are rules specifying a time period when initiatives on the same issue (or simply another initiative) are not allowed. In many jurisdictions, the rules of decision making in such votes include specific majority rules (e.g. double majorities in federal states). The initiative committee may have some scepticism about the freedom and fairness of the ballot process itself and choose to appeal to a court.

182. *Implementation.* It is not unusual for the work of a citizens' initiative committee to continue even after the day of decision. It may become involved in a post-referendum appeal process, or it may begin to look forward to a future referendum or alternative political strategy. When the proposal is accepted by a majority at the ballot box, this may produce even more work for the original drafter of the new law or amendment to the constitution. In this case, a lengthy process follows during which (in most cases) the authorities will have the main responsibility for implementing the decision.

Table 6.1. Summary: the steps, actors and events involved in direct democracy procedures

	Step	Actor(s)	Event
1	Knowledge	EMB, educational and non-governmental organizations	Efforts to guarantee that information is provided on available procedures
2	Idea	Group of citizens and/or organizations	Depending on the exact procedure, this may include a totally new idea or a reaction to a new law
3	Organization	Group of citizens	The (in)formal establishment of an initiative/demand/recall committee
4	Draft	Committee, EMB	Agreement on a text (and possibly translations) for a new/change of law or amendment to the constitution
5	Title	Committee, EMB, legislative body	Setting a title for the proposal and the whole process to come
6	Registration	Committee, EMB	The formal step to register an initiative/demand/recall with the authorities
7	Legality (check)	Designated authority	Legality or constitutionality checks may take place at one or several points of the process, undertaken by one or several designated authorities
8	Launch	Committee	With the official start of signature gathering, the initiative/demand/recall enters its most critical phase
9	Signature collection	Citizens, committee, authorities	The signature-gathering process has to consider certain rules, options and restrictions
10	Submission	Committee, EMB	Delivery of the signatures that have been gathered to the authorities
11	Validation	Authorities	The authorities check the eligibility and validity of the signatures delivered
12	Verification	EMB	After the validity check, the initiative/demand/recall may be verified and either directly qualified for the ballot (demand/recall) or sent to the legislative body or government for consideration (initiatives)

	Step	Actor(s)	Event
13	Interaction	Legislature, government, president	Initiative proposal is now an 'official' matter. The legislative or governmental body may have the right to put an alternative proposal on the ballot and to make recommendations. As an element of interaction the initiative committee may have the right to withdraw its initiative in order to find a compromise
14	Certification	Designated authorities	Setting the ballot (time, final rules, campaign assistance)
15	Campaign	Citizens, groups, political parties	Campaign regulations for free and fair direct democracy procedures may be applicable
16	Voting	Registered electors	Voting may take different forms (personal voting, remote voting, e-voting) and can cover a period of several days or weeks
17	Appeal	Committee, authorities	In the event of irregularities, an appeal procedure may start. Otherwise the decision of the voters is final
18	Implementation	Authorities, others	Implementation of a new law or amendment to the constitution, to create new dynamics, possible hurdles and sometimes even the need for the initiative committee to remain active

183. The administrative procedures are critical to citizen- and user-friendly practice. The authorities have a role to play at almost every step of the process, including offering advice and support to the electorate. The most important actors, however, are the proponents/initiators of the process. Designers of citizen-triggered direct democracy procedures need to consider several aspects of the legal context, including the roles of both proponents and authorities. Consequently, direct democracy procedures should be assessed from at least three different perspectives – those of the administrators (the EMB, the courts etc.), the users (citizen groups) and the designers (politicians, legal experts).

184. Before an idea becomes an initiative, and an initiative qualifies for the ballot, a series of preconditions must be fulfilled, including:

- there must be basic legal provisions in place;

- there must be administrative readiness and infrastructure to deal with initiatives/ demands and recalls; and

- potential proponents must be free and able to launch an initiative process.

In sum, because citizen-triggered direct democracy procedures carry great expectations on the part of the citizens, careful design and good administrative practice are essential if such procedures are to lead to a ballot.

CHAPTER 7

Direct democracy votes: information, campaigning and financing

185. The conduct of referendum, initiative and recall campaigns raises a number of important issues which must be considered in addition to those that involve placing a proposal before the people or qualifying an initiative for the ballot. Mechanisms must be put in place to ensure that voters have enough information on the issue to allow them to make an informed decision. Both those supporting a measure and those opposing it must have sufficient opportunity to place their arguments before the electorate. These objectives require access to the media – both electronic and print media – and the expenditure of money – either public or private. This chapter discusses the issues involved in organizing, administering and financing referendum, initiative or recall campaigns.

The principle of fairness

186. A commonly stated goal of campaign regulation and finance laws is to create and maintain a 'level playing field'. But it is not an easy matter to define exactly what this is or how it can be created and maintained throughout the course of a campaign which will often be hotly contested. When the government places an issue before the electorate, government ministers often take public positions on the issue to be voted on, or become involved directly in the campaign. In the 2005 referendum in France on the EU Constitutional Treaty, for example, the president of the republic took the decision put the issue to the ballot and then actively campaigned for a 'Yes' vote (see box 7.1). In such circumstances the government is, by definition, not a neutral party. Similarly, the provincial government of Quebec called and organized the 1995 referendum on sovereignty. But all its actions were intended to secure a 'Yes' result, not to ensure neutrality. The federal government of Canada was also not a neutral party in this referendum. Although it had no formal role in the organization or conduct of the referendum, its officials and representatives were heavily involved in the campaign in a variety of ways. Some jurisdictions attempt to mandate government neutrality. In

the case of Spain (see box 7.1), during the 2005 referendum on the EU Constitutional Treaty, the EMB, the Central Electoral Board, acted to restrain the campaign activities of the government. In the Republic of Ireland, the courts have consistently ruled that the government and its officials must refrain from assuming an active role in referendum campaigns, and that public funds cannot be spent in support of one side of an issue.

Box 7.1. Determining the role of government: the 2005 referendums on the EU Constitutional Treaty in Spain and France

Spain was the first European country to put the proposed EU constitution to a vote of the electorate in February 2005. France held its referendum on the same issue a few months later. Neither country was legally required to hold such a referendum, but in both instances a political decision was taken to put the treaty to a popular vote.

In Spain, the government is not allowed to campaign either in favour of or against any specific outcome in a referendum that it has called. Article 50 of the Spanish electoral law explicitly forbids the government and other public officials to influence the vote of the electorate in any way. But governmental neutrality is not so easily achieved, or maintained, in a partisan campaign. Approval of the constitution was seen as crucial for the government, which launched a wide-reaching information dissemination campaign, complete with its own motto, 'First with Europe'. Prominent journalists and celebrated actors, singers and football players were employed to read articles from the constitution to the Ode to Joy from Beethoven's Ninth Symphony, the anthem of the European Union. Activities such as these led the supervisory body, the Central Electoral Board, to rule that 'the government should limit itself objectively to inform about the content of the treaty, eliminating all value judgements or mottos such as "First with Europe"' or 'any declarations which, directly or indirectly, influence the position or attitude of the citizens' (*Boletin oficial del Estado*, 3 February 2005).

In France, there is no legal requirement that the government remain neutral in a referendum campaign, nor was there any pretence of political neutrality in the referendum on the Constitutional Treaty. The referendum was called by the president of the republic, who campaigned actively for a 'Yes' vote along with other members of the government. The campaign in France was difficult because the major parties were divided on the issue, and the EU constitution quickly became caught up in other issues of French domestic politics. While French voters ultimately rejected the Constitutional Treaty in the referendum, the consequences of that rejection were unclear until well after the conclusion of the campaign. The difficulty of providing balanced information to the voters in a heated political atmosphere, with the president actively engaged in the campaign,

---

quickly became apparent. A televised address by the president in support of the treaty on the eve of the referendum failed to save it from defeat, and may in fact have prompted some voters to support the 'No' side. Thus, the defeat of the constitution was interpreted not only as a rejection of some specific provisions of the treaty but also as a defeat for both the governing party and the president who had campaigned on its behalf.

187. Initiative campaigns in US states are sometimes criticized because of the disproportionate amounts of money spent by one side or the other. For example, an individual, group or organization that has been able to bear the high costs of qualifying a proposal for the ballot is often able to spend far more money in a campaign to secure its passage than opponents are able to raise to defeat it. It is, however, also true that the expenditure of money does not in itself ensure the passage or defeat of any referendum proposal, and that groups or organizations that pursue such a strategy can just as easily fail to persuade the public. Regulations that limit the amount of money that can be spent on a campaign are intended to create a more equal balance between the groups active in a campaign. A less interventionist form of regulation simply requires disclosure of the sources of funding, but does not place limits on the amount that can be spent on a campaign. Public subsidies are another means of ensuring that a degree of balance is maintained between the two sides (see below), but they do not limit or control the raising or expenditure of funds from private sources.

188. Access to the media through which voters will obtain information on ballot propositions can also be a contentious matter. In countries where some media, such as television stations, are state-controlled, parties or groups on one side of an issue may be able to obtain preferential treatment or greater access. In countries where media are privately owned, groups with more resources may hold the advantage, particularly when the prices charged by newspapers, radio or television stations for access to their facilities are high. Such media themselves sometimes become involved in campaigns by taking editorial positions on an issue, thereby complicating further the question of fair access. In some jurisdictions, the media are required to provide 'equal time' to both sides of a referendum campaign. Alternatively, public funds may be used to subsidize media access in order to ensure that the voters hear both sides of an issue over the course of a campaign.

189. The answer to difficulties such as those described above could be found in tighter regulation of direct democracy campaigns. Measures can be taken to ensure that the amount of money spent in a campaign falls within defined limits, that campaigners for both sides of an issue have sufficient access to the media, and that voters hear the arguments put forward on both sides. But such regulations are difficult to formulate and sometimes even more difficult to enforce. For example, attempts to limit

disproportionate media access by one side in a referendum or initiative campaign may run up against free speech guarantees in countries that have a constitutional charter of rights. Attempts to limit disproportionate spending by one side in a campaign may be difficult to enforce if expenditures are indirect or difficult to track. It is sometimes assumed that campaigning can be regulated by making each side responsible for its campaign activities. But the various groups and individuals who become involved in initiative and referendum campaigns are not always directly affiliated with a formal campaign organization such as a political party or umbrella committee. Thus at least part of campaign activity can easily fall outside of any regulatory regime that might be imposed. One example of a regulatory regime which attempts to balance some of these concerns may be found in Colombia (see box 7.2).

Box 7.2. Organizing and financing direct democracy in Colombia

In Colombia, the electoral authority, the National Electoral Council, has the responsibility to receive the registration of initiatives, check the validity of signatures, organize the administration of the process, count the votes and announce the result. It also has some functions relating to the dissemination of information, advertising and financing.

The general norm is that any group or individual can promote the collection of signatures and the participation of citizens, or support a particular position on an initiative or referendum question. When they pay for advertising, they are required to reveal the name of the person who is financing the activity. Similarly, the promoters of an initiative must draw up detailed accounts showing the source and destination of private contributions. Two weeks after the vote, a financial report must be presented which is signed by a certified public accountant.

The National Electoral Council is able to set the maximum amount of private money that can be spent in campaigns. This amount is set by law in January each year. For the October 2003 referendum promoted and carried out by the government of President Álvaro Uribe, a fixed amount of 274 million Colombian pesos (equivalent at the time to 93,000 USD) was allowed. There is no public financing for referendum or initiative campaigns in Colombia. Each political party decides in its internal regulations on its own activities in direct democracy campaigns.

The media are regulated by the principle of equal treatment. When a media outlet accepts advertising from any interested party in a campaign it must give all other interested parties the same financial terms. Additionally, the distribution of television slots and advertising space as well as the electoral organization campaign are stipulated at the institutional level. With regard to the television slots prescribed for referendums, the promoters, the political parties and other groups with legal status will have the right to at least two slots on each national television channel within 30 days prior to the voting. The time assigned to the promoters cannot be less than the time assigned to the political parties and political movements. Moreover, the government, if it so wishes, may have three slots to set out its position on the matter. For the October 2003 referendum, the National Electoral Council drew up a resolution setting out the maximum limits on the number of radio slots, notices in the newspapers and billboards.

The national registrar, who is also the secretary of the National Electoral Council, must arrange for the referendum text to be published in three publications that have a wide circulation. In the same way, the National Electoral Council must conduct an objective campaign, putting forward the points in favour of and against the proposal, which includes a special audience with the interested parties. It is also required to circulate widely invitations to participate in the voting. According to a ruling of the Constitutional Court, advertising space must also be given to those who are promoting abstention in the referendum.

Access models

190. In jurisdictions where referendums and initiatives are more widely used, different 'access models' have evolved that can help to illustrate alternative approaches to the regulation of campaign finance and media access in referendum, initiative and recall campaigns. The models commonly used to regulate campaign activities might be thought of as representing points on a continuum running from a high degree of regulation to little or no regulation. The Republic of Ireland and Uruguay (see boxes 7.3 and 7.4) might be thought of as representing nearly opposite points on the continuum with regard to their attitudes to the regulation of referendum campaign activities. When the electoral authorities or an independent regulatory commission attempt to restrain or manage campaign activity, to control or facilitate media access, or to impose limits on campaign spending, a high degree of regulation might be said to exist. In contrast, where such controls or limits do not exist, or where they are easily evaded, groups, individuals or organizations are free to campaign for or against an issue with little or no restriction on their activities. More nuanced positions also exist whereby some types of controls or limits are imposed but not others. For example, a regulatory authority may provide a certain level of free or heavily subsidized public access to the media to both sides in a campaign in order to ensure that voters hear both sides of the debate, but it may also permit the unrestricted purchase of additional advertising by those groups that can afford it.

Box 7.3. Regulating direct democracy: the Republic of Ireland's Referendum Commission

A non-partisan commission oversees the conduct of referendum campaigns in the Republic of Ireland. A new referendum commission is set up for each referendum. It is chaired by a judge or former judge of the High Court. Other members of the commission are the Clerks of the Dáil and Seanad (the two houses of the parliament), the ombudsman, and the Comptroller and the Auditor General. The Referendum Commission is independent in its actions and is supported by a secretariat from the Office of the Ombudsman. Each referendum commission prepares independent and unbiased information about the referendum and makes that information available to the public. The commission publishes and distributes leaflets and brochures giving general information about the referendum. It also promotes debate and discussion about the referendum and advertises the referendum in the media.

High Court decisions in the Republic of Ireland have established that the government and its officials cannot participate directly in referendum campaigns, and that public resources cannot be used in support of one side in a campaign. Under the Referendum Act of 1998, the Referendum Commission initially had the role of setting out the arguments both for and against referendum proposals. Following amendment of the Referendum Act in 2001, it no longer has this responsibility. The 2001 act also removed from the commission the statutory function of fostering and promoting debate or discussion on referendum proposals. At present, the primary role of the Referendum Commission is to explain the subject matter of referendum proposals, to promote public awareness of the referendum and to encourage the electorate to participate. Putting forward the arguments for and against a proposal is left to the political parties and the other individuals and groups active in the campaign.

Box 7.4. Uruguay: a 'maximum freedom' model

Uruguay has wide experience in the use of instruments of direct democracy. Its referendum law is designed to provide complete freedom to all groups and individuals participating in a referendum or initiative campaign. There is no framework to regulate campaign advertising, whether it appears in the print or electronic media. All campaign materials are designed and circulated by individuals or groups who choose to become active in a campaign. Of course, these parties use this freedom to promote their own positions, and there is no law either to regulate the accuracy of the information provided or to ensure any kind of balance between the different sides. Turnout in referendums in Uruguay is very high because voting is compulsory. In the 2004 popular initiative on the defence of water as a human right, 90 per cent of eligible voters participated.

The state does not participate in any way, either in the regulation of campaign activities or in the financing of referendum and initiative campaigns. The instigators of an initiative are responsible for all costs relating to signature collection, as well as the costs of producing materials to be used in the campaign. There are no limits on campaign expenditure, nor are there requirements that an accounting of contributions and expenses be provided to the electoral authority. However, there is a ban on all campaign activity for 48 hours prior to the referendum vote.

The absence of any form of regulation in Uruguay could be seen as creating a risk that citizens will be poorly informed or uninformed regarding the issues of a campaign, or that many will be uninterested. However, the Uruguay model is defended not as one which is lax in regulation but as one that provides 'maximum freedom' which, in the view of its proponents, is the true goal of direct democracy.

Campaign structure and organization

191. In some jurisdictions, referendum, initiative or recall campaigns are highly structured according to rules set down in legislation or by the electoral authorities. For example, groups or individuals who wish to participate actively in a campaign may be required to join or affiliate with one of two 'umbrella committees' – one representing the 'Yes' side and the other the 'No' side. Activities channelled through such committees are more easily regulated. However, it may be difficult to force all the individuals or groups who wish to become involved in a campaign to affiliate with such committees, particularly in jurisdictions where certain types of political activity are protected by a constitutional charter of rights. In addition, some types of campaign activity may be beyond the reach of any regulatory regime, particularly if they emanate from outside the jurisdiction of the regulatory authority. Moreover, if a government, either acting on its own or through a political party, is active in a referendum campaign, it may be difficult to force it to affiliate with an umbrella committee or to abide by any external set of rules.

192. Campaign activities in initiatives, recalls and referendums are sometimes, as in elections, channelled through political parties. Since political parties are often subject to specific rules regarding campaign activities, finance and so on, they can be convenient organizations around which to structure a referendum campaign. However, campaign

activities in a referendum or initiative may not necessarily be partisan in character: opinion on the particular issue may not be divided on party political lines, and political parties are not always the prime movers behind an initiative or referendum proposal. Moreover, in some circumstances parties may be internally divided on a referendum issue or initiative proposal, with some of their members campaigning on one side and some members on the other. In the 1994 referendum in Sweden on membership of the EU, for example, members of the governing Social Democratic Party campaigned on both sides of the issue. It is difficult under these conditions to hold parties responsible for the activities of all of their supporters who may wish to participate in the campaign.

193. In the absence of a structure that requires campaign activities to be channelled through either umbrella committees or political parties, referendum, initiative or recall campaigns could be wide open to campaigning by any organization, individual or group that wishes to participate. Such a model may be favoured by those who prefer to allow direct democracy to find its own means and methods of communication with the electorate over the course of a campaign. A wide-open, essentially unregulated, model does not specify what the role of government should be in a campaign (active or neutral), does not seek to level the playing field with regard to expenditure or media access, and does not attempt to channel all campaign activities through political parties or formal campaign organizations such as umbrella committees (see box 7.4).

Campaign finance

194. The role played by money in initiative and referendum campaigns – as in elections – remains a source of contention in many jurisdictions. If there is little regulation or disclosure of contributions or expenditures, there is a risk that the side that is able to raise and spend the most money will have an unfair advantage. However, experience in some of the US states suggests that excessive expenditure by one side or the other can sometimes precipitate a backlash among voters. The side which spends the most money in a campaign does not always win. Nevertheless, the funding of initiative and referendum campaigns and/or the control and regulation of campaign expenditures present challenges in many jurisdictions. At a minimum, the expenditure of more money by one side will make the electorate more aware of its position than of that of its opponents.

195. One of the simplest and most basic models of campaign finance regulation in referendum or initiative campaigns provides for disclosure of monies spent on the campaign and the nature of such expenditures. Where all campaign activities are channelled through umbrella committees, it is a relatively simple matter to require such committees to file financial reports during or at the end of the campaign; but where other types of groups are active in a campaign it may be difficult to track all of their expenditures and activities. And disclosure of campaign contributions and expenditures does not necessarily imply any controls or limits on such expenditures. As mentioned above, the disclosure or reporting of expenses does not in itself act to provide a more level playing field, although it may achieve greater transparency in campaign activity.

Box 7.5. Online disclosure in Oregon

In 2006 the US state of Oregon developed an Internet-based system to allow citizens to track the flow of money used in election campaigns more easily. Campaign committees are required to disclose their contributions and expenditures on a database called OreStar. Citizens and the news media can use OreStar to easily 'follow the money' to see who is influencing the campaign and how the money is being spent.

196. Models that range from relatively little control of private expenditure in campaigns to those that provide for some form of public subsidy to both sides might be considered. In an entirely privatized model, there is a danger that either too much or too little money will be spent on the task of informing voters about the issues of a referendum or initiative proposal. The case of excessive expenditure by one side (sometimes the proposers of an initiative or recall) creating the conditions for an unequal contest has been mentioned above, but the opposite problem can also exist. If a system relies entirely on private expenditure by parties or groups to inform voters, it is equally possible that too little money will be spent to accomplish the task of informing the electorate on both sides of the issue. This may lead to lower turnout if voters fail to become engaged in the debate, or it may lead to poorly informed or erroneous choices. Thus, many advocate that the state or the electoral authorities should also play a role in the process of disseminating information in order to facilitate the process of engaging voters and to ensure that they are well informed on the issue(s) of the referendum. In the 1999 Australian referendum on becoming a republic, the government funded a public education campaign organized and run by a neutral expert group (see box 7.6).

197. One way in which the state or the electoral authorities can become involved in the financing of referendum or initiative campaigns is through the provision of public subsidies in some form. Generally, to qualify for a subsidy, an organization will have to be part of a formal campaign structure, for example, a legally registered political party or an official committee established for a particular referendum campaign. As is the case in elections, subsidies may be given on the basis of the share of the vote obtained in a previous election or as a lump sum. The expenditure of such subsidies, when granted to a group or organization, would then have to be accounted for at the end of a campaign through the filing of an official report with the electoral authorities, along with the return of any unexpended funds. A regime of this type has the advantage of ensuring that adequate funds will be available for the purposes of informing voters, but it does not attempt to direct or control the expenditure of such funds.

198. Another method may be to provide for a portion of campaign expenditure to be reimbursed by a public authority. A registered party, group or organization is free

to raise and spend its own funds, but may also apply for reimbursement of a certain amount or a certain type of expense. Public funds may also, in some instances, be granted directly to official campaign organizations. In the case of the 1999 Australian referendum, grants of 7.5 million Australian dollars (AUD) were made to each of the officially sanctioned 'Yes' and 'No' committees (see box 7.6).

Box 7.6. Providing public education: the 1999 Australian constitutional referendum

In November 1999, Australians voted on a proposal to end the role of the British monarchy in Australia and to replace the monarch as head of state with a president chosen by parliament. In Australia, all constitutional amendments must be approved by the voters in a mandatory referendum, and passage requires both an overall national majority of the votes cast and a majority in at least four of the six states. Voting is compulsory, both in elections and in referendums.

To ensure that the proposal received sufficient debate and discussion in the campaign, the Australian parliament authorized a subsidy of 7.5 million AUD to each of the two officially sanctioned umbrella committees supporting the 'Yes' and 'No' sides, respectively. An official pamphlet summarizing the 'Yes' and 'No' arguments was prepared under the direction of the Australian Electoral Commission and delivered at public expense to every household. In addition, an allocation of 4.5 million AUD was made to a neutral expert group for the purpose of funding a public education campaign.

The purpose of these various public subsidies was to ensure that Australian voters were adequately informed regarding the proposed constitutional change and the arguments for and against it. However, individuals and groups were also free to promote their own views over the course of the campaign. In spite of these attempts to provide balance, there were several incidents of litigation during the campaign.

---

199. A more tightly regulated model might demand that any public funds be expended in a strictly neutral manner, rather than leaving such expenditure to the discretion of a party or umbrella committee. This may be accomplished by turning the task of disseminating information over to a neutral body, perhaps the electoral authority itself or a subsidiary body created for this purpose. It may be the task of such a body to prepare and distribute materials presenting the arguments for and against the referendum or initiative question in a balanced manner. Under provisions such as these, representatives of both sides of the issue might be invited to prepare, submit, and/or review materials

which are to be disseminated to voters during the campaign. In some jurisdictions, this takes the form of a booklet or brochure which is distributed to every household within the electoral region. This type of model seeks to ensure that adequate information is made available to all voters and that it is presented in a balanced or neutral manner. However, such balance or neutrality is often difficult to achieve, and one or more of the parties may be inclined to challenge such a claim of 'neutrality'.

Access to the media

200. One of the most important issues in the management and administration of referendum and initiative campaigns is that of access to the media. It is largely through the media – the newspapers, radio and television – that voters are able to follow the campaign discourse and learn about the issues involved. In the privatized or unregulated models discussed above, access to the media depends largely on the financial resources available to particular campaign groups and organizations. Those that have substantial private resources or receive large contributions will be able to purchase television time, radio spots and newspaper advertisements accordingly. Attempts by electoral authorities to ensure a more level playing field will most likely involve the limitation of such open access, subsidies to groups or organizations with fewer resources, or the provision of 'free' time through public access. In countries with state-owned or -controlled television stations, such access may be provided directly as a public service, as is sometimes done in elections. In many countries, political advertising on radio or television is not allowed. Where the media are privately owned, access may be facilitated either by means of financial subsidy or through licensing regulations regarding the public service obligations of private media.

201. However, the provision of public access to television or radio time also raises issues of neutrality and balance. If groups or organizations are able to write their own television or radio copy and present their own point of view directly, others may demand the same right. Where umbrella committees have been sanctioned, access can be restricted to persons appointed by such committees to speak for their organizations. Where political parties are involved, the issue may be more complicated when parties are divided, or when more than one person claims the right to speak for the party. The editors of news programmes that report on campaigns may not feel compelled to give equal weight to both sides or may report on the campaign in a manner that is considered unsatisfactory by one side or the other. The increasing use of the Internet in political campaigns also presents a challenge, since this resource remains largely unregulated.

202. In general, the principle of 'equal access' to the media is considered important to ensuring that referendum and initiative campaigns present arguments in a manner that is fair to both sides. But it is not easy in practice to do this. Public-service broadcasters may attempt in their news programmes to present both sides of an argument within a neutral framework, but the results are often seen by the voters as uninteresting, and can sometimes have the effect of robbing the campaign of spontaneity and a sense of

political engagement. Where multiple media channels exist, equal access may be possible in some instances but not in others. Regulatory authorities that have faced these types of dilemma have on occasion found themselves in court, defending themselves against alleged restrictions on the rights of freedom of speech or freedom of the press.

Voter participation and information

203. Direct democracy requires a well-informed citizenry. Voters acquire the necessary information regarding a referendum proposal or initiative over the course of the campaign. When an issue is a partisan one, information is likely to come through the political parties. In the case of citizens' initiatives, which are often undertaken by groups or organizations formed for the purpose, these groups or organizations may become the primary sources of information for voters. Surveys taken in the aftermath of a campaign often show that 'insufficient information' is one of the most common complaints of citizens. Many jurisdictions in which direct democracy procedures are used have developed mechanisms to provide information to voters. In others, voters will often have to depend on interested groups to provide that information through advertising and other means, and information emanating from these sources will inevitably reflect opposing positions. The assumption is that, as in a jury trial, hearing both sides of an argument will provide voters with sufficient information to arrive at an informed decision.

204. In some jurisdictions this problem is addressed by having neutral authorities provide 'balanced' information. In the Republic of Ireland, for example, an independent Referendum Commission (see box 7.3) is charged with the responsibility of disseminating unbiased information to the public through its own publications, and of promoting debate and discussion of the issue(s) over the course of the campaign. However, this mechanism proved insufficient in the case of the first (2001) referendum on the Treaty of Nice, and the relative lack of information concerning the treaty was one of the factors leading to the low turnout which was widely blamed for the proposal being defeated. Changes in the law regarding the function and powers of the commission were made following that referendum, and the Referendum Commission mounted a more substantial public information campaign during the second (2002) referendum. The mainstream political parties also ran much stronger campaigns. While many other factors certainly came into play, the level and quality of the information made available to voters may well have been the deciding factor accounting for the opposite results of these two referendums. Turnout in the 2001 referendum was 35 per cent of the Irish electorate, while that in 2002 was 49 per cent.

205. The role of an electoral commission or other public authority in an initiative or referendum campaign is often to encourage voters to participate. Voter turnout may be higher when the initiative or referendum occurs concurrently with an election, although this also means that the issue of the referendum may receive less attention from voters, and that turnout may fluctuate with the type of election being held. In the United

States, for example, turnout is generally higher in presidential elections than in state or congressional elections, but propositions may be on the ballot paper in either case in those states which use direct democracy procedures. Voter information guides (see e.g. box 7.7) are intended both to stimulate voter turnout and to inform voters about the content of ballot propositions and the arguments for and against them. In Switzerland, turnout fluctuates considerably between referendums depending on the level of interest in a particular issue, the amount of publicity it receives, and the number of items on the ballot paper (see the case study following chapter 1).

Box 7.7. Informing the voters: voter information booklets in California and Oregon

In some jurisdictions, the government or an independent electoral authority assumes a role in providing information directly to the public, sometimes in the form of a pamphlet or brochure giving information on both sides of an issue. California and Oregon are two of the US states that have such a provision.

In California, the secretary of state is legally responsible for publishing a *Voter Information Guide*, which contains information regarding every proposition on the ballot. Included in the booklet is a summary of the proposal, a statement by the legislative analyst regarding its meaning and consequences, and unedited statements by groups supporting and opposing the proposition. Added to the latter are rebuttal statements by each of the supporting and opposing groups. The intention is to provide voters with a source of information which is balanced between the two sides over and above that which comes directly from the campaign.

Similarly, Oregon publishes a state-sponsored *Voter's Pamphlet*. It contains an impartial statement explaining the measure written by a committee of five members including two proponents of the measure, two opponents and a fifth member chosen by the first four committee members, or, if they fail to agree on a fifth member, appointed by the secretary of state. In Oregon, any group or individual who wishes to do so may, upon payment of a 500 USD fee or the filing of a petition containing 1,000 signatures, also include a statement in the *Voter's Pamphlet*.

Conclusion

206. Any jurisdiction that is considering the adoption of an initiative, referendum or recall law will need to consider regulatory, finance and media access issues. One of the principal sources of variation between different models is the role played by government. In different circumstances the government may be the proposer of a ballot proposition,

an active campaigner on its behalf, or a neutral regulator. An unregulated model does not attempt to organize or control any campaign activities, and is sometimes justified in terms of allowing the maximum amount of democratic freedom to all individuals or groups who wish to become involved in a campaign. A 'light regulation' model may require disclosure of campaign contributions and expenses, may provide for some limited form of public subsidy to campaign groups, and/or may require the state or an independent authority to provide some type of basic information to the electorate. Heavier models of regulation may try to channel campaign activities through officially sanctioned groups or organizations, to impose limits on campaign spending, and/or to provide subsidized or free access to the media in order to ensure that the public is well informed on the competing positions. More heavily regulated models place greater responsibility on the government acting as a neutral party, or on an independent electoral authority or commission, and in this way seek to ensure that the arguments on both sides of an issue are given equal treatment throughout a campaign.

207. Heavier models of regulation are sometimes defended and justified on grounds of fairness, or the need to create a level playing field for the competing sides. Others may emphasize the responsibility to provide voters with adequate information or the need to protect essential freedoms of speech and the press. While some of these goals are difficult to achieve in practice, they nevertheless reflect differing philosophies about how initiative, referendum or recall campaigns ought to be run or managed. Those considering the adoption of a referendum, initiative or recall law will need to consider the types of regulatory activities that may be applicable in different jurisdictions. Certain types of rules or limitations may not be suitable in some settings, particularly if they are at odds with the prevailing political culture, or if they conflict with other established constitutional provisions, such as a charter of rights. Some types of regulation may prove unenforceable, or may be evaded or challenged in a court. The choice of an appropriate regulatory regime that will be regarded as fair by all sides competing in a referendum or initiative campaign is an important goal, but it is not always easy. The Republic of Ireland, for example, has experimented a great deal with different regulatory mechanisms, but has been required to make changes to its model on several occasions as a result of legal challenges, uneven results, or the impracticality of certain regulatory measures. Its use of an independent referendum commission and its emphasis on government neutrality provide one of the best examples of both the risks and the benefits of tighter regulation.

Direct democracy in the Republic of Uganda

Jennifer Somalie Angeyo, Mugyenyi Silver Byanyima and Alfred Lock Okello Oryem

Introduction

The cornerstones of direct democracy in Uganda are mainly questions of law rather than practice. The authority of government and its organs is vested in the people, who express their will and consent on who shall govern them and how they shall be governed through regular, free and fair elections of their representatives or through referendums and the provision for recall – the instruments of direct democracy. The constitution entrenches the right to choose both the actors and the method of governance while at the same time allowing the rights of referendum and recall. Ugandan voters thus regularly choose who governs them and how they shall be governed, and may at any time, at will, recall those chosen, and from time to time decide their destiny on various questions through elections and referendums.

The promulgation of at least the current constitution came against a background of protracted and exhaustive soul-searching, consultative gathering of the people's views, and lengthy national debate. The provisions of the constitution have been tested for over ten years.

Historical background

Scholars of African history will largely agree that the Republic of Uganda would not have taken its present form without the advent of colonialism in the 19th and 20th centuries, which eventually precipitated the struggle for independence in the 1950s and the achievement of independence in 1962. Prior to that, Uganda was a group of kingdoms, chiefdoms, and tribal, clan or family groupings. What little forms of direct democracy there were could be traced to a few of the chiefdoms and tribal groupings, with the bulk of the kingdoms largely practising authoritarian governance by royal decree. Pre-colonial Uganda therefore hardly provides a fertile ground for searching for the roots of direct democracy. Periods of democratic, quasi-democratic, military and pseudo-military government punctuated the history of the independent Uganda of the 1960s, 1970s and 1980s. Any search for direct democracy practices during those periods will attract numerous different schools of thought, and a number of myths.

Consequently, this case study is confined to the period leading up to the constitution of 1995 and since then, which has seen and is still seeing the progressive cementing of direct democracy.

The early 1990s saw a new wave of demands for constitutional reforms in Uganda, eventually leading to the establishment of the Uganda Constitutional Commission, commonly referred to as the Odoki Commission. The commission traversed the country seeking the views of the people of Uganda on necessary constitutional reform. Its report produced the 1994 Constituent Assembly of directly elected delegates, and it was these delegates who debated on behalf of the people and subsequently promulgated what is now the 1995 constitution of Uganda.

In general, the term 'direct democracy' usually refers to citizens making decisions on policy and law without going through their elected representatives and legislatures. The supporters of direct democracy argue that democracy is more than merely a procedural matter (i.e. voting).

The legislative framework and direct democracy in Uganda

The procedures for direct democracy discussed below include the right to amend laws and the constitution through *referendums* and also the right of *recall*.

The government of Uganda finances both the referendum and the recall process. All monies required to defray expenses that may be incurred in the discharge of the functions of the Electoral Commission are charged to the Consolidated Fund. The Electoral Commission's funds may, with prior approval of the minister responsible for finance, include grants and donations from sources within or outside Uganda. The Electoral Commission must 'give equal facilitation to all sides in a referendum'.

Citizen-initiated procedures

Referendums. The voters have the right to demand a referendum. This is subject to an enabling law that must be passed by parliament as a mechanism for the citizens' demand to be accommodated and the referendum conducted. Under article 255 of the constitution, parliament shall by law make provision:

(a) for the citizens' right to demand the holding by the Electoral Commission of a referendum, whether national or in any particular part of Uganda, on any issue; and

(b) for the holding of a referendum by the Electoral Commission if the government refers any contentious matter to a referendum.

The result of the referendum is binding on all organs and agencies of the state and all persons and organizations in Uganda. However, a referendum does not affect the fundamental human rights and freedoms guaranteed in the constitution or the power of the courts to question the validity of the referendum.

The right of agenda initiative. Rule 105 of the Rules of Parliament allows private citizens to propose new laws or amendments to existing laws by submitting to parliament a private member's bill. The parliament has passed several such bills.

Referendums on change of the political system

Under article 69 of the constitution (1995), the people of Uganda shall have a right to choose and adopt a political system of their choice through free and fair elections and referendums. A political system is defined there subject to the constitution and shall include the Movement political system; the multiparty political system; and any other representative political system. Under article 70 of the constitution, the Movement political system is broadly based, inclusive and non-partisan and shall conform to the principles of participatory democracy – democracy, accountability and transparency; access to all positions of leadership by all citizens; and individual merit as a basis for election to political office.

The constitution also spells out when the referendum on a change of political system should be held. Article 74 of the constitution provides as follows:

'74. (1)   A Referendum shall be held for the purpose of changing the political system:

   (a) if requested by a resolution supported by more than half of all members of parliament; or

   (b) if requested by a resolution supported by the majority of the total membership of each of at least one half of all district councils; or

   (c) if requested through a petition to the Electoral Commission by at least one-tenth of the registered voters from each of at least two-thirds of the constituencies for which representatives are required to be directly elected under paragraph (a) of clause (1) of article 78 of this Constitution.

   (2)   The political system may also be changed by the elected representatives of the people in parliament and district councils by resolution of parliament supported by not less than two-thirds of all members of parliament upon a petition to it supported by not less than two-thirds majority of the total membership of each of at least half of all district councils.

   (3)   The resolution or petitions for the purposes of changing the political system shall be taken only in the fourth year of the term of any parliament.'

Referendums on amendment of the constitution

Mandatory referendums are held to approve or reject certain types of constitutional amendment. Article 260 of the constitution provides that an act of parliament seeking to amend any of the provisions of the constitution must be supported at the second and third readings in parliament by not less than two-thirds of all members of parliament, and it must have been referred to a decision of the people and approved by them. Other specific constitutional amendments under article 261 are not subject to referendum but must be ratified by at least two-thirds of the members of the District Council in at least two-thirds of all the districts of Uganda.

Provisions for recall

The constitution and the enabling Parliamentary and Local Governments Act provide for recall of elected representatives by the electorate subject to the procedures and grounds shown in table 1. However, under the Presidential Election Act, recall of the president is not possible. The recall of a member of parliament has to be initiated by a petition in writing setting out the grounds for a recall and signed by at least two-thirds of the registered electors of the constituency and shall be delivered to the speaker of parliament.

Table 1. Summary of the grounds for recalls at national level

Article of the constitution	Scope of effect	Provision of the law
84	Recall of elected members of parliament	A member of parliament may be recalled for misconduct, desertion, or mental or physical incapacity by a petition signed by at least two-thirds of the registered electors of his or her constituency.
185	Recall of elected district chairpersons and speakers of parliament	A district chairperson or speaker may be removed for misconduct, abuse of office, or mental or physical incapacity by a resolution supported by not less than two-thirds of all members of the District Council.

The use of direct democracy in Uganda

Referendums on political systems

Uganda held a referendum on a political system in 2000. Under article 271 (3) of the constitution, and during the last month of the fourth year of the term of parliament, a referendum was held on 29 June 2000 to determine the political system the people of Uganda wished to adopt. A total of 4.9 million voters participated (51 per cent); 91 per cent voted for the Movement political system and 9 per cent voted for a multiparty system.

The second referendum on a change of the political system, called by parliament for 28 July 2005, was for a change away from the Movement political system to a multiparty political system. The result of this referendum was that, with a turnout of 47 per cent of registered electors, 90 per cent of those voting voted 'Yes' in favour of a multiparty system. A series of meetings were held, culminating in the formation of the 'Yes' and 'No' sides for purposes of the 2005 referendum. In accordance with the Referendum and Other Provisions Act 2005, and in consultation with both sides, the referendum question was formulated as follows: 'Do You Agree To Open Up The Political Space To Allow Those Who Wish To Join Different Organizations/Parties To Do So To Compete For Political Power?' The 'Yes' side chose a tree as their symbol, while the 'No' side chose a 'closed house', as depicted below.

Yes   No

The 2005 referendum was a landmark in the political history and democratic process of Uganda as it ushered in a new era of multiparty politics. Uganda is currently governed under a multiparty political system and subsequent elections have been conducted under the multiparty dispensation.

Challenges and lessons learned

Both referendums held in Uganda were conducted successfully. In both, voter participation was somewhat constrained by the fact that the voters are more accustomed to voting for individuals than for sides represented only by symbols.

Voter apathy affects turnout in most of the key stages of the process. Voters may make a last-minute attempt to turn out for activities such as registration and display of the electoral register; thus the Electoral Commission has to intensify the sending out of reminder messages and/or increase the numbers of registration venues and personnel, and/or even extend the period unless it is constrained by a constitutional deadline.

In both referendums on change of the political system, some sections of the public made a deliberate attempt to derail the referendum campaigns by calling on the electorate or the parties to boycott the referendum. However, this did not prevent the enthusiastic section of the public from participating in the two referendums.

Both referendums required intensive voter education since the referendum process is quite distinct from that for general elections. The electorate has to be informed about the differences between a referendum and an election. Most voters tend to associate the symbols with individuals. Voter education messages are disseminated through the electronic and print media and usually one person per parish is appointed by the Electoral Commission to conduct voter education and the dissemination of information. Other channels for voter education include commercial advertising through bill-boards, street poles and banners; printed materials like handbooks, manuals, booklets, posters, fliers, leaflets and handbills; mobilization materials like mobile shows or films or drama groups; rallies, and so on.

In an effort to improve its voter education, the Electoral Commission has undertaken to diversify the methods of voter education by using non-commercial methods such as drama groups and mobile units, using district registrars as part of the voter education process and decentralizing the voter education. This is, however, subject to the availability of funds.

It is worth noting that (a) timely enactment and amendment of the legal framework of operation and (b) funding are important issues for the successful conduct of a given referendum. This also enables the stakeholders in the process to be involved at the earliest opportunity. The referendum process is much more demanding financially than the recall process. This is because a referendum is a universal adult suffrage exercise involving all registered electors in the country and key components such as the display of the electoral registers for all the polling stations, the printing of ballot papers for all registered electors, ballot box procurement, and so on. Recall processes, by contrast, involve only the electorate from a given area. Moreover, the grounds for a recall are often not substantiated or the legal requirements are not complied with, and most attempts to initiate a recall do not succeed on grounds of non-compliance with the law. Petitions under the Local Governments Act, however, have had a degree of success, resulting in a recall, in contrast to recalls under the Parliamentary Election Act.

The concept of direct democracy is still evolving in Uganda and is yet to be appreciated by the citizens, especially in the rural setting, despite the legal framework in place. This challenge can be overcome by both civic and voter education, although the process is constrained by limited resources.

Direct democracy in Uruguay

Rodolfo González Rissotto and Daniel Zovatto*

Uruguay has one of the longest and richest traditions in the use of direct democracy mechanisms. Since the first half of the 20th century, it has been able to combine and articulate representative democracy alongside direct democracy. Since 1934 the constitution has stated that national sovereignty is expressed directly by means of elections, popular initiatives and referendums, and indirectly, by means of representative powers.

Terminological variations

Several types of direct democracy mechanisms are in use in Latin America, and there are several ways to describe them. National constitutions often use different terminology to refer to similar mechanisms. The most common terms include 'popular legislative initiative' (*iniciativa popular legislativa*); 'referendum', '*plebiscito*' (a referendum on constitutional matters), or the more direct translation, 'popular consultation' (*consulta popular*); recall (*revocatoria de mandato*); and 'open town meeting' (*cabildo abierto*). As a result of the variations in usage, it is not possible to arrive at a common terminology for the purpose of cross-country comparison that is faithful to the diverse set of concepts currently in use throughout the region.

The language used in this case study classifies the mechanisms of direct democracy into three types – *popular consultations* (by far the most commonly used term), *popular legislative initiatives*, and *recall votes*. Given that these mechanisms are interconnected (for instance, a legislative initiative can lead to a popular consultation), the classification is somewhat loose and is intended merely to enhance the clarity of the description of the various mechanisms in the region.

---

* Parts of this case study are based on earlier work by Daniel Zovatto, published in Payne, J. Mark et al., *Democracies in Development: Politics and Reform in Latin America* (Washington, DC: Inter-American Development Bank, International Institute for Democracy and Electoral Assistance and Rockefeller Center for Latin American Studies, Harvard University, 2007).

The Latin American context

The transition towards democracy in Latin America over the past three decades can be broken down into two main periods, the first covering the 1980s – considered a 'lost decade' in economic terms, but fairly progressive in the sense of democratic advance – and the second taking place throughout the 1990s, characterized by the crisis of representation in the political party system and a growing discontent with politics. A twofold approach was used to deal with both these situations in several countries throughout the region, including constitutional reforms and the option of direct democracy mechanisms. Thus now, when parliaments and political parties are the object of mistrust in pubic opinion, some sectors see mechanisms of civic participation as a viable option for enhancing representation, boosting participation and keeping political parties stable. Debate over the potential benefits and risks of these mechanisms has become established on the Latin American political agenda.

Direct democracy mechanisms were incorporated into the great majority of the reformed constitutions which were adopted in Latin American countries throughout the 1990s. They were adopted for two main reasons. The first was the crisis in the party system, which produced an increasing gap in political representation – a gap which was filled, in some countries, by neo-populist leaders who achieved power by criticizing representative democracy and promising to solve national problems by means of participative democracy and a direct relation with the people (presidents Alberto Fujimori in Peru and Hugo Chávez in Venezuela, among others). The other was that, in countries that were in extreme institutional crisis, the dominant elite incorporated mechanisms of direct democracy as a safety valve to prevent the collapse of the democratic system (Paraguay and Colombia, among others).

Despite these provisions, over the past three decades, most countries in Latin America have made only modest use of mechanisms for direct citizen participation at the national level. Historically, direct democracy mechanisms have been used for a variety of reasons, ranging from demagogic manipulation to the defence of conservative or traditionalist interests and the implementation of reforms sought by voters.

Overall, direct democracy mechanisms have been applied in only 11 of the 16 countries in which they are provided for in the constitution. Of these 11 countries, only two – Uruguay (in terms of frequency) and Ecuador (in terms of number of issues voted on) – show extensive use of these mechanisms.

The usage of direct democracy mechanisms: the case of Uruguay

In Uruguay, direct democracy mechanisms predated the process of democratic restoration. After the return of democracy, the only innovation was the ability of the citizens to repeal laws by means of a referendum.

The usage of direct democracy mechanisms throughout Latin America has often led to mixed, and at times unanticipated, results. For instance, in two extreme cases where authoritarian regimes resorted to these mechanisms to keep themselves in power – Chile in 1988 and Uruguay in 1980 – their use backfired. In Uruguay, in 1980 the military regime drew up a charter that would have provided for a strong, continuing role for the military along the lines of the 1976 constitutional decrees, including legitimizing the new role of the National Security Council (Cosena, the Consejo de Seguridad Nacional). The document would also have greatly reduced the roles of the General Assembly and the political parties. A *plebiscito* held on 30 November 1980, however, rejected the new military-drafted constitution.

In regard to the electoral participation of the citizens in the processes of direct democracy, Latin America had an average voter turnout of 68.13 per cent over the period 1978–2007. Uruguay has one of the highest turnouts of the region – on average 87.4 per cent over the same period.

The constitutional framework

The constitution of Uruguay provides for the use of referendums at both national and sub-national levels and may be used to repeal or abrogate laws. The recall does not exist.

The referendum is the mechanism by which citizens who are entitled to vote express their decision to ratify or reject a duly approved law within a year of its coming into force. The referendum can also be used to oppose a decree issued by a sub-national assembly, such as the *Junta Departamental*.

The popular initiative is the power granted to the electorate to propose constitutional, legal or municipal-type regulations or to oppose the validity of a law or decree of the *Junta Departamental*.

The constitution also provides for yet another type of popular consultation, which is the referendum on constitutional matters, called the *plebiscito*. This is the procedure by which citizens approve or reject a proposed constitutional reform. This is the last stage of a process at the end of which, in order for the change to be valid, the electorate has to be consulted.

Article 79 of the constitution states that 'Twenty-five percent of the total number of persons eligible to vote may, within one year of its promulgation, lodge a referendum petition against the laws and exercise the right of initiative before the legislative power', and sets out the limits to its application as follows: 'These instruments cannot be applied with regard to laws which establish taxes. Neither can they be applied in cases in which the initiative is restricted to the executive power'.

The application of the provisions for direct democracy

Popular consultations encompass both *plebiscitos* and referendums. In Uruguay this process may be initiated by the executive branch, the legislative branch or the citizenry. In Latin America, the results of popular consultations carried out to ratify constitutional reforms are in all cases binding. In only a few countries, such as Uruguay, which requires a minimum turnout of 35 per cent of registered electors, is a minimum level of participation necessary for the approval of binding consultations. Furthermore, in Uruguay, the results of popular consultations called to ratify laws are also always binding.

As table 1 shows, between 1980 and 2007, 12 popular consultations took place in Uruguay, of which nine were to approve or reject constitutional reforms. The consultations that took place in 1989, 1992 and 2003 sought to annul legislation: the first was rejected and the law remained in effect, but in the other two cases the laws were repealed.

Table 1. The use of mechanisms of direct democracy in Uruguay, 1980–2007

Date	Mechanism	Topic	Decision	Outcome
Nov. 1980	*Plebiscito*	New constitution proposed by the military regime	Rejected	Rejection generated pressure on the military to start the liberalization process of the regime. The government was in favour of the new constitution. **The government's position lost.**
Apr. 1989	Referendum	To repeal the law of expiration, which was an amnesty law for members of the military and police officers	Rejected	The law was kept, giving popular support to a very controversial decision. The government favoured the expiration law. **The government's position won.**
Nov. 1989	*Plebiscito*	Constitutional reform to establish procedures and criteria that should be used to periodically increase pensions	Approved	Promoted by the national Commission of Retirees. A new system of readjustment of pensions established in the constitution came into effect. The government opposed it. **The government's position lost**.
Dec. 1992	Referendum	Proposal to repeal a law that would partially privatize the state telephone company	Approved	Expression that the sentiments of the electorate prevailed. The government opposed the abolition of the law. **The government's position lost**.
Aug. 1994	*Plebiscito*	Constitutional reform to separate in the ballots national and municipal elections	Rejected	Both the government and the opposition favoured the reform but the citizens rejected it. **The government's position lost.**
Nov. 1994	*Plebiscito*	Constitutional reform to establish regulations to protect retirees	Approved	Constitution was reformed to include protections for this group of citizens. The government opposed the reform. **The government's position lost.**
Nov. 1994	*Plebiscito*	Constitutional reform that sought to assign 27% of the budget to education	Rejected	The government opposed the constitutional reform. **The government's position won**.

Date	Mechanism	Topic	Decision	Outcome
Dec. 1996	*Plebiscito*	Constitutional reform aimed at modifying the electoral system	Approved	Important reforms to the electoral system took place by eliminating the simultaneous double vote, and replacing it with primary and general elections. The government favoured the reform. **The government's position won**.
Oct. 1999	*Plebiscito*	Constitutional reform forbidding employees of state companies from running for candidates	Rejected	The government opposed the reform. **The government's position won**.
Oct. 1999	*Plebiscito*	Constitutional reform to establish a fixed percentage for the budget of the judicial branch	Rejected	The government opposed the reform. **The government's position won**.
Dec. 2003	Referendum	Appeal against Law no. 17.448 of 2002, which authorized ANCAP* to associate with private enterprises and eliminated the import monopoly for fuel as of 2006	Approved	Binding. ANCAP is not able to associate with other private enterprises for those purposes established in the law. The government opposed the repeal; however, the citizens repealed it. **The government's position lost.**
Oct. 2004	*Plebiscito*	Constitutional reform to include a series of regulations regarding the right to use water resources	Approved	Water resources cannot belong to private citizens or companies, and all drinking water supply services must belong to the state companies. The government opposed the reform. **The government's position lost**.

* Administración Nacional de Combustibles, Alcoholes y Portland

Funding of the mechanisms of direct democracy and publicity

The funding of direct democracy mechanisms such as referendums and popular initiatives is the sole responsibility of their promoters and advocates. The state does not take part, directly or indirectly, in the funding, except in those cases that originate in the Electoral Court, and events leading to a call for elections.

There is no regulation on questions of advertising and propaganda in referendums (or acts of adhesion), popular initiatives, and *plebiscitos* to ratify constitutional reforms. Thus, all types of propaganda and advertising are allowed through any of the mass media, whether intended for the general public or for paying subscribers. The propaganda is designed by the interested parties and advocates for or against the referendum or *plebiscito*, and they can address any issue they deem relevant and linked to the direct democracy mechanism they are promoting.

The role of civil society

The constitutions of several Latin American countries allow citizens to initiate constitutional reforms, thus giving them a significant decision-making role. Each country requires a certain percentage of registered electors to sign a petition to take the process forward. To date this mechanism has been used only in Uruguay. Reform initiatives launched by civil society organizations in 1989, 1994 and 1999 aimed at increasing the budget or benefits for pensioners and in the education and judicial sectors (see the table).

Popular initiatives have also led to referendums to overturn laws in Uruguay. A coalition of left and centre-left parties and an ad hoc civil society movement sponsored the ultimately unsuccessful 1989 referendum aimed at revoking the amnesty law, which had been designed to protect members of the armed forces from prosecution for human rights violations committed during the military regime (1973–85). Although the legal outcome was accepted, the dispute over the memory and history, as well as over compensation, is still ongoing.

The 1992 referendum, which successfully overturned a law that would have partially privatized the state-owned telephone company, was spearheaded by a similar coalition of forces working in tandem with the labour unions representing telephone workers. The 2003 referendum to repeal this law was promoted by the workers' union of the state fuel company, with the support of parties on the left. The participation of Uruguayan civil society organizations was limited, since in both cases ad hoc social movements sought alliances with political parties as opposed to these civil society organizations.

In terms of the effect these mechanisms have had, in general their use at national level has not given civil society a major role. Until now, and only in a few cases, their role has mainly been that of controlling and restraining rather than creating and innovating. The strengthening of citizen control over the government or any other bodies of the representative system has had limited efficacy.

The behaviour of the citizenry

During the past 30 years in Latin America, citizens' behaviour with respect to direct democracy has varied, with no overall trend having emerged. It is clear that Latin Americans frequently fail to vote in a manner that focuses on the particular issue put before them; rather, they use the vote as an opportunity to vent their frustration at the poor performance of the government in power. In some cases popular consultations have served as a means of expressing overall disenchantment with politics and politicians.

One example is the unequivocal rejection by Uruguayan citizens of the 1994 'mini' constitutional reform, which had the backing of all the major political parties. It was apparent that the outcome had little to do with the specific content of the issues presented to the public.

The complexity of economic and financial issues at the national level means that it is difficult to address them through mechanisms of direct democracy, as these require a high level of citizen participation. As a result, constitutions in most Latin American countries have expressly excluded such matters from popular consultations.

Case Study: Direct democracy in Uruguay

However, in Uruguay (and Ecuador) these mechanisms have been used by civil society organizations tied to centre-left parties seeking to impose limits on economic reforms. The paradigmatic case is the 1992 referendum in Uruguay to repeal the law enacted by the government to partially privatize the state-owned telephone company. However, a similar attempt several years later to overturn a law regulating the distribution of electricity and gas failed, as did a challenge to the private retirement and pension system. In 2003, a referendum repealed a law that allowed Uruguay's national fuel agency to set up joint ventures to refine and distribute petroleum products.

Conclusion

Direct democracy mechanisms must be seen as instruments for consolidating the democratic system, and which complement but do not replace the institutions of representative democracy. While such mechanisms can help to strengthen political legitimacy, and open up channels for participation that foster reconciliation between the citizens and their representatives, political parties and the legislative branch must remain the central institutions where citizens articulate and combine their preferences. Hence, parties and legislators must be strengthened in order to improve the quality and legitimacy of democratic representation. Although in the beginning some people saw participatory democracy as something opposed to representative democracy, it is now generally accepted that they are complementary formulas. Even so, people sometimes attribute over-dimensioned functions to direct democracy mechanisms and have excessive expectations of them – functions and expectations that are beyond the capabilities of direct democracy.

CHAPTER 8

CHAPTER 8

Direct democracy in today's world: a comparative overview

208. The instruments of direct democracy are found in all regions of the world, although their usage varies considerably from one country to another. Many countries have provisions for one or more direct democracy procedures in their laws or constitutions, but make use of them only in exceptional circumstances. Others use these instruments more routinely and have integrated them more completely into political life. Throughout the world today, use of the instruments of direct democracy is increasing. In this chapter, the patterns of legal provision for, and the practice of, direct democracy in all regions of the world are examined, highlighting those countries with the most experience of using these instruments and processes.

Africa

209. Referendums in African countries are most often called by the authorities, although a few countries (e.g. Uganda) also have provisions for citizens' initiatives or recall. Most referendums have dealt with constitutional issues, and the device has been employed in a number of instances to ratify a new constitution, as in Benin (1990) and Mali (1992). A referendum in South Africa in 1992 ended apartheid and began the process of transition to a multiracial democracy.

Table 8.1. Frequency of usage of direct democracy mechanisms at the national level in Africa

Frequency of usage at national level	Country or territory	Referendum	Citizens' initiatives	Agenda initiatives	Recall
	ALGERIA	•			
	MOROCCO	•			
	COMOROS	•			
	MADAGASCAR	•			
	TANZANIA, UNITED REPUBLIC OF				
	TOGO	•	•	•	
	CONGO, REPUBLIC OF THE	•			
	EQUATORIAL GUINEA	•			
	NIGER	•		•	
	BENIN	•		•	
	BURKINA FASO	•		•	
	BURUNDI	•			
	CENTRAL AFRICAN REPUBLIC	•			
	CONGO, DEMOCRATIC REPUBLIC OF THE	•		•	
	GHANA	•			
	LIBERIA	•	•	•	
	SUDAN	•			
	BOTSWANA	•			
	CAMEROON	•			
	CHAD	•			
	DJIBOUTI	•			
	GAMBIA	•			
	GUINEA	•			
	SENEGAL	•			
	SOMALIA	•			•
	SOUTH AFRICA	•			
	CÔTE D'IVOIRE	•			
	MALI	•			
	MAURITANIA	•			

Frequency of usage at national level	Country or territory	Referendum	Citizens' initiatives	Agenda initiatives	Recall
	NAMIBIA	•			
	RWANDA	•			
	SEYCHELLES	•			
	SIERRA LEONE	•			
	SWAZILAND	•			
	UGANDA	•	•	•	•
	ERITREA			•	
	ETHIOPIA	•			•
	GABON	•			
	GUINEA-BISSAU				
	KENYA				
	LIBYAN ARAB JAMAHIRIYA				
	MALAWI	•			
	SÃO TOMÉ AND PRINCIPE	•			
	TUNISIA	•			
	ZAMBIA	•			
	ZIMBABWE				
	ANGOLA	•			
	CAPE VERDE	•	•	•	
	LESOTHO	•			
	MAURITIUS	•			
	MOZAMBIQUE	•			
	NIGERIA	•			•

Algeria

210. Referendums in Algeria have been used principally to deal with constitutional issues. A referendum in 1962 authorized the drafting of a new constitution, and a vote in 1963 ratified that document. Further constitutional reforms were approved in referendums in 1976, 1989 and 1996. A referendum in 1999 provided for an amnesty for guerrilla fighters in an effort to end the civil war, and a 2005 referendum (known as the 'Peace Referendum') approved a presidential plan for national reconciliation. In the Peace Referendum, 97 per cent of those participating voted in favour of President Abdelaziz Bouteflika's Charter for Peace and National Reconciliation. Turnout in the 2005 referendum was 80 per cent.

Madagascar

211. In 1992, voters in Madagascar approved a new constitution by a vote of 73 per cent to 27 per cent. Turnout in this referendum was 65 per cent. The 1992 constitution institutionalized direct democracy procedures by providing for presidential plebiscites and obligatory referendums on changes to the constitution. In 2007, voters in Madagascar approved a package of constitutional reforms that included provisions for wider presidential emergency powers and changes in language rights. With a turnout of 43 per cent in this referendum, the proposed constitutional changes were approved by 75 per cent of those participating.

Uganda

212. The 1995 constitution made provisions for direct democracy in Uganda. Under article 255 of the constitution, parliament is required to protect the right of citizens to demand the holding of a referendum on any issue and to provide for the holding of a referendum by the Electoral Commission upon a reference by the government. Citizens are also able to initiate a referendum on change in the political system through a petition to the Electoral Commission signed by 10 per cent of all registered electors in two-thirds of the parliamentary constituencies. There are also provisions for the recall of elected members of parliament by two-thirds of the registered electors in a constituency. In 2000, Ugandans voted in a referendum to determine the type of political system, and in 2005 a second referendum approved a change to a multiparty system (see the case study following chapter 7).

The Americas

Table 8.2. Frequency of usage of direct democracy mechanisms at the national level in the Americas

Frequency of usage at national level	Country or territory	Referendum	Citizens' initiatives	Agenda initiatives	Recall
	URUGUAY	•	•	•	
	GUATEMALA	•		•	
	HAITI				
	ECUADOR	•	•	•	•
	PANAMA	•			
	VENEZUELA	•	•	•	•
	CHILE	•			
	COLOMBIA	•	•	•	•

Frequency of usage at national level	Country or territory	Referendum	Citizens' initiatives	Agenda initiatives	Recall
	BOLIVIA	•	•	•	•
	BRAZIL	•		•	
	PERU	•	•	•	
	CANADA	•			
	COSTA RICA	•	•	•	
	ANGUILLA				
	BERMUDA	•			
	CUBA	•			
	PARAGUAY	•		•	
	SAINT KITTS AND NEVIS	•			
	ARGENTINA	•		•	
	ARUBA				
	BAHAMAS	•			
	DOMINICAN REPUBLIC				
	FALKLAND ISLANDS (MALVINAS)				
	GUYANA				
	HONDURAS	•		•	
	JAMAICA				
	NETHERLANDS ANTILLES				
	SURINAME	•			
	ANTIGUA AND ARUBA	•			
	BARBADOS				
	BELIZE				
	CAYMAN ISLANDS				
	DOMINICA	•			
	EL SALVADOR	•			
	GRENADA	•			
	MEXICO				
	MONSERRAT				
	NICARAGUA	•	•	•	
	SAINT LUCIA	•			
	SAINT VINCENT AND THE GRENADINES	•			

Frequency of usage at national level	Country or territory	Referendum	Citizens' initiatives	Agenda initiatives	Recall
	TRINIDAD AND TOBAGO				
	TURKS AND CAICOS ISLANDS				
	UNITED STATES OF AMERICA				
	VIRGIN ISLANDS, BRITISH				

North America

213. Direct democracy procedures in North America are found primarily at the state and local level in the United States. There is a particularly vigorous usage of all types of direct democracy practices in many of the western US states. Direct democracy is less widely practised in Canada, although there have been several important referendums at the federal and provincial levels.

Canada

214. There have been only three national referendums or plebiscites in Canada, one of which was a vote on a set of proposed changes to the constitution in 1992. There is a federal referendum law which allows the federal government to hold a referendum on any issue, but there are no provisions at the national level for citizens' or agenda initiatives, or for the recall of elected officials. Referendums have also taken place in Canada at the provincial and territorial levels. A referendum was held in the Northwest Territories on the creation of the new territory of Nunavut in 1992. Quebec held referendums on sovereignty in 1980 and 1995, and also held its own referendum on the 1992 constitutional proposals. As is typical within the British parliamentary tradition, the results of a referendum can never be binding. It is up to Parliament or the provincial legislatures to decide whether, and how, to act on the result of any referendum.

The United States

215. There are no provisions for direct democracy of any kind at the national level in the United States. However, there is a very active usage of direct democracy procedures in many of the US states. Nearly all employ direct democracy procedures for amending state constitutions. Twenty-four states have provisions for citizens' initiatives, and 18 states allow recall of elected officials. Citizens' initiatives are more widely used in the western states, particularly California, Colorado, North Dakota and Oregon. (On

Oregon, see the case study following chapter 4.) Recall is less frequently used, but the recall of the governor of California in 2003 was an important event in that state (see box 5.1). There has been an active debate in the United States about potential misuses of direct democracy, but it remains popular with voters in most of the states where it is most widely used.

Central and South America

216. Many Latin American countries have incorporated provisions for the use of direct democracy into their constitutions. Initially, direct democracy instruments were employed mainly for the ratification of national constitutions, but they have come to be used for a wider range of issues. In Latin America, they have been most successfully employed in countries where the institutions of representative democracy are most solid. Among the countries that have used instruments of direct democracy more extensively in recent years are Chile, Colombia, Ecuador, Panama, Uruguay and Venezuela. Mexico does not employ direct democracy at the national level, but there is some use of direct democracy processes in some Mexican states.

Uruguay

217. Nowhere in Latin America have the instruments of direct democracy been used more often than in Uruguay, which established a semi-representative or semi-direct system of government in its constitution of 1934 (see the case study following chapter 7). Since the 1973–85 dictatorship, referendum issues have included the revocation of amnesty laws (in 1989), measures to safeguard pensions (1989), the privatization of state-owned companies (1992), constitutionally fixed budgets for the education system (1994), legal restrictions on workers' claims against their employers (1998) and the privatization of water assets (2004). The Uruguayan experience of direct democracy has often suggested that voters remain politically loyal to the parties that they support.

Panama

218. The first referendum in Panama, held in 1983, proposed a number of amendments to the 1972 constitution, such as the replacement of the 505-member National Assembly of Municipal Representatives by a national legislature of 70 members. The proposals were approved by 88 per cent of those participating – a result that strengthened the authoritarian regime of Manuel Noriega. In 1992, a referendum was held on further constitutional reforms. A third referendum was held in 1998 in which 64 per cent of the voters rejected a proposal to change the constitution so as to allow immediate re-election of the president. In 2006 Panama held a national referendum on a proposal to enlarge the Panama Canal.

Ecuador

219. The first referendum to take place in Ecuador was organized by the military regime in 1978, during the country's transition to democracy. A new constitution was approved but further constitutional reforms stagnated until 1984, when President León Febres proposed to strengthen presidential powers so as to enable him to call referendums on constitutional reform. In 1995, during a period of conflict with the legislature, President Sixto Durán called for a consulta hoping to gain power to dissolve the parliament. This proposal was firmly rejected by the voters. A constitutional crisis triggered the next use of direct democracy, in 1997, removing President Abdalá Bucarám from office and appointing Fabián Alarcón Rivera as an interim replacement. In both the 1995 and 1997 referendums, a number of other policy and reform proposals were also placed on the ballot paper, including the abolition of the right to strike in the public sector, the privatization of social insurance, and judicial reforms. Most of these proposals were not approved by the voters.

Chile

220. A national plebiscite took place in 1978, five years after Augusto Pinochet seized power in a military coup. The next plebiscite, also called by Pinochet, was held in 1980 to decide on a new constitution, which was to become the foundation for the new government. The new constitution obliged Pinochet to seek continued endorsement in yet another plebiscite or to call new elections within a period of eight years. In 1988, therefore, Pinochet called one of the most important referendums to have been held in Latin America to date. The opposition gained 56 per cent of the votes, thus putting an end to a dictatorship that had lasted for 15 years. Counting on a strong economy and controlled media, Pinochet had hoped to legitimize his position through a 'democratic' vote. Ironically, he had to accept defeat in and by a plebiscite that he himself had instituted. Chile's fourth national plebiscite was held the following year. Centring on constitutional reform, that referendum confirmed and furthered the transition to democracy.

Colombia

221. In Colombia, constitutional provisions for direct democracy were introduced in 1991. The reform of the earlier constitution was largely motivated by a general crisis in democratic institutions – a crisis deepened by the ever-increasing numbers of political murders carried out by drug cartels and guerrilla movements. Colombia has seen a number of different kinds of referendum since 1991. The most (in)famous took place in 2003, when President Álvaro Uribe presented the electorate with 15 different proposals in a single referendum. The proposals covered a wide range of political and administrative issues – action against corruption, reductions in government expenditure and increases in state funding for sanitation and education – but only the proposal on anti-corruption measures reached the turnout quorum of 25 per cent. The low turnout in the 2003 referendum sparked extensive debate on the principles and procedures of direct democracy.

Venezuela

222. The 1998 elections, in which Hugo Chávez was elected president, were a turning point for direct democracy in Venezuela. In 2004 the opposition convened a presidential recall, which Chávez survived (see the case study following chapter 1). His promise to include instruments of direct democracy in the constitution, so as to overcome the supposed limitations of representative democracy, had been central to Chávez's electoral platform. In April 1999, he held a referendum asking voters to authorize elections for a new assembly. The Venezuelan constitution was then reformed through a plebiscite held in December 1999. The new constitution stated that Venezuelan citizens have the right to a wide range of direct democracy instruments such as plebiscites, consultas, referendums, constitutional initiatives, indirect legislative initiatives, recalls and powers to revoke existing laws.

Asia

223. While few Asian countries use direct democracy procedures extensively, a mixture of different instruments and procedures exists in a number of countries. The 1987 constitution in the Philippines was ratified in a referendum, and institutionalized a number of direct democracy instruments including provisions for both citizens' and agenda initiatives. Kyrgyzstan and Taiwan have provisions for referendums called by the authorities, as well as agenda initiatives and recall. In Taiwan, in addition to many local referendums, two referendums on international issues have been called by the government, each on the same day as presidential elections. In March 2004, one referendum question referred to the intensification of defence, and the other to reopening peace discussions with Beijing; neither vote was valid since the participation rate of 45 per cent of registered electors did not meet the turnout quorum of 50 per cent. On 22 March 2008, in the referendum on support for Taiwan's bid for membership of the United Nations, the 'Yes' side did not receive a majority of votes cast.

Table 8.3. Frequency of usage of direct democracy mechanisms at the national level in Asia

Frequency of usage at national level	Country or territory	Referendum	Citizens' initiatives	Agenda initiatives	Recall
	PHILIPPINES	•	•	•	
	MALDIVES	•			
	CAMBODIA				
	KYRGYZSTAN	•		•	•
	KOREA, REPUBLIC OF	•			

Frequency of usage at national level	Country or territory	Referendum	Citizens' initiatives	Agenda initiatives	Recall
	AZERBAIJAN	•			
	IRAN, ISLAMIC REPUBLIC OF	•			
	UZBEKISTAN	•			
	BANGLADESH	•			
	TAJIKISTAN	•			
	INDONESIA				
	KAZAKHSTAN	•			
	PAKISTAN	•			
	TAIWAN	•	•		•
	TURKMENISTAN	•	•	•	
	BURMA				
	MONGOLIA	•			
	NEPAL				
	SINGAPORE	•			
	SRI LANKA	•			
	THAILAND	•		•	
	VIET NAM	•			
	AFGHANISTAN	•			
	BHUTAN				
	BRUNEI DARUSSALAM				
	CHINA				
	INDIA				
	JAPAN	•			
	KOREA, DEMOCRATIC PEOPLE´S REPUBLIC OF				
	LAO PEOPLE´S DEMOCRATIC REPUBLIC				
	MALAYSIA				
	TIMOR-LESTE	•			

The Philippines

224. A number of referendums were held in the Philippines under the authoritarian regime of President Ferdinand Marcos. Following Marcos' downfall, a new constitution was approved by the voters in a referendum on 2 February 1987. The 1987 constitution recognized the right of the people to exercise by 'direct initiative' many powers previously reserved to the government. These included powers to repeal national and local laws, to propose new laws, and to propose amendments to the constitution. In keeping with this provision, the Congress in 1989 adopted an Initiative and Referendum Act setting out the procedures under which 10 per cent of registered electors, including a minimum of 3 per cent in each electoral district, can initiate a vote on an issue. In addition to the national provisions, the possibility of local-level recall is detailed in Book One of the Local Government Code of the Philippines, which states 'the power of recall for loss of confidence shall be exercised by the registered voters of a local government unit to which the local elective official subject to such recall belongs'.

Thailand

225. On 19 September 2006 a military junta toppled the democratically elected government of Prime Minister Thaksin Shinawatra. The leaders of the coup annulled the 1997 constitution and appointed a Constitution Drafting Assembly to write a new constitution. By the end of June 2007 a proposed new constitution was published, and the Constitution Drafting Assembly announced that a national referendum would take place on 19 August. Copies of the draft constitution, comprising more than 300 articles, were published and sent to all Thai families on 31 July. Thus, a very short period of 19 days was provided for informing the voters on a lengthy and complex document. The result of the referendum was an endorsement of the new constitution as 58 per cent voted 'Yes' and 42 per cent 'No'. However, only about 58 per cent of the eligible electors participated in the referendum.

Japan

226. According to article 96 of the Japanese constitution, amendments to the constitution may be adopted by a two-thirds majority of both houses of the Diet and are then to be submitted to a vote of the people. No referendums have been held in Japan to date under this provision. There are, however, initiative and referendum practices at the local level, and local referendums have been held to deal with issues such as nuclear power plants, waste processing plants, the construction of dams and the location of US military bases.

Europe

Table 8.4. Frequency of usage of direct democracy mechanisms at the national level in Europe

Frequency of usage at national level	Country or territory	Referendum	Citizens' initiatives	Agenda initiatives	Recall
◀ ◀ ◀ ◀	SWITZERLAND	•	•		
◀	ITALY	•	•	•	
	LIECHTENSTEIN	•	•	•	•
	FRANCE	•			
	IRELAND, REPUBLIC OF	•			
	DENMARK	•			
	SLOVENIA	•	•	•	
	ROMANIA	•		•	
	ESTONIA	•			
	GREECE	•			
	LATVIA	•	•	•	
	LITHUANIA	•	•	•	
	SWEDEN	•			
	NORWAY	•			
	SAN MARINO			•	
	SLOVAKIA	•	•	•	
	SPAIN	•		•	
	ANDORRA	•			
	HUNGARY	•	•	•	
	ICELAND	•			
	POLAND	•		•	
	ARMENIA	•			
	MALTA	•	•		
	PORTUGAL	•		•	
	TURKEY	•			
	ALBANIA	•	•	•	
	AUSTRIA	•		•	
	BELARUS	•	•	•	•
	BULGARIA	•			
	CYPRUS (NORTH)	•			

Frequency of usage at national level	Country or territory	Referendum	Citizens' initiatives	Agenda initiatives	Recall
	GEORGIA	•	•	•	
	GIBRALTAR	•			
	LUXEMBOURG	•			
	UKRAINE	•	•		
	CYPRUS				
	FINLAND	•			
	MACEDONIA, THE FORMER YUGOSLAV REPUBLIC OF	•	•	•	
	MOLDOVA, REPUBLIC OF	•	•	•	
	RUSSIAN FEDERATION	•	•		
	BOSNIA AND HERZEGOVINA				
	CROATIA	•	•		
	CZECH REPUBLIC	•			
	MONTENEGRO	•		•	
	NETHERLANDS	•		•	
	SERBIA	•	•	•	
	UNITED KONGDOM OF GREAT BRITAIN AND NORTHERN IRELAND	•			
	BELGIUM				
	GERMANY				
	GUERNSEY				
	HOLY SEE (VATICAN CITY STATE)				
	JERSEY	•			
	MAN, ISLE OF				
	MONACO				
	SAINT HELENA				

227. Historically, referendums have been an important part of the political process in Europe. A number of referendums were held in France during the Revolutionary and Napoleonic periods, and a tradition of direct democracy became established. Switzerland has had provisions for direct democracy in its constitution since 1778, and uses direct democracy procedures extensively in its politics at both the national and the cantonal levels. With the advent of the EU, the usage of direct democracy has become more widespread in Europe. Referendums have been used by a number of European countries as part of the process of deciding whether to join the EU, and in others to ratify major EU treaties. Provisions for both citizens' initiatives and agenda initiatives are found widely throughout Europe, although recall is less common. Liechtenstein, however, has provisions in its constitution for all four of these instruments, and uses direct democracy procedures extensively. Historically, direct democracy has not been associated with the British political tradition, but referendums have been employed selectively in the UK in recent years.

Switzerland

228. Switzerland is generally acknowledged to be the world leader in the use of direct democracy (see the case study following chapter 1). Typically, Swiss citizens vote on several initiatives, constitutional proposals or treaties three or four times each year. For most types of referendum, a double majority – that is, a popular majority and a majority of the cantons – is required if the referendum is to pass. Direct democracy instruments are also extensively used in the Swiss cantons and at the local level. Experience in Switzerland has shown that initiatives and referendums can be fully integrated into the political system in a way that enhances democracy at all levels. In recent years, referendums have dealt with subjects such as immigration, genetically modified foods, health care, taxes and transport, to mention only a few of the many subjects which have been treated in citizens' initiatives or other types of popular vote.

France

229. The tradition of direct democracy in France dates back to the period following the French Revolution. The constitution of the Fifth Republic was adopted by means of a referendum in 1958. Since then, a number of referendums have been held under article 11 of the constitution, which empowers the president of the republic to 'submit to a referendum any government bill which deals with the organization of the public authorities, or with reforms relating to the economic or social policy of the Nation'. Referendums have been held in France on the Maastricht Treaty (1992), the length of the president's term of office (2000) and the EU Constitutional Treaty (2005).

The Republic of Ireland

230. In the Republic of Ireland, all constitutional amendments must be submitted to a referendum. Because they have been entrenched in the constitution, this has meant

that issues such as divorce and abortion have been the subject of referendum votes. The courts in the Republic of Ireland have also ruled that major treaties that involve any transfer of sovereignty or jurisdiction in constitutional areas must be submitted to a referendum. Thus, EU treaties such as those of Maastricht (1992), Nice (2001 and 2002) and Lisbon (2008) have been submitted to referendum votes. Because of the importance of these referendums to its national politics, the Republic of Ireland has developed an extensive process for the regulation of referendum campaigns. Government activity is severely restricted, and a Referendum Commission is responsible for providing public information about the subject of the referendum and encouraging participation.

Italy

231. Italy has a rare constitutional provision for the 'abrogative referendum' in which 500,000 voters or five regional councils can demand a referendum on total or partial repeal of an existing law. No such referendums are allowed for tax or budget laws, amnesties, pardons, or ratification of international treaties. There is also a provision in the Italian constitution for agenda initiatives, which can be proposed by 50,000 citizens, and can be sent to a referendum by the parliament if it so decides. This provision is little used, but since 1974 there have been many abrogative referendum votes dealing with subjects such as advertising, media ownership, party finance, the drug laws and electoral reform. A turnout quorum of 50 per cent of eligible electors is required for the passage of a proposal, and the parliament has two months to change or amend a law following the passage of an abrogative measure.

Denmark

232. The Danish constitution provides for mandatory referendums on constitutional amendments and on the delegation of sovereignty to international authorities. There is also a provision under which one-third of the members of parliament can demand a referendum on a bill passed by the parliament. It is also possible for the authorities to call referendums on other issues. There are no provisions for citizens' initiatives or recall. Denmark has had a number of important referendums in recent years on issues of European integration, including referendums on the Maastricht Treaty (1992) and on the adoption of the euro (2000).

The Middle East

233. Among the institutions of direct democracy, only referendums (or plebiscites) called by the authorities are found in the Middle East. The countries that have made the most use of this device are Egypt and Syria.

Table 8.5. Frequency of usage of direct democracy mechanisms at the national level in the Middle East

Frequency of usage at national level	Country or territory	Referendum	Citizens' initiatives	Agenda initiatives	Recall
	EGYPT	•			
	SYRIAN ARAB REPUBLIC	•			
	IRAQ	•			
	YEMEN	•			
	BAHRAIN	•			
	QATAR	•			
	ISRAEL				
	JORDAN				
	KUWAIT				
	LEBANON				
	OMAN				
	PALESTINE				
	SAUDI ARABIA				
	UNITED ARAB EMIRATES				

Egypt

234. Most referendums in Egypt have dealt with constitutional issues or with presidential powers. Referendums were held to secure the dissolution of the parliament (1987, 1990) and to confirm Hosni Mubarak as president (1981, 1987, 1993, 1999). A controversial referendum held in 2007 ratified extensive constitutional reforms, including a ban on religious political parties, the adoption of a new election law and procedures, the possibility for the president to dissolve the parliament unilaterally and the establishment of a new anti-terrorism law. Although 75 per cent of those participating approved the changes, the 2007 referendum saw a turnout of only 27 per cent.

Syria

235. Referendums in Syria have been used mainly to confirm the president in office or to approve his policies. Referendums (1971, 1978, 1985, 1991 and 1999) maintained the presidency of Hafez el-Assad. In 2000, a referendum was employed to confirm his son, Baschar el-Assad, as president. In 2007, President Assad was retained in office for a

second seven-year term. The 'Yes' vote in this referendum was 97 per cent, and turnout was reported to be 95 per cent of the electorate.

Oceania

236. Australia requires a referendum for amendments to the constitution, and instruments of direct democracy are also used in several of the Australian states. New Zealand has used instruments of direct democracy quite extensively, and adopted a new provision for 'citizen initiated referendums' in 1993. Palau and the Federated States of Micronesia have extensive provisions for direct democracy, including citizens' initiatives and recall.

Table 8.6. Frequency of usage of direct democracy mechanisms at the national level in Oceania

Frequency of usage at national level	Country or territory	Referendum	Citizens' initiatives	Agenda initiatives	Recall
	NEW ZEALAND	•	•	•	
	AUSTRALIA	•			
	PALAU	•	•		•
	MICRONESIA, FEDERATED STATES OF		•		•
	COOK ISLANDS	•	•		
	MARSHALL ISLANDS	•	•		
	NIUE	•			
	SAMOA	•			
	TOKELAU				
	KIRIBATI	•			•
	TIMOR-LESTE	•			
	TUVALU				
	FIJI				
	NAURU	•			
	PAPUA NEW GUINEA				
	PITCAIRN ISLANDS				
	SOLOMON ISLANDS				
	TONGA				
	VANUATU	•			

New Zealand

237. New Zealand has a long tradition of practising direct democracy. For many years, a referendum on liquor legislation was held automatically concurrent with each general election. In 1992 and 1993, referendums were held which resulted in a change in the electoral system from the British-style single-member plurality representation to a Mixed Member Proportional system. In 1993, the parliament adopted a Citizen Initiated Referenda Act which permitted 10 per cent of New Zealand citizens to propose a non-binding initiative on any issue. Under this legislation, a number of initiative petitions have been started, and three votes have been held to date (see box 3.2).

Palau

238. Palau is one of the world's youngest and smallest nations. It has about 20,000 inhabitants and 13,000 voters. The constitution provides for several direct democracy instruments, such as citizens' initiatives called by 10 per cent of the registered electors to enact or repeal national laws (except on appropriations); citizen's initiatives on constitutional amendments, which can be called by 25 per cent of the registered electors; and mandatory referendums on constitutional amendments. A double majority – a majority of the votes cast plus a majority in 12 of 16 states – is required for constitutional amendments. The constitution also provides for the recall of MPs, called by 25 per cent of the number of persons who voted in the most recent election for the MP concerned. Up to 2008, 23 referendums have been conducted, eight of them since independence in 1994. Between 1982 and 1993, Palau held eight referendums on the "Compact of Free Association with the United States" setting an example where persistence may lead to an eventual affirmation. In 2004 six referendums on constitutional amendments on the same day dealt with dual citizenship, joint election of the president and vice-president, limited terms for MPs, a unicameral parliament, uniform compensation for MPs, and a convention for constitutional amendments. All were passed except for the proposal for a unicameral parliament.

Australia

239. Amendments to the Australian constitution must be approved in a referendum. A double majority, comprising a majority of the national electorate and a majority in four of the six states, is required for an amendment to be adopted. The government may also hold non-binding referendums on other issues. Referendums are employed in the same manner in several of the Australian states. There are no provisions in Australia for citizens' or agenda initiatives, or for the recall of elected officials. In 1999, Australians voted in a referendum on a proposed constitutional amendment to replace the queen with a president to be chosen by parliament. The proposal was rejected by 55 per cent to 45 per cent. Voting in both elections and referendums in Australia is compulsory.

240. As this survey shows, the instruments of direct democracy are most widely used at the national level in Europe and Latin America. Switzerland and Uruguay are

the two countries in these regions, with the most extensive usage and the most fully developed integration of direct democracy with other political institutions. While there is no provision for direct democracy at the national level in the United States, the use of all forms of direct democracy is widespread in the US states, and these have been important laboratories for the development of direct democracy institutions and practices. There is also considerable use of the referendum in Australia at both the national and the state levels, and great interest in New Zealand with the adoption of a law providing for citizen initiatives. The usage of direct democracy in Asia, Africa and the Middle East has been more sporadic, and has generally been limited either to presidential plebiscites or the approval of a new constitution. Nevertheless, the spread of democracy has increased interest in these types of instruments in all parts of the world, and it is likely that their usage will increase as more countries gain experience with new forms of citizen engagement and democratic practice.

CHAPTER 9

CHAPTER 9

Recommendations and best practices

241. In this final chapter, strategies are considered that might be of relevance to those jurisdictions that are considering the adoption of one or more of the instruments of direct democracy, or those that are seeking to make existing institutions and processes perform more effectively. Such recommendations draw upon both positive and negative experiences with direct democracy institutions and practices. Procedures that work well in one jurisdiction may not necessarily be suitable in another. In some cases choices must be made between institutions, laws or procedures that involve difficult trade-offs between different objectives. For example, measures that may be intended to preserve the integrity of some direct democracy instruments may make those instruments more difficult to use. Nevertheless, the experience drawn from a wide variety of different political and social contexts around the world can help to inform those choices. Drawing on information in the preceding chapters, a number of best practices are suggested that may apply to direct democracy institutions and the administrative and electoral processes associated with them.

Referendums

242. Mandatory referendums are usually restricted to what are generally considered very important political issues. Too many referendums may reduce both the efficient working of the polity and political stability. Referendums are costly, as they require money, time and political attention. Hence, *the use of such resources needs to be considered carefully.*

243. Optional referendums called by the authorities are sometimes criticized from a democratic point of view because they have been initiated for political and tactical reasons: the referendum instrument has been used not to strengthen popular sovereignty but rather to bypass popular control or even to extend or maintain control by elites. In order to improve democratic legitimacy it is, in general, *recommended to regulate*

DIRECT DEMOCRACY HANDBOOK

the use of referendums either in the constitution or in ordinary, general and permanent legislation and to avoid ad hoc decisions – in particular in jurisdictions that lack a long democratic tradition and a broad consensus on the democratic rules of the game.

244. It is important to determine how the referendum fits within the legal system and political culture of the jurisdiction. The *advantages* of regulating referendums in the constitution or ordinary legislation are transparency and greater popular control, which contribute to the democratic legitimacy of referendums initiated by the political authorities. The *disadvantage* of regulating referendums in the constitution is reduced flexibility, particularly if the constitutional regulation is exhaustive and prohibits any calling of optional referendums. Thus, a balance has to be found between democratic legitimacy on the one hand and political efficiency and stability on the other.

245. The *alternatives presented to the voters on each and every issue have to be considered carefully.* The clearest result is obtained if the voters are asked to choose between two alternatives. If a choice between more than two alternatives is really wanted, a vote where the alternatives are rank-ordered could be applied.

246. The *wording of the ballot text* can have an important effect on the result and on its legitimacy. In general, the ballot text should be as precise and clear as possible and should have only one goal and one possible interpretation.

247. *Regulation should be considered on how referendums are to be organized* and who shall be responsible for ensuring that voting procedures are carried out in accordance with the law. In general, in order to avoid deliberate manipulation by the political authorities, good practice is to apply the same rules in national elections and referendums.

248. A critical issue to be considered is *when a referendum is judged to have passed.* General rules about turnout and approval quorums have to be made clear in advance of the referendum. Legitimacy, transparency, fairness and popular acceptance of referendum results are improved if such quorums are specified in the constitution or in ordinary legislation, and not decided upon in an ad hoc way just before each and every referendum.

249. The question of *whether a referendum is to be considered as binding or is consultative only* should also be carefully considered and, if possible, specified in a referendum law. A government that calls a consultative referendum and then ignores the result is open to criticism on democratic grounds. A binding referendum however means that sovereignty has in effect been transferred to the people. Consideration should also be given to the length of time within which the result should be implemented, and whether a second referendum on the same issue is possible. Governments that have called more than one referendum on an issue because they were dissatisfied with the outcome are also subject to criticism for manipulation.

250. Although high turnout is often seen as an indicator of the democratic legitimacy

of a referendum, *specifying a certain turnout quorum may not accomplish this goal* because it may encourage opponents to abstain. The risk of a small and active minority dominating a large and passive majority may be handled by means other than turnout quorums, such as opening genuine opportunities for vigorous information campaigns and political mobilization of the voters by political parties, social movements and ad hoc campaign groups.

251. Careful consideration has to be given to *how far the rules, norms and principles of good practice are specified* in the constitution or in ordinary legislation regulating referendums. A balance has to be found between a large amount of specific and detailed regulation, which may limit flexibility and transparency, and an almost complete absence of regulations, which may open the door to arbitrariness and even deliberate manipulation.

252. In the hands of the political authorities, a referendum holds both dangers and democratic possibilities. If the political authorities have the power to determine when referendums are held, if they can decide on which political issues a vote is called, if they control the campaign and the information provided for the voters, and if they can interpret the referendum result as they like, referendums become merely a political tool used to serve the needs of the governing party rather than the interests of democracy.

Citizens' initiatives

253. There are several types of initiative procedures designed to be concluded by a referendum vote – citizens' initiatives and citizen-demanded referendums (a) to abrogate or repeal an existing law, and (b) to reject a bill that has already passed in the legislature but is not yet in force (not promulgated). Some countries provide for only one or the other of these instruments (e.g. Italy has only the abrogative referendum). The citizens' initiative, by offering a new proposal, can best serve a function of political articulation, whereas the citizen-demanded referendum functions more as an instrument of political control. A broad range of these democratic functions can best be realized by providing for both types of procedure.

254. *Restrictions on the subjects that are admissible* for initiative instruments are often specified in law. An initiative procedure for constitutional amendments should be allowed since constitutions, as 'fundamental laws', should be based on the consent of the people and therefore should be open for discussion and change by parts of the citizenry. With respect to legislation on ordinary political issues, restrictions should not be too narrowly defined; otherwise initiative provisions would hardly ever be used and could cause frustration rather than offering opportunities. If subject restrictions are employed it is most important that they are clearly formulated and cannot be subject to too much legal uncertainty. A particularly sensitive area is financial matters. If the budget and/or taxes are to be excluded it should be made clear that this will not exclude all legal or political measures which imply some financial costs.

255. Initiative procedures should be designed in such a way as to offer realistic opportunities for their use. A critical choice is the *threshold of signatures required* for qualifying a proposal for the ballot. In jurisdictions which require the signatures of 10 per cent or more of registered electors, there is usually very little initiative activity. A lower threshold, perhaps 5 per cent or less, should be more appropriate to the democratic function of the procedures and more conducive to providing additional channels of political participation to supplement representative structures.

256. A second major choice refers to the *requirements for a valid referendum vote beyond the usual majority of votes cast.* For constitutional amendments, qualified majorities are often required, sometimes specified as double majorities referring to sub-national units. For ordinary legislation, additional approval quorums are sometimes used in order to secure broad legitimation of the referendum decision. Some jurisdictions require approval of the ballot question by a certain percentage of all registered electors; in other cases a specific turnout of electors must be reached. In practice, however, a turnout quorum may encourage the 'No' side to recommend abstention from voting. There are also good arguments for not having additional approval requirements which tend to count undecided voters as 'No'.

257. Finally, there is the question of whether a referendum vote should be *binding.* There are few jurisdictions (such as New Zealand) which treat the ballot on an initiative proposal as non-binding. A binding outcome seems to be most appropriate for votes on important issues. Otherwise the citizens' action in voting does not seem to be taken seriously.

Agenda initiatives

258. When introducing or practising an agenda initiative mechanism it is of critical importance to clearly differentiate this mechanism from petitions. To avoid confusion with other possible direct democracy mechanisms (including the citizens' initiative or the citizen-demanded referendum), key requirements for an agenda initiative must be legally defined and agreed in advance.

259. In contrast to petitions, which may just deal with general issues or claims, it is recommended that *an agenda initiative should address a statutory or constitutional issue* by means of a fully formulated draft law or proposed constitutional amendment.

260. Consideration should be given to the *threshold level for qualification* of an agenda initiative. A low level may encourage the legislative body to ignore the issue raised, while a very high threshold will make it difficult to qualify.

261. Because agenda initiatives enable and regulate an institutional dialogue between citizens and authorities, some *public financial or logistical support* for an agenda initiative effort should be provided.

Recalls

262. The recall, like other direct democracy procedures, has to balance the principles of participation and effective governance. The rights of citizens as well the rights of the officials involved in the recall process must be protected. The *difficulty of harmonizing recall procedures with effective institutions of representative democracy* is one reason why recall is not used to the same extent as other instruments of direct democracy. Frequent recall votes may undermine representative democracy. However, making the process overly difficult to use may limit its effectiveness as a means for citizens to exercise control over their representatives. The recall interacts with other institutions and rules of representative and of direct democracy; thus the decision to introduce it in a particular institutional setting must consider its possible impact in that setting.

263. Where recall procedures are permitted, a number of related questions must be anticipated. *When an official is recalled, provision must be made for a replacement to be chosen*, and this may require an additional election to be held. Holding a replacement election simultaneously with the recall confuses the recall with issues of electoral politics and may have the effect of turning the recall into a competitive election. If a replacement is simply appointed, the effect may be to supplement a direct democracy process with one that is less democratic. While the mechanics of the recall process are often difficult to manage in practice, the logic of recall is consistent with the underlying principles of direct democracy.

Procedures

264. *Knowledge* about the instrument(s) available is essential. In jurisdictions where such instruments have only been introduced recently, or where they are used very seldom, a public awareness programme should be undertaken, which may include use of the Internet, printed materials, educational efforts and media coverage.

265. The first persons to draft, deposit, sign and register an initiative/demand/recall document are the proponents. In order to be able to register a citizen-triggered instrument, and to become entitled to certain rights and duties, most countries require the establishment of a *designated committee*, which needs to fulfil certain conditions.

266. *Official assistance* should be provided to these designated committees. Such assistance should include drafting of the text and title, and translation services in multilingual jurisdictions. The formulation of the title should follow specific rules, including the need for clarity and unity of subject matter.

267. As the *signature-collecting process* is key to a citizen-initiated procedure, it is recommended that clear rules be set up for this step and applied uniformly. These rules should not contain unnecessary hurdles to free signature gathering or limit the available time frame excessively. Regulations regarding the use of paid signature gatherers should be considered.

268. Rules for *checking the signatures* vary considerably between jurisdictions. While one country may apply a full check of all the signatures submitted, others provide for only random checks. In order to strengthen institutional trust, any system of random checks must be statistically valid.

269. Critical to a citizen- and user- friendly practice are the *administrative procedures*. The authorities have a role to play at almost each step of the process, including offering advice and support to the electorate. Because citizens have great expectations of direct democracy procedures, careful design and good administrative practice are essential to allowing a proposal to qualify for the ballot.

Campaigns

270. Regulation of the *timing* of referendum votes, that is, when the referendum can take place, should allow for an adequate period for the campaign. General and permanent rules for the length of referendum campaigns may improve democratic legitimacy, whereas specific ad hoc rules may allow more governmental flexibility and efficiency. In general, ad hoc rules should be used as little as possible. In some jurisdictions, referendums or votes on citizens' initiatives are held at the same time as general elections, while in others they are held at different times. These decisions often affect both the voting turnout and the amount of attention a measure receives during the campaign.

271. *Communicating information to the public* about the content of a referendum proposal is vital for the legitimacy of the referendum result, and the process for communicating information must be carefully considered. On the one hand, a main principle of good practice in this respect is to ensure a level playing field for those in favour of and those against the proposal. On the other hand, the fundamental principle of freedom of expression should also be respected. Thus, in some jurisdictions, public funds or free media access are provided to ensure that citizens have sufficient information on a proposal. In others, this function is left entirely to political parties or other private actors in the campaign.

272. The creation of *official campaign committees* should be considered. Where official 'Yes' and 'No' committees assume responsibility for all campaign activities, a more manageable structure of the initiative or referendum campaign may be achieved. This may give the authorities greater regulatory control over the structure of the campaign, but it is viewed by some as an unwarranted restraint on free expression of opinion.

273. Many jurisdictions provide at least some minimal legal regulation of *campaign finances* by requiring disclosure of campaign contributions and the filing of financial reports with the authorities. However, disclosure of contributions and finances is not the same as restraint of campaign expenditures. If the objective is to create a level playing field, then either limits on the amount of money that can be spent by one side in a campaign or some form of public subsidy may be considered.

Annex A

World survey of direct democracy in 214 countries and territories*

Country or territory	Legal provisions for mandatory referendums (national level)	Legal provisions for optional referendums (national level)	Legal provisions for citizens' initiatives (national level)	Legal provisions for agenda initiatives (national level)	Legal provisions for recall (national level)	Are referendum results binding?	What can be brought to a referendum?	Legal provisions at the regional level	Legal provisions at the local level	Has there been a national referendum since 1980?
AFGHANISTAN		•					B			
ALBANIA		•	•	•		A	B	•	•	•
ALGERIA		•				A	B			•
ANDORRA	•	•		•		S	B	•		•
ANGOLA		•				B	0			
ANGUILLA										
ANTIGUA AND BARBUDA	•					A	B			
ARGENTINA		•		•		S	0	•	•	•
ARMENIA	•	•				A	B		•	•
ARUBA										
AUSTRALIA	•	•				S	B	•		•
AUSTRIA	•	•		•		S	B	•	•	•
AZERBAIJAN	•	•				A	B		•	•
BAHAMAS	•					A	C			•
BAHRAIN		•				A	B			•
BANGLADESH	•					A	C			•
BARBADOS										

* As per data collected by January 2008.

Country or territory	Legal provisions for mandatory referendums (national level)	Legal provisions for optional referendums (national level)	Legal provisions for citizens' initiatives (national level)	Legal provisions for agenda initiatives (national level)	Legal provisions for recall (national level)	Are referendum results binding?	What can be brought to a referendum?	Legal provisions at the regional level	Legal provisions at the local level	Has there been a national referendum since 1980?
BELARUS	•	•	•	•	•	A	B	•	•	•
BELGIUM									•	
BELIZE										
BENIN	•	•		•		S	B			•
BERMUDA	•						O			•
BHUTAN										
BOLIVIA	•	•	•	•	•	A	B	•	•	•
BOSNIA AND HERZEGOVINA								•	•	
BOTSWANA	•					A	C			•
BRAZIL		•		•		A	B	•	•	•
BRUNEI DARUSSALAM										
BULGARIA		•				S	B	•	•	
BURKINA FASO		•		•		A	B			
BURMA										
BURUNDI	•	•				A	C			•
CAMBODIA										
CAMEROON		•				A	B			
CANADA		•				N	B	•	•	•
CAPE VERDE		•	•	•		A	B		•	
CAYMAN ISLANDS										
CENTRAL AFRICAN REPUBLIC	•	•				A	B			•

Legend

•	Indicates existence of provision or referendum	S	Sometimes
	Indicates no existence of provision or inability to find provision	C	Constitutional changes only
		O	Other issues only
A	Always	B	Both constitutional and other issues
N	Never		

203

Country or territory	Legal provisions for mandatory referendums (national level)	Legal provisions for optional referendums (national level)	Legal provisions for citizens' initiatives (national level)	Legal provisions for agenda initiatives (national level)	Legal provisions for recall (national level)	Are referendum results binding?	What can be brought to a referendum?	Legal provisions at the regional level	Legal provisions at the local level	Has there been a national referendum since 1980?
CHAD	•	•				A	B			•
CHILE		•				S	C		•	•
CHINA										
COLOMBIA	•	•	•	•	•	S	B	•	•	•
COMOROS		•				A	B			•
CONGO, REPUBLIC OF THE	•	•				A	C			•
CONGO, DEMOCRATIC REPUBLIC OF THE	•			•			C			•
COOK ISLANDS		•					B			•
COSTA RICA	•	•	•	•		S	B	•	•	•
CÖTE DÍVOIRE	•	•				A	B			•
CROATIA	•	•	•			A	B	•	•	•
CUBA	•	•						•	•	
CYPRUS										•
CYPRUS (NORTH)		•				S	B			•
CZECH REPUBLIC	•					A	0		•	•
DENMARK	•	•				S	B		•	•
DJIBOUTI	•	•				A	C			•
DOMINICA	•					A	C			
DOMINICAN REPUBLIC										
ECUADOR	•	•	•	•	•	A	B	•	•	•
EGYPT	•	•					B			•
EL SALVADOR	•						0		•	
EQUATORIAL GUINEA		•				A	B			•
ERITREA										
ESTONIA	•	•				A	B		•	•
ETHIOPIA	•				•	A	0	•		•
FALKLAND ISLANDS										•
FIJI										

Country or territory	Legal provisions for mandatory referendums (national level)	Legal provisions for optional referendums (national level)	Legal provisions for citizens' initiatives (national level)	Legal provisions for agenda initiatives (national level)	Legal provisions for recall (national level)	Are referendum results binding?	What can be brought to a referendum?	Legal provisions at the regional level	Legal provisions at the local level	Has there been a national referendum since 1980?
FINLAND		•				N	B		•	•
FRANCE		•				A	B	•	•	•
GABON	•	•				A	C			•
GAMBIA	•					A	C			•
GEORGIA		•	•		•	A	B			•
GERMANY								•	•	
GHANA	•					A	C	•	•	•
GIBRALTAR	•						B			•
GREECE		•				A			•	
GRENADA	•						C			
GUATEMALA	•	•			•	A	B	•	•	•
GUERNSEY										
GUINEA	•	•				A	B			•
GUINEA-BISSAU										
GUYANA										
HAITI										•
HOLY SEE (VATICAN CITY STATE)										
HONDURAS	•	•			•	S	B		•	
HUNGARY	•	•	•		•	S	B		•	•
ICELAND	•	•				N	B			
INDIA										
INDONESIA										
IRAN, ISLAMIC REPUBLIC OF		•				A	B			•

Legend

•	Indicates existence of provision or referendum	S	Sometimes
	Indicates no existence of provision or inability to find provision	C	Constitutional changes only
		O	Other issues only
A	Always	B	Both constitutional and other issues
N	Never		

Country or territory	Legal provisions for mandatory referendums (national level)	Legal provisions for optional referendums (national level)	Legal provisions for citizens' initiatives (national level)	Legal provisions for agenda initiatives (national level)	Legal provisions for recall (national level)	Are referendum results binding?	What can be brought to a referendum?	Legal provisions at the regional level	Legal provisions at the local level	Has there been a national referendum since 1980?
IRAQ	•					A	C	•	•	•
IRELAND, REPUBLIC OF	•	•				A	B			•
ISRAEL										
ITALY		•	•	•		A	B	•	•	•
JAMAICA										
JAPAN	•					A	C	•	•	
JERSEY		•				N	B			
JORDAN										
KAZAKHSTAN		•				S	B			•
KENYA										•
KIRIBATI	•				•	A	B	•	•	•
KOREA, DEMOCRATIC PEOPLE'S REPUBLIC OF										
KOREA, REPUBLIC OF	•	•				S	B	•	•	•
KUWAIT										
KYRGYZSTAN		•		•	•	A	B		•	•
LAO PEOPLE'S DEMOCRATIC REPUBLIC										
LATVIA	•	•	•	•		A	B			•
LEBANON										
LESOTHO	•	•					B			
LIBERIA	•	•	•			A	C			•
LIBYAN ARAB JAMAHIRIYA										
LIECHTENSTEIN		•	•	•	•	A	B			•
LITHUANIA	•	•	•	•		S	B			•
LUXEMBOURG		•				S	O			•

Country or territory	Legal provisions for mandatory referendums (national level)	Legal provisions for optional referendums (national level)	Legal provisions for citizens' initiatives (national level)	Legal provisions for agenda initiatives (national level)	Legal provisions for recall (national level)	Are referendum results binding?	What can be brought to a referendum?	Legal provisions at the regional level	Legal provisions at the local level	Has there been a national referendum since 1980?
MACEDONIA, THE FORMER YUGOSLAV REPUBLIC OF	•	•	•	•		A	O		•	•
MADAGASCAR	•	•					B			•
MALAWI	•					A	C		•	•
MALAYSIA										
MALDIVES		•				N	B			•
MALI	•	•				A	B			•
MALTA	•	•	•			S	B	•	•	•
MAN, ISLE OF										
MARSHALL ISLANDS	•	•	•							•
MAURITANIA	•	•				A	B			•
MAURITIUS	•					A	C			
MEXICO								•		
MICRONESIA, FEDERATED STATES OF			•		•					•
MOLDOVA, REPUBLIC OF	•	•	•	•			B	•	•	•
MONACO										
MONGOLIA		•				A	B			
MONTENEGRO	•			•					•	•
MONTSERRAT										
MOROCCO	•	•				A	B			•

Legend

•	Indicates existence of provision or referendum	S	Sometimes
	Indicates no existence of provision or inability to find provision	C	Constitutional changes only
		O	Other issues only
A	Always	B	Both constitutional and other issues
N	Never		

Country or territory	Legal provisions for mandatory referendums (national level)	Legal provisions for optional referendums (national level)	Legal provisions for citizens' initiatives (national level)	Legal provisions for agenda initiatives (national level)	Legal provisions for recall (national level)	Are referendum results binding?	What can be brought to a referendum?	Legal provisions at the regional level	Legal provisions at the local level	Has there been a national referendum since 1980?
MOZAMBIQUE	•	•				A	B			
NAMIBIA		•					B			
NAURU	•						C			
NEPAL										•
NETHERLANDS		•		•		N	O	•	•	•
NETHERLANDS, ANTILLES										•
NEW ZEALAND	•	•	•	•		S	B		•	•
NICARAGUA		•	•	•			B			
NIGER	•	•		•		A	B			•
NIGERIA	•				•	S	B	•	•	
NIUE	•						C			
NORWAY		•				N			•	•
OMAN										
PAKISTAN		•					B			•
PALAU	•		•		•	S	B			•
PALESTINE										
PANAMA	•					A	B		•	•
PAPUA NEW GUINEA								•		
PARAGUAY	•	•		•		S	B			
PERU	•	•	•	•		A	B	•	•	•
PHILIPPINES	•	•	•	•		A	B	•	•	•
PITCAIRN ISLANDS										
POLAND	•	•		•		A	B	•	•	•
PORTUGAL		•		•		S	O	•	•	•
QATAR		•				A	B			•
ROMANIA	•	•		•		A	B	•	•	•
RUSSIAN FEDERATION	•	•	•			A	B	•	•	•
RWANDA	•	•				A	B			•
SAINT HELENA										

Country or territory	Legal provisions for mandatory referendums (national level)	Legal provisions for optional referendums (national level)	Legal provisions for citizens' initiatives (national level)	Legal provisions for agenda initiatives (national level)	Legal provisions for recall (national level)	Are referendum results binding?	What can be brought to a referendum?	Legal provisions at the regional level	Legal provisions at the local level	Has there been a national referendum since 1980?
SAINT KITTS AND NEVIS	•					A	B	•		•
SAINT LUCIA	•						C			
SAINT VINCENT AND THE GRENADINES	•					A	C			
SAMOA	•						C			•
SAN MARINO				•						•
SÃO TOMÉ AND PRINCIPE		•					C			•
SAUDI ARABIA										
SENEGAL	•	•				A	B			•
SERBIA	•	•	•	•		A	B	•	•	•
SEYCHELLES	•	•				A	B			•
SIERRA LEONE	•					A	B			•
SINGAPORE	•	•					B			
SLOVAKIA	•	•	•	•		S	B	•	•	•
SLOVENIA	•	•	•	•		A	B		•	•
SOLOMON ISLANDS										
SOMALIA	•	•			•		B			•
SOUTH AFRICA		•				N	O	•		•
SPAIN	•	•		•		S	B	•	•	•
SRI LANKA	•	•				A	B			•
SUDAN	•	•				A	B	•		•
SURINAME		•								•

Legend

•	Indicates existence of provision or referendum	S	Sometimes
	Indicates no existence of provision or inability to find provision	C	Constitutional changes only
		O	Other issues only
A	Always	B	Both constitutional and other issues
N	Never		

Country or territory	Legal provisions for mandatory referendums (national level)	Legal provisions for optional referendums (national level)	Legal provisions for citizens' initiatives (national level)	Legal provisions for agenda initiatives (national level)	Legal provisions for recall (national level)	Are referendum results binding?	What can be brought to a referendum?	Legal provisions at the regional level	Legal provisions at the local level	Has there been a national referendum since 1980?
SWAZILAND	•	•				S	B			
SWEDEN		•				N	B	•	•	•
SWITZERLAND	•	•	•			A	B	•	•	•
SYRIAN ARAB REPUBLIC	•	•				A	B			•
TAIWAN	•	•	•		•	A	B	•	•	•
TAJIKISTAN	•	•				A	B			•
TANZANIA, UNITED REPUBLIC OF										•
THAILAND		•		•		A	B	•	•	•
TIMOR-LESTE		•				S	B			
TOGO	•	•	•	•			B			•
TOKELAU										•
TONGA										
TRINIDAD AND TOBAGO										
TUNISIA	•	•				A	B			•
TURKEY	•	•				A	C			•
TURKMENISTAN		•	•	•			B		•	•
TURKS AND CAICOS ISLANDS										
TUVALU										
UGANDA	•	•	•	•	•	A	B	•	•	•
UKRAINE	•	•	•			A	B	•	•	•
UNITED ARAB EMIRATES										
UNITED KINGDOM OF GREAT BRITAIN AND NORTHERN IRELAND		•				S	B	•	•	
UNITED STATES OF AMERICA								•	•	
URUGUAY	•		•	•		A	B	•	•	•

Country or territory	Legal provisions for mandatory referendums (national level)	Legal provisions for optional referendums (national level)	Legal provisions for citizens' initiatives (national level)	Legal provisions for agenda initiatives (national level)	Legal provisions for recall (national level)	Are referendum results binding?	What can be brought to a referendum?	Legal provisions at the regional level	Legal provisions at the local level	Has there been a national referendum since 1980?
UZBEKISTAN	•	•					B			•
VANUATU	•					A	C			
VENEZUELA	•	•	•	•	•	A	B	•	•	•
VIET NAM		•					O			
VIRGIN ISLANDS, BRITISH										
YEMEN	•					A	B			•
ZAMBIA	•					A	C			
ZIMBABWE										•

* The UN name is Myanmar

Legend

•	Indicates existence of provision or referendum	S	Sometimes
	Indicates no existence of provision or inability to find provision	C	Constitutional changes only
		O	Other issues only
A	Always	B	Both constitutional and other issues
N	Never		

Annex B

Glossary

Abrogative referendum – A vote of the *electorate* which may repeal a law or decree that has been agreed and promulgated by the legislature and already implemented.

Ad hoc referendum – A vote of the *electorate* called by a person or group within the executive or the legislature but not otherwise provided for by law.

Agenda initiative – A *direct democracy procedure* which enables citizens to submit a proposal which must be considered by the legislature but is not necessarily put to a vote of the electorate.

Approval quorum – A requirement for passage of a *proposal* which takes the form of a specified number of votes or a percentage of the *electorate* in support of the *proposal* .

Ballot text – Text which appears on the ballot paper for a vote of the *electorate* under a *direct democracy procedure*, typically in the form of a question or a series of options. For a *referendum* it may be a specified question text, or a question seeking agreement or rejection of a text; for an *initiative*, a question asking for agreement or rejection of a proposal identified by the title of the *citizens' initiative*; for a *recall*, a question asking for agreement or rejection of the early termination of the period in office of a specified office holder.

Binding referendum – A vote of the *electorate* where, if a *proposal* passes, the government or appropriate authority is compelled to implement it.

Citizens' demand – A *direct democracy procedure* that allows citizens to initiate a *referendum* to repeal an existing law (*abrogative referendum*) or a law recently adopted by a legislature (*rejective referendum*).

Citizens' initiative – A *direct democracy procedure* that allows citizens to initiate a vote of the *electorate* on a *proposal* outlined by those citizens. The *proposal* may be for a new law, for a constitutional amendment, or to repeal or amend an existing law.

Consultative referendum – A vote of the *electorate* the outcome of which is in legal terms only advisory for a government or appropriate authority.

Counter-proposal – A *proposal* agreed by the legislature to be presented to a vote of the *electorate* as an alternative to the *proposal* contained in a *citizens' initiative.*

Direct democracy procedure – A legal arrangement which gives citizens the right to be directly involved in the political decision-making process. It may take one of three forms:

- citizens voting on a public policy *proposal* originated elsewhere (*referendum*);
- citizens setting the agenda by originating a public policy *proposal* themselves (*initiative*); and
- citizens requesting and voting on the early termination of the period in office of one of the personnel of government (*recall*). Also known as a direct democracy instrument and a direct democracy mechanism.

Double majority – A requirement for a *proposal* to pass which includes both a majority of the total votes cast and a majority of the votes in a specified number of sub-national areas.

Electoral management body (EMB) – An organization or body which has been founded for the sole purpose of, and is legally responsible for, managing some or all of the essential (or core) elements of the conduct of elections, and of *direct democracy procedures.*

Electorate – The total number of electors registered to vote.

Initiative – A procedure which allows citizens to put forward a proposal. One form (*citizens' initiative*) leads to a vote of the *electorate*, a second (*agenda initiative*) to the consideration by the legislature or other specified authority.

Legality check – The scrutiny by a public authority of the constitutionality and legality of a *proposal.*

Mandatory referendum – A vote of the *electorate* which is required under circumstances defined in the constitution or in legislation. Also known as an obligatory referendum.

Optional referendum – A vote of the *electorate* which is not required by the constitution or by law.

Plebiscite – Sometimes used as a synonym for a *referendum* called by the authority, often the executive.

Proponents – The citizens who first sign and deposit an *initiative proposal*.

Proposal – The complete text of a referendum or *initiative proposal*. Sometimes called a measure or proposition.

Qualified majority – A majority requirement demanding that for a *proposal* to be passed, it must receive a proportion of the vote in excess of 50 per cent plus 1 – for example two-thirds or three-quarters.

Quorum – See *approval quorum* and *turnout quorum*.

Recall – A *direct democracy procedure* that allows a specified number of citizens and/or an appropriate authority to demand a vote of the *electorate* on whether an elected holder of public office should be removed from that office before the end of her/his term.

Referendum – A *direct democracy procedure* consisting of a vote of the *electorate* on an issue of public policy such as a constitutional amendment or a draft law. Also known as *popular consultation* or a *plebiscite*.

Referendum question – See *ballot text*.

Registration of a citizens' initiative – The act of depositing an *initiative* for publication and collection of signatures, whereby the legal process of the *initiative* is officially started.

Registered committee – The *proponents* of a *referendum, initiative* or *recall* when they are officially registered in the form of a committee.

Rejective referendum – A vote of the *electorate* which may veto a law or decree that has been agreed by the legislature but has not yet come into force. Also known as a facultative referendum.

Submission – The act of depositing collected *signatures* with the proper authority in a *citizens' initiative* or *citizens' demand* process.

Turnout quorum – A specified minimum voter turnout required for a vote of the *electorate* to be valid.

Verification – The declaration of acceptance by the proper authority that the *submission* contains at least the required number of valid signatures and complies with the law, regulations and procedural rules.

Annex C

Bibliography and further reading

Chapters 1, 7 and 8

Bowler, Shaun, Donovan, Todd and Tolbert, Caroline J. (eds), *Citizens as Legislators: Direct Democracy in the United States* (Columbus, Ohio: Ohio State University Press, 1998)

Bowler, Shaun and Donovan, Todd, *Demanding Choices: Opinion, Voting, and Direct Democracy* (Ann Arbor, Mich.: University of Michigan Press, 1998)

Budge, Ian, *The New Challenge of Direct Democracy* (Cambridge: Polity Press, 1996)

Butler, David and Ranney, Austin (eds), *Referendums Around the World: The Growing Use of Direct Democracy* (Basingstoke and London: Macmillan, 1994)

Cronin, Thomas, *Direct Democracy: The Politics of Initiative, Referendum and Recall* (Cambridge, Mass. Harvard University Press, 1989)

European Commission, 'Ratification of the Treaty Establishing a Constitution for Europe', 2005, <http://europa.eu.int/constitution/referendum_en.htm>

Gallagher, Michael and Uleri, Pier Vincenzo (eds), *The Referendum Experience in Europe* (Basingstoke and London: Macmillan, 1996)

Gerber, Elisabeth, *The Populist Paradox: Interest Group Influence and the Promise of Direct Legislation* (Princeton, NJ: Princeton University Press, 1999)

Gundelach, Peter and Siune, Karen (eds), *From Voters to Participants* (Aarhus: Institute for Political Science, University of Aarhus, 1992)

Hamon, Francis, *Le Référendum: Étude Comparative* [Referendums: a comparative study] (Paris: LGDJ, 1995)

Haskell, John, *Direct Democracy or Representative Government?* (Boulder, Col.: Westview Press, 2001)

Jahn, Detlef and Storsved, Ann-Sofie 'Legitimacy Through Referendum: The Nearly Successful Domino Strategy of the EU Referendums in Austria, Finland, Sweden and Norway', *West European Politics*, 18 (1995), pp. 18–37

Jenssen, Anders Todal, Pesonen, Pertti and Gilljam, Mikael (eds), *To Join or Not to Join: Three Nordic Referendums on Membership in the European Union* (Oslo: Scandinavian University Press, 1998)

Johnston, Richard, Blais, André, Gidengil, Elisabeth and Nevitte, Neil, *The Challenge of Direct Democracy: The 1992 Canadian Referendum* (Montreal: McGill-Queens University Press, 1996)

Kobach, Kris, *The Referendum: Direct Democracy in Switzerland* (Aldershot: Dartmouth, 1993)

Kriesi, Hanspeter, *Citoyenneté et démocratie directe* [Citizenship and direct democracy] (Zürich: Seismo, 1993)

LeDuc, Lawrence, *The Politics of Direct Democracy: Referendums in Global Perspective* (Peterborough, Ont. and Orchard Park, NY: Broadview Press, *c.* 2003)

Lupia, Arthur and McCubbins, Matthew, *The Democratic Dilemma: Can Citizens Learn What They Need To Know?* (New York: Cambridge University Press, 1998)

Qvortrup, Mads, *A Comparative Study of Referendums: Government by the People* (Manchester: Manchester University Press, 2002)

Rourke, John T., Hiskes, Richard P. and Zirakzadeh, Cyrus, *Direct Democracy and International Politics: Deciding International Issues Through Referendums* (Boulder, Col.: Lynne Rienner, 1992)

Setälä, Maija, *Referendums and Democratic Government* (New York: St Martin's Press, 1999)

Simpson, Alan, *Referendums: Constitutional and Political Perspectives* (Wellington: Victoria University of Wellington, Department of Political Science, 1992)

Szcerbiak, Aleks and Taggart, Paul (eds), *Choosing Union: the 2003 EU Accession Referendums*, special issue of *West European Politics*, 27/4 (2004)

Suski, Markku, *Bringing in the People: A Comparison of Constitutional Forms and Practices of the Referendum* (Dordrecht: Nijhoff, 1993)

Chapter 2

Garry, John, Marsh, Michael and Sinnott, Richard, '"Second-order" versus "Issue-voting" Effects in EU Referendums', *European Union Politics*, 6/2 (2005), pp. 201–21

Morel, Laurence, 'The Rise of the "Politically Obligatory" Referendums: The 2005 French Referendum in Comparative Perspective', *West European Politics*, 30/5 (2007), pp. 1041–67

Morel, Laurence, 'The Strategic Use of Government-Sponsored Referendums in Liberal Democracies', in Matthew Mendelsohn and Andrew Parkin (eds), *Referendum Democracy: Citizens, Elites, and Deliberations in Referendums Campaigns* (New York: Palgrave, 2001)

Setälä, Maija, 'On the Problems of Responsibility and Accountability in Referendums', *European Journal of Political Research*, 45/4 (2006), pp. 699–721

Setälä, Maija, 'Referendums in Western Europe: A Wave of Direct Democracy?', *Scandinavian Political Studies*, 22/4 (1999), pp. 327–40

Uleri, Pier Vincenzo, 'Introduction', in Michael Gallagher and Pier Vincenzo Uleri (eds), *The Referendum Experience in Europe* (Basingstoke and London: Macmillan, 1996)

Chapter 3

Auer, Andreas and Bützer, Michael (eds), *Direct Democracy: The Eastern and Central European Experience* (Aldershot: Ashgate, 2001)

Butler, David and Ranney, Austin (eds), *Referendums around the World: The Growing Use of Direct Democracy* (Basingstoke and London: Macmillan, 1994)

Gallagher, Michael and Uleri, Pier Vincenzo (eds), *The Referendum Experience in Europe* (Basingstoke and London: Macmillan, 1996)

Kaufmann, Bruno et al. (eds), *Guidebook to Direct Democracy in Switzerland and Beyond* (Amsterdam: IRI Europe, 2005 and 2008)

Kriesi, Hanspeter, *Direct Democratic Choice: The Swiss Experience* (Lanham, Md and Boulder, Col.: Lexington Books, 2005)

LeDuc, Lawrence, *The Politics of Direct Democracy: Referendums in Global Perspective* (Peterborough, Ont. and Orchard Park, NY: Broadview Press, *c.* 2003)

Moeckli, Silvano, *Direkte Demokratie: Ein internationaler Vergleich* [Direct democracy: an international comparison] (Bern: Haupt, 1994)

Schiller, Theo, *Direkte Demokratie: Eine Einführung* [Direct democracy: an introduction] (Frankfurt and New York: Campus, 2002)

Chapter 4

Auer, Andreas, 'European Citizens' Initiative', in Bruno Kaufmann et al., *Initiative for Europe Handbook 2007: A Roadmap for Transnational Democracy* (Brussels: IRI Europe, 2007), pp. 69–76

Berg, Carsten et al., *Initiative for Europe Handbook 2008: The Guide to Transnational Democracy* (Brussels: IRI Europe, 2008)

Cuesta, Victor, *La iniciativa popular en el derecho constitutional europeo comparado* [The popular initiative in comparative European constitutional law] (Florence: European University Institute, 2005)

Ferro, Miguel Sousa, *Alea Iacta Est: Popular Legislative Initiative* (Bruges: College of Europe, Law Department, 2006)

Held, David, 'The Changing Contours of Political Community: Rethinking Democracy in the Context of Globalization', in Barry Holden (ed.), *Global Democracy: Key Debates* (London: Routledge, 2000)

Kaufmann, Bruno, *The Initiative and Referendum Monitor 2004/2005: IRI Europe Toolkit to Free and Fair Referendums and Citizens' Initiatives* (London: The Creative Element, 2004)

Kaufmann, Bruno et al., *The Initiative and Referendum Institute Europe Guidebook to Direct Democracy in Switzerland and Beyond*, 2009 edn (Marburg/Brussels: IRI Europe, 2008)

Pallinger, Zoltán Tibor et al. (eds), *Direct Democracy in Europe: Developments and Prospects* (Wiesbaden: VS Verlag für Sozialwissenschaften, 2007)

Schiller, Theo, 'Direct Democracy in Europe: Towards a European Initiative Right and a First Pan-European Referendum', Paper presented at the IRI Europe Forum, Warsaw, 15 February 2006

Chapter 5

Barczak, M., 'Representation by Consultation? The Rise of Direct Democracy in Latin America', *Latin American Politics and Society*, 43/3 (2001), pp. 37–59

Butler, David and Ranney, Austin, *Referendums Around the World: The Growing Use of Direct Democracy* (Washington, DC: American Enterprise Institute, 1994)

Cronin, T., *Direct Democracy: The Politics of Initiative, Referendum and Recall* (Cambridge, Mass. Harvard University Press, 1989)

Kornblith, Miriam, 'The Referendum in Venezuela: Elections versus Democracy', *Journal of Democracy*, 16 (January 2005), pp. 124–37

LeDuc, Lawrence, *The Politics of Direct Democracy: Referendums in Global Perspective* (Peterborough, Ont. and Orchard Park, NY: Broadview Press, *c*. 2003)

Zovatto, Daniel, 'Direct Democracy Institutions in Latin America', in J. Payne, D. Zovatto, F. Carrillo and A. Allamand, *Democracies in Development: Politics and Reform in Latin America* (Washington, DC: International Development Bank and International IDEA, 2002), pp. 249–65

Chapter 6

Büchi, Rolf, *Kohti osallistavaa demokratiaa* [Towards participatory democracy] (Helsinki: Like Förlag, 2007)

Donovan, Todd and Karp, Jeffrey A., 'Popular Support for Direct Democracy', Paper presented for the 20th IPSA World Conference in Fukuoka, 2006

Gross, Andreas, *Auf der politischen Baustelle Europa: Eine europäische Verfassung für eine transnationale Demokratie eröffnet auch der Schweiz neue Integrationsperspektiven* [On the political construction of Europe: a European constitution for transnational democracy opens up a new perspective on integration for Switzerland as well] (Zürich: Realotopia, 1996)

Held, David et al., *Global Transformations: Politics, Economics and Culture* (Cambridge: Polity Press, 1999)

Kaufmann, Bruno, Erne, Roland, Gross, Andreas and Kleger, Heinz, *Transnationale Demokratie: Impulse für ein demokratisch verfasstes Europa* [Transnational democracy: the drive for a democratically constituted Europe] (Zürich: Realotopia, 1995)

Kaufmann, Bruno and Filliez, Fabrice, *The European Constitution: Bringing in the People. The Options and Limits of Direct Democracy in the European Integration Process* (Brussels: IRI Europe, 2004)

Kaufmann, Bruno and Waters, M. Dane, *Direct Democracy in Europe: A Comprehensive Reference Guide to the Initiative and Referendum Process in Europe, sponsored by the Initiative and Referendum Institute Europe* (Durham, NC: Carolina Academic Press, 2004)

Morel, Laurence, 'Le choix du référendum: Leçons françaises. L'émergence d'un référendum politiquement obligatoire' [The choice of referendum: lessons from France. The emergence of the politically mandatory referendum], Paper presented at the ECPR General Conference in Budapest, 2005

Patomäki, H., 'Republican Public Sphere and the Governance of Globalizing Political Economy', in M. Lensu and J.-S. Fritz (eds), *Value Pluralism, Normative Theory and International Relations* (Basingstoke and London: Macmillan; and New York: St Martin's Press, 2000), pp. 160–95

Sauger, Nicolas and Laurent, Annie, *Le Référendum de ratification du Traité constitutionnel européen: Comprendre le 'Non' français* [The referendum to ratify the European Constitutional Treaty: understanding the French 'No'], Les Cahiers du Cevipof, 42 (Paris: Centre de Recherches Politiques de Sciences Po, 2005)

Schiller, Theo, '"Secondary Democracy" in the European Union and the Role of Direct Democracy', in Norbert Kersting and Lasse Cronqvist (eds), *Democratization and Political Culture in Comparative Perspective* (Wiesbaden: VS Verlag für Sozialwissenschaften, 2005)

Internet sources

Initiative and Referendum Institute Europe (IRI), <http://www.iri-europe.org/>

University of Zurich, Centre for Research on Direct Democracy, <http://www.c2d.ch>

Annex D

About the authors

Main authors

Virginia Beramendi is the head of mission for International IDEA's Andean Region Programme in Bolivia. She has been the manager of the Direct Democracy project since its inception and is also the project manager of the Building Resources in Democracy, Governance and Elections (BRIDGE) Project for Latin America. Before moving to Bolivia, she was the manager of the Administration and Cost of Elections (ACE) Comparative Data Project, in which position she established a global network of partner organizations and conducted training on election management and research. She was also the 'Media and Elections' topic supervisor for the electronic *ACE Encyclopedia* and worked as a researcher for International IDEA handbooks such as *Funding of Political Parties and Election Campaigns* (2003) and *Mujeres en el Parlamento: Más allá de los números* [Women in parliament: beyond numbers] (2002). She holds an MPhil in development studies from Cambridge University, UK, and a BA (Hons) degree in communication studies and sociology from Anglia Ruskin University, UK.

Andrew Ellis is currently the director of operations for International IDEA in Stockholm, having previously been head of the Electoral Processes Programme. From 1999 to 2003 he acted as senior adviser for the National Democratic Institute (NDI) in Indonesia, working on constitutional reform, electoral process and decentralization issues. He is the co-author of International IDEA's *Electoral System Design: The New International IDEA Handbook* (2005) and *Electoral Management Design: The International IDEA Handbook* (2006), and has written numerous papers on issues of institutional framework design. Other major assignments include acting as chief technical adviser to the Palestinian Election Commission in 1996, and designing and planning the European Commission's electoral assistance programme in Cambodia for the 1998 elections. Andrew is a former vice-chair and secretary general of the UK Liberal Party and chief executive of the UK Liberal Democrats.

Bruno Kaufmann has worked with democracy, conflict and development issues since the mid-1980s. After a term with the Berne Declaration, a Swiss development non-governmental organization, he became the coordinator of a European citizens' network preparing a 'transnational constitution with direct-democratic rights'. Ten years later he became the first director of the Initiative and Referendum Institute Europe, a non-partisan research and educational institute with its headquarters at Marburg University, Germany. As a journalist he has worked at the Swiss Broadcasting Company, the daily *Tagesanzeiger* newspaper and the weekly *Die Weltwoche* before joining the special editorial team for international reform issues at *Die Zeit* in Hamburg in 1998. Since 2001 he has covered European and international affairs for the Swiss Broadcasting Company and has been a columnist on publications such as *Nordis, OpenDemocracy, Gazette* and *European Voice*. Bruno has served as an expert for numerous national governments and international organizations including the European Union, the German parliament, the Council of Europe and International IDEA, where he joined the expert team on global direct democracy assessment in 2004. He has an MA in social sciences from the University of Gothenburg, Sweden.

Miriam Kornblith, a Venezuelan sociologist and political scientist, is a professor and researcher at the Institute of Political Studies at the Central University of Venezuela in Caracas. She has published extensively on electoral processes, political and institutional reform and the contemporary political system of Venezuela. She is currently the director of the Latin American and Caribbean programme at the National Endowment for Democracy in Washington, DC. From 1998 to 1999 she was the vice-president and member of the National Electoral Council of Venezuela, and from August 2003 to January 2005 a substitute member of the council. She is the author of 'The Referendum in Venezuela: Elections versus Democracy', *Journal of Democracy*, 16 (January 2005), pp. 124–37.

Lawrence LeDuc is professor of political science at the University of Toronto, Canada. His books include *The Politics of Direct Democracy: Referendums in Global Perspective* (Broadview Press, c. 2003); *Comparing Democracies 2* (with Richard G. Niemi and Pippa Norris, Sage, 2002); and *Absent Mandate: Canadian Electoral Politics in an Era of Restructuring* (with Harold D. Clarke, Jane Jenson and Jon H. Pammett, Gage Educational, 3rd edn 1996). Other recent publications include chapters in Alain-G. Gagnon and Brian Tanguay (eds), *Canadian Parties in Transition* (Broadview Press, c. 2007); Henry Milner (ed.), *Making Every Vote Count: Reassessing Canada's Electoral System* (Broadview Press, c. 1999); and David Farrell and Rüdiger Schmitt-Beck (eds), *Do Political Campaigns Matter?* (Routledge, 2002). He is a member of the editorial boards of *Electoral Studies*, the *Journal of Elections, Public Opinion and Parties* and the *European Journal of Political Research*.

Paddy McGuire is the senior vice-president of Public Policy for Strategies 360, a public affairs and lobbying company. He was previously Oregon deputy secretary of state, overseeing the Oregon Elections Division, worked in the administration of President

Bill Clinton and ran the Clinton campaign in Oregon in both 1992 and 1996. Prior to that he served as executive director of the Democratic Party of Oregon. He is a graduate of Hamilton College, New York, USA, and has a certificate from the Kennedy School of Government at Harvard University, USA.

Theo Schiller is currently a professor at the Institute of Political Science, Philipps University in Marburg, Germany (emeritus since 2007), director of the Centre for Citizens' Participation and Direct Democracy, and chair of the Council of the Initiative and Referendum Institute Europe. Between 1997 and 2001 he was vice-president of Philipps University. His publications include *Direkte Demokratie: Eine Einführung* [Direct democracy: an introduction] (Campus-Verlag, 2002); *Direkte Demokratie: Forschungen und Perspektiven* [Direct democracy: research and perspectives] (co-edited with V. Mittendorf, Westdeutscher Verlag, 2002); and *Direct Democracy in Europe: Developments and Prospects* (co-edited with Z. T. Pallinger, Bruno Kaufmann and Wilfried Marxer, VS Verlag für Sozialwissenschaften, 2007). Forthcoming in 2008 are (co-edited with Maija Setälä): *Referendums and Direct Democracy* (Routledge) and *Direct Democracy in Local Politics in Europe* (VS Verlag für Sozialwissenschaften).

Palle Svensson is a professor in political science at the University of Aarhus, Denmark. He has written on democratic theory, political participation and Scandinavian politics, most recently on referendums in Denmark and turnout in Danish elections. He has also acted as an adviser to the Danish government on democratization and elections and as an electoral observer in various African countries. His recent publications include 'Voting Behaviour in the European Constitution Process', in Z. T. Pallinger et al. (eds), *Direct Democracy in Europe* (VS Verlag für Sozialwissenschaften, 2007); *Folkets røst: Demokrati og folkeafstemninger i Danmark og andre europæiske lande* [The voice of the people: democracy and popular consultations in Denmark and other European countries] (Aarhus Universitetsforlag/Magtudredningen, 2003); and 'Five Danish Referendums on the European Community and European Union: A Critical Assessment of the Franklin Thesis', *European Journal of Political Research*, 41/6 (2002).

Contributors

Jennifer Somalie Angeyo has worked as a legal officer with the Electoral Commission of Uganda since 1998 and as a senior legal officer specializes in legal advisory work, and drafting legal documents, contracts, guidelines, *Gazette* notices and proposals for legislation. She holds an LLB degree from Makerere University, Uganda, and a postgraduate diploma in legal practice from the Law Development Centre, Kampala, Uganda. She also holds a master's degree in computer science, and has experience in conducting needs assessment studies for information and communications technology (ICT) in tertiary institutions and the drafting of ICT policies with an emphasis on ethical and legal issues. Jennifer has participated as a technical assignee in observer missions to the electoral commissions of Rwanda and Kenya, and is currently part of a pan-African research network of researchers and institutions (LOG-IN Africa) assessing the current state and outcomes of e-local governance initiatives in Africa.

Nadja Braun is the head of the Legal Department at the Swiss Federal Chancellery (the EMB). Previously she was a legal adviser to and project manager of the Swiss e-voting project in the Section of Political Rights at the Federal Chancellery. She studied at the universities of Berne and Helsinki, completing her doctorate on ballot secrecy in 2005. Her interests and work revolve around constitutional law, good governance, direct democracy, e-voting, electoral systems, administrative law and human rights. Her professional affiliations include the Council of Europe, International IDEA and the Initiative and Referendum Institute Europe. She was a contributor to International IDEA's *Voting from Abroad: Handbook on External Voting* (2007) and her recent publications include the *Guidebook to Direct Democracy in Switzerland and Beyond* (with Bruno Kaufmann and Rolf Büchi, Marburg, 2007); *Stimmgeheimnis* [Voting secrecy] (Reihe: Abhandlungen zum schweizerischen Recht, 708) (Bern, 2005); 'E-voting: Swiss E-Voting Pilot Projects: Evaluation Analysis and How to Proceed', in Robert Krimmer (ed.), *Electronic Voting 2006* (with Daniel Brändli, Bonn, 2006), pp. 27–36; and 'E-Voting: Switzerland's Projects and their Legal Framework in a European Context', in Alexander Prosser and Robert Krimmer (eds), *Electronic Voting in Europe: Technology, Law, Politics and Society* (Bonn, 2004), pp. 43–52.

Mugyenyi Silver Byanyima is currently working with the Electoral Commission of Uganda as a senior election officer in charge of the Mid-Western Region, comprising nine districts, and is the secretary of the Contracts Committee of the Electoral Commission and a member of the Quality Control Committee. He has worked as returning officer for the Lira and Buliisa districts, and participates in preparing election budgets and programmes.

Rodolfo Gonzáles Rissotto has been minister of the Electoral Court of Uruguay since 1996. Along with other ministers, he has served as editor of the new Electoral Law of Uruguay. He has also been executive director of the Information and Research Center of Uruguay (CIIDU), director of the Department of Electoral Research of the Democracy Center of Uruguay (CELADU), and head of the Ministry of Education and Culture. In addition, he was a leader of the Adults National Commission and the National Commission of Fellowship. Dr Gonzalez has also served as drafts coordinator of Uruguay with the Ministry of Education and the Organization of American States (OAS), presided over the Uruguayan delegation at the Education Committee of the Southern Common Market (Mercado Común del Sur, MERCOSUR), and is a former vice-minister and minister of defence. A historian and former visiting professor at the Pontifícia Universidade Católica de São Paulo (PUC/SP), Brazil, he has published in many Latin American publications. He is also a consultant for several international organizations such as International IDEA, UNESCO, PARLATINO, and the Inter-American Institute for Human Rights (Instituto Interamericano de Derechos Humanos,

IIDH) Center for Electoral Promotion and Assistance (Centro de Asesoría y Promoción Electoral, CAPEL).

Algis Krupavicius has been a professor of politics at the Kaunas University of Technology, Kaunas, Lithuania since 2001 and since 1999 has been director of the university's Policy and Public Administration Institute. Since 2006 he has been a member of the Lithuanian Commission of Science Awards, and he is currently a member of the European Science Foundation. His many publications include 'The End of Communism and the New Party System', in Jean Blondel et al., *Governing New European Democracies* (Palgrave Macmillan, 2007); two chapters on Lithuania and the Baltic states in A. Kulik and S. Pshizova (eds), *Political Parties in Post-Soviet Space: Russia, Belarus, Ukraine, Moldova and the Baltics* (Praeger, 2005); and 'Lithuania', in Bruno Kaufmann and M. Dane Waters (eds), *Direct Democracy in Europe: A Comprehensive Reference Guide to the Initiative and Referendum Process in Europe* (Carolina Academic Press, 2004).

Humberto de la Calle Lombana is a lawyer with extensive experience in constitutional and administrative law. As minister of the interior, he acted on behalf of the Colombian government in the sessions of the Constitutional Assembly of 1991. He has been the director of the Colombian EMB, the National Electoral Council, worked as a consultant in electoral matters, been a university professor and has written various books and essays. He chaired the Permanent Council of the OAS when the Inter-American Democratic Charter was being discussed, and was elected vice-president of Colombia in 1994.

Krisztina Medve is a member of the National Election Office of Hungary, specializing in electoral law and constitutional law. She has worked in the field of elections for seven years and has taken part in several domestic and international projects, while participating in the conduct of parliamentary and local governmental elections and national referendums. She graduated recently as a lawyer specializing in European law, focusing primarily on European parliamentary elections.

Alfred Lock Okello Oryem holds an LLB (Hons) degree from Makerere University, Uganda, and a postgraduate diploma in legal practice from the Law Development Centre, Kampala, Uganda. He currently divides his time between many projects, including his work for the head of the Legal and Public Relations Department of the Electoral Commission of Uganda, his position as chief legal and public relations adviser to the Electoral Commission, and his membership of the Association of African Election Authorities. He is a member of the Association of African Election Authorities and was one of the African Union election monitoring/observers team in Harare, Zimbabwe, for the Upper House/Senate elections there.

Daniel Zovatto is International IDEA's regional representative for Latin America. From 1986 to 1996 he was the executive director of the IIDH's CAPEL specialist centre, based in San José, Costa Rica. In 1994–1996 he also held the position of deputy executive director of the same institution. He graduated from the School of Law and

Social Sciences, National University of Cordoba, Argentina. He holds postgraduate degrees in international studies, from the Diplomatic School of the Ministry of Foreign Affairs, Spain; in human rights, from the School of Law, Institute of Human Rights, Complutense University, Madrid, Spain; and in public administration, from the John F. Kennedy School of Government, Harvard University, USA. He also holds a PhD in international law from the School of Law, Complutense University. He has been a visiting professor at several universities in Latin America, Europe and North America, and is an international speaker and frequent contributor of articles to many Latin American newspapers and political science journals.

About International IDEA

What is International IDEA?

The International Institute for Democracy and Electoral Assistance (International IDEA) is an intergovernmental organization that supports sustainable democracy worldwide. Its objective is to strengthen democratic institutions and processes. IDEA acts as a catalyst for democracy building by providing knowledge resources, expertise and a platform for debate on democracy issues. It works together with policy makers, donor governments, UN organizations and agencies, regional organizations and others engaged in the field of democracy building.

What does International IDEA do?

Democracy building is complex and touches on many areas including constitutions, electoral systems, political parties, legislative arrangements, the judiciary, central and local government, and formal and traditional government structures. International IDEA is engaged with all of these issues and offers to those in the process of democratization:

- knowledge resources, in the form of handbooks, databases, websites and expert networks;

- policy proposals to provoke debate and action on democracy issues; and

- assistance to democratic reforms in response to specific national requests.

Areas of work

International IDEA's notable areas of expertise are:

- *Constitution-building processes*. A constitutional process can lay the foundations for peace and development, or plant seeds of conflict. International IDEA is able to provide knowledge and make policy proposals for constitution building that are genuinely nationally owned, are sensitive to gender and conflict-prevention dimensions, and responds effectively to national priorities.

- *Electoral processes.* The design and management of elections has a strong impact on the wider political system. International IDEA seeks to ensure the professional management and independence of elections, adapt electoral systems, and build public confidence in the electoral process.

- *Political parties.* Political parties form the essential link between voters and the government, yet polls taken across the world show that political parties enjoy a low level of confidence. International IDEA analyses the functioning of political parties, the public funding of political parties, and their management and relations with the public.

- *Democracy and gender.* International IDEA recognizes that if democracies are to be truly democratic, then women—who make up over half of the world's population—must be represented on equal terms with men. International IDEA develops comparative resources and tools designed to advance the participation and representation of women in political life.

- *Democracy assessments.* Democratization is a national process. IDEA's State of Democracy methodology allows people to assess their own democracy instead of relying on externally produced indicators or rankings of democracies.

Where does International IDEA work?

International IDEA works worldwide. It is based in Stockholm, Sweden, and has offices in Latin America, Africa and Asia.

Index

Burundi, 176, 203
Bush, George W., 47
Bustamante, Cruz, 113

C

California (US state), direct democracy in
  agenda initiatives, 84
  citizens' initiatives, 11, 75, 132, 180
  criticism of, 24
  constitutional amendment, 69
  frequency of use, 24
  Proposition 71, 22–24, 75–76
  recall, 11, 16, 111–113, 180–181
  regulation, 19, 54, 132
  Voter Information Guide, 157
California Institute for Regenerative Medicine, 75, 157
Cambodia, 183, 203
Cameroon, 176, 203
campaigning. *See direct democracy campaigns*
Canada, direct democracy in. *See also names of individual provinces*
  citizens' initiatives, 78
  constitutional amendment, 180
  electoral reform, 128
  frequency of use, 49, 179–180
  Nunavut Territory, referendum on the creation of, 180
  Quebec referendum, 55, 145
  regulation, 203
Cape Verde, direct democracy in
  agenda initiatives, 85
  citizens' initiatives, 63, 73
  constitutional amendment, 67, 89
  frequency of use, 177
  regulation, 203
Carter Center, 36, 38
Cayman Islands, 179, 203
Central African Republic, 176, 203
Chad, 176, 204
Chávez, Hugo, 34–37, 74, 167, 183
Chile, direct democracy in
  constitutional amendment, 5
  frequency of use, 178
  Pinochet, Augusto, use by, 24, 45, 47, 49, 167,

181–182
  regulation, 52, 204
China, 184, 204
Chr. Michelsen Institute, 22
Chulalongkorn University, 53
Chulanont, Surayud, 53
Citizens Initiated Referenda Act (New Zealand), 74–75, 131–132, 191–192
CNE. *See Consejo Nacional Electoral*
Coalition for Stem Cell Research and Cures, 76
Colorado (US State), direct democracy in
  citizens' initiatives, 75, 180
  recall, 111
Colombia, direct democracy in
  agenda initiatives, 13, 85
  amnesty, referendum on 15
  citizens' initiatives, 63, 67, 73–74, 78
  consultative referendum, 13
  frequency of use, 178, 181
  history, 182
  recall, 13, 115–116
  regulation 13, 17, 19, 54, 148, 167, 181–182, 204
  taxation, referendum on, 15
Comoros, 176, 204
Congo, Democratic Republic of, direct democracy in
  agenda initiatives, 85
  frequency of use, 176
  regulation, 204
Consejo Nacional Electoral (CNE), 35–37
constitutional amendment, 2,3, 6, 15, 17, 21, 34, 43–45, 47–48, 50-51, 56, 60, 63–69, 73, 75, 77, 79, 84–85, 88–90, 94–98, 126, 140–142, 154, 163, 181, 184–185, 188–189, 191–192, 197–198, 213
constitutional reform, referendums on, 12, 34, 38–39, 49, 51, 91, 161,167–171, 177–178, 181–182, 190
Cook Islands, 191, 204
Costa Rica, direct democracy in
  agenda initiatives, 85
  citizens' initiatives, 63, 67
  frequency of use, 73, 179
  regulation, 88, 204

E